THE
TREASURY
 of
AMERICAN
PRAYER

THE
TREASURY
of
AMERICAN
PRAYER

James P. Moore Jr.

DOUBLEDAY

New York London Toronto Sydney Auckland

ⅅ

DOUBLEDAY

Copyright © 2008 by James P. Moore Jr.

Published in the United States by Doubleday,
an imprint of The Doubleday Publishing Group,
a division of Random House, Inc., New York.

DOUBLEDAY is a registered trademark and the
DD colophon is a trademark of Random House, Inc.

Book design by Kathryn Parise

LIBRARY OF CONGRESS CATALOGING-IN-PUBLICATION DATA
Moore, James P.
The treasury of American prayer / by James P. Moore Jr. — 1st ed.
p. cm.
ISBN 978-0-385-52462-9
1. Prayers. I. Title.
BL560.M665 2008
204'.330973—dc22

2008009888

PRINTED IN THE UNITED STATES OF AMERICA

1   3   5   7   9   10   8   6   4   2

First Edition

This book is dedicated to

Father Benedict Groeschel, CFR,

whose devotion to

God, country, and humanity

has inspired countless individuals around the world.

CONTENTS

PART TWO

PROLOGUE

For more than a decade I have been absorbed in the riveting saga of American prayer. I have climbed into people's attics, combed rare book rooms, and scoured for rare manuscripts in such far-away places as Europe and Australia. I even have traveled to historic American sites to re-create in my mind's eye, with the help of detailed memoirs and historic documents, certain key historic events in which prayer took on critical dimensions.

What consistently has amazed me is the dynamic and integral role that prayer has played in forging the direction of our country over time. It was prayer that came to bind our Founding Fathers together against all odds when they first met in Philadelphia. It was in the midst of prayer that Martin Luther King Jr. was transformed through an "epiphany" that reinforced his commitment to lead the civil rights movement. If it had not been for prayer, such diverse personalities as J. C. Penney and Johnny Cash could well have committed suicide, and their lasting legacies never would have been realized. Other Americans such as Harriet Tubman, Conrad Hilton, Elvis Presley, Thomas Merton, and even Abraham Lincoln arguably would have lived far different lives without it.

What I have compiled here are the very private thoughts of

American philosophers, farmers, athletes, statesmen, mothers, laborers, scientists, industrialists, and others in their relationships with God. Some are simple, straightforward entreaties; others are elaborate invocations. All of them, however, provide keys to understanding the inner sanctums of the individuals who have made America what it is today.

The prayers of these Americans are intimate snapshots of how they dealt with the gamut of human emotions, conditions, and events in their lives. They found comfort, hope, and an ability simply to endure by turning to God in their often unpredictable lives.

While the language of these prayers may vary from era to era, the essence remains the same. Americans from all walks of life and faiths have found their existences incomplete without being able to reach out to a higher power. It is through the words of their prayers that they find purpose in a larger context and from a greater perspective.

Considering the days in which we live, we cannot help but recognize the implicit influence of prayer. Our members of Congress begin their daily deliberations in prayer. Our president opens his cabinet meetings with prayer. Even our Supreme Court commences its proceedings with the words "God save the United States and this Honorable Court."

Indeed, prayer has been an indispensable staple in the lives of Americans, helping to reinforce faith, community, human justice, and much more. The record is clear and not inconsequential that the course of U.S. history would have been forged in far different ways if it had not been for the spiritual company of prayer.

While the Founding Fathers spoke very clearly about the separation between church and state, eschewing the state-sponsored religion then so prevalent in Europe, they did not distance themselves from the need for prayer. Even with the influences of the Enlightenment, they were not about to abandon the virtues and the culture of prayer into which they had been born. That is why they called upon the public to pray for both support and thanksgiving during the Revolutionary War and why they laid the groundwork for the country's future leaders to promote prayer in both word and deed. This is also why they ended their Declaration of Independence with the words "with a firm reliance on the protection of Divine Providence, we mutually pledge to each other our Lives, our Fortunes, and our sacred Honor."

This treasure trove of American prayers, providing a composite of the spiritual traditions of diverse faiths and backgrounds, offers only a glimpse of the spiritual fervor that has distinguished us as a people since the days of early Native America. Each prayer is accompanied by a description to place it in its proper context and to give some insight into its author. While the inclusion of some of the invocations has a largely historic purpose, most are inspirational and have a lasting resonance even at the beginning of the twenty-first century.

Some of the prayers have not been published in more than a 150 years. Others have never been seen in print. Still others will be recognized instantly as lyrics to favorite hymns or will be familiar because they have been incorporated into various literary or musical works.

These prayers have been written largely by Americans. There are exceptions, however, when a particular invocation holds special significance in U.S. history, such as "Amazing Grace," or when it has been adapted in some way as an American composition, such as the U.S. Navy hymn.

While compiling a book of this kind calls for many solitary hours, it is only a strong and dedicated team rowing in the same direction that can bring the work to fruition. First, I would like to thank Bill Barry, who in his role as Vice President and Director of Religious Publishing at Doubleday suggested this latest venture as part of the American Prayer Project. Most important, however, I am enormously grateful to Andrew Corbin, an extraordinary editor and friend, and to John Burke and Gary Jansen, for their kindness and guiding hands. I would also like to thank Nora Reichard and Maggie Carr for their meticulous work in finalizing the manuscript for publication.

Morton Janklow and Luke Janklow, my literary agents, as well as Claire Dippel of Janklow and Nesbit, have been invaluable counselors and supporters and have helped to steer me in the proper direction. I also am indebted to my right hand, Carlos Rosales-Coronado, for his steadfast and critical assistance, as well as to James L. Bayless Jr. who has been a part of the American Prayer Project for more than a decade.

I also want to acknowledge the encouragement and help that have been given to me by Father Benedict Groeschel, Al and Jackie Kingon, Peter Allen, Suzette Perkins, Holly Peppe, Eva and Alma Saloum, Christopher Brueningsen, Dean Alan Jones of Grace Episcopal Cathedral, Elizabeth Bayless, Robert and Louise Parsley, Wendy Smith, Father William J. Byron, Michael and Karen Yukevich, Russ and Ellen Swank, Ken and Judy Ravitz, Jeff Wieser, Arthur and Kathryn Taylor, Denise Blake, Anthony Masalonis, Clark Lobenstine and the Interfaith Conference of Metropolitan Washington, Jan DuPlain, the Stiner Family, the Fleming Family, Marie Gallo, Eugene and Magda Herzberger, Arthur Schwartz, the Templeton Foundation, Mitzi Budde and her terrific team at the Payne Library of the Virginia Theological Seminary, the Georgetown University community, Dean Samuel T. Lloyd and the Washington National Cathedral. I have been enormously grateful for the steadfast support—for this project and throughout my life—of my mother, Dorothy R. Moore, and my brothers, Terence E. Moore and Gregory S. Moore.

The Treasury of American Prayer is an important part of the American Prayer Project, which was launched with the publication of *One Nation Under God: The History of Prayer in America* (Doubleday) and later released in paperback as *Prayer in America.* The book also generated a remarkable narration of the book (Random House Audio) in which I was joined in reading by such extraordinary friends and associates as Senator John McCain; the late, great journalist Hugh Sidey and memorable actor Roscoe Lee Browne; former astronaut Colonel Frank Borman; actors Ben Vereen and David Conrad; former U.S. Senate Chaplain Lloyd John Ogilvie; House Chaplain Daniel P. Coughlin; businesswoman Kathryn Hauser; Breck and Lily Morton; and novelist Gail Buckley, among others.

The book also inspired the public television miniseries *Prayer in America* (the Duncan Group) as well as a five-part program for public, private, and parochial middle schools and high schools across the United States (Questar) for which I served as consulting producer. In addition, the book helped to inspire the music CD *The Many Voices of One Nation Under God* (PBA Music Publishing).

The Treasury of American Prayer represents a rich and broad look into the spiritual heritage of our country. At the same time, it provides an invaluable resource in understanding how and why Americans have turned to prayer. It is this historic measure that serves as prologue to understanding the country we have inherited.

At the outset of the twenty-first century, Americans face war, economic recession, and terrorism as well as the effects of natural and man-made disasters of every kind. The sheer magnitude of what we face seems so overwhelming at times that we lose perspective and the necessary fortitude to endure and to thrive.

By reflecting on the prayer life and most private thoughts of Americans as they dealt with their own challenges over the generations, we can gain invaluable insights into how we should handle the complexities of our own modern world. Most profoundly, we can take comfort, as our forebears did, in knowing that throughout our personal struggles and victories alike, no matter where our journey takes us, we are not alone.

❊ PART ONE ❊

LOVE AND DEVOTION

Renewed Wonderment

>Earth our mother, breathe forth life
>All night sleeping
>Now awaking
>In the east
>Now see the dawn.
>
>Earth our mother, breathe and waken
>Leaves are stirring
>All things moving
>New day coming
>Life renewing
>
>Eagle soaring, see the morning
>See the new mysterious morning
>Something marvelous and sacred
>Though it happens every day
>Dawn the child of God and Darkness

This prayer has been handed down for generations among members of the Pawnee tribe in modern-day Kansas. It is an invocation of renewal and wonderment at the beginning of each new day.

Prayer of Chief Seattle

Earth mother, star mother,
You who are called by
A thousand names,
May all remember
We are cells in your body
And dance together
You are the grain
And the loaf
That sustains each day,
And as you are patient
With our struggles to learn
So shall we be patient
With ourselves and each other.
We are radiant light
And sacred dark
—the balance—
You are the embrace that heartens
And the freedom beyond fear.
Within you we are born
We grow, live, and die—
You bring us around the circle
To rebirth, Within us you dance
Forever.

Composed by Chief Seattle in the early nineteenth century, this tribute gives glory to creation and nature's continual regeneration. Chief Seattle was the leader of the Suquamish and Duwamish tribes, located in today's Washington State. The city of Seattle was named in his honor.

Prayer at Dawn

Blessed be the light of day
And the Holy Cross, we say;
And the Lord of the Verity
And the Holy Trinity.
Blessed be th' immortal soul
And the Lord who keeps it whole,
Blessed be the light of day
And He who sends the night away.

Each morning as they crossed the Atlantic, Christopher Columbus and his men were awakened by this chant sung by one of the young mates on board. It was one in a series of prayers that was invoked at specific times during the day, creating discipline among the men while they praised God in hopes of safe passage.

Rise, O My Soul

Rise, O my soul, with thy desires to heaven,
And with divinest contemplation use
Thy time where time's eternity is given,
And let vain thoughts no more thy
Thoughts abuse;

To thee, O Jesu, I direct my eyes;
To thee my hands, to thee my humble knees;
To thee my heart shall offer sacrifice;
To thee my thoughts, who my thoughts only sees;
To thee my self—my self and all I give;
To thee I die; to thee I only live.

Having led one of the more colorful and accomplished lives among the courtiers of Queen Elizabeth I, Sir Walter Raleigh wrote this prayer when he was imprisoned in the Tower of

London for unproven crimes. Although he would never set eyes on the New World, he was a critical force in the British settlement of Virginia. His deep faith would endear him to many of America's earliest colonists, and this invocation would become part of *The Book of Common Prayer* of America's Episcopal Church.

En Este Nuevo Día

En este neuvo día
gracias te tributamos,
oh, Dios omnipotente,
Señor de todo lo creado . . .

Por ti nacen las flores
y reverdece el campo,
los arboles dan fruta
y el sol nos da sus rayos . . .

Dirige Dios immenso
y guia nuestros pasos
para que eternamente
tu santa ley sigamos.

On This New Day
(English Translation)

On this new day
thanks we pay in tribute
oh, omnipotent God,
Lord of all creation . . .

For you the flowers grow
and the countryside turns green,
and trees give fruit
and the sun gives us your rays . . .

Immense God direct
and guide our steps
so that eternally
We follow your holy law.

When the Franciscan priests of Spain established their missions throughout the western United States, they composed hundreds of "alabados" for their indigenous congregations. These prayers were set to melodies that echoed the sounds of Jewish and Arabic chants mixed with Flamenco music. Not only did these hymns express praise to God, but they also taught the faithful the tenets of their religious faith.

Love and Adoration

O my Lord, my love, how wholly delectable thou art! Let him [Jesus] kiss me with the kisses of his mouth, for his love is sweeter than wine: how lovely is thy countenance! How pleasant are thy embraces! My heart leaps for joy when I hear the voice of thee my Lord, my love, when thou sayest to my soul, thou art her salvation. O my God, my king, what am I but dust! A worm, a rebel, and thine enemy was I, wallowing in the blood and filth of my sins, when thou didst cast the light of Countenance upon me, when thou spread over me the lap of thy love, and saidest that I should live . . .

John Winthrop, the single greatest influence in founding and governing the Massachusetts Bay Colony in its early years, wrote a series of prayers in the daily entries of his diary. In time his affection for Christ became all the more profound, as this prayer shows. He believed that the more he prayed, the more he came to be "enamored."

For Love of Others

Lord, make my Tongue, a *Tree of Life!*

Living Christianity's Golden Rule was central to the faith of Reverend Cotton Mather and to his leading a loving, redemptive life. Although he would become a catalyst in advancing the Salem witch trials, he nonetheless firmly believed in the message of his spiritual ejaculation.

A Crumb of Dust

Lord, can a crumb of dust the earth outweigh,
Outmatch all mountains, nay the crystal sky?
Imbosom in't designs that shall display
And trace into the boundless deity?
Yea, hand a pen whose moisture doth glid o'er
Eternal glory with a glorious glore.

If it is pen had of an angel's quill,
And sharpened on a precious stone ground tight,
And dipped in liquid gold, and moved by skill
In crystal leaves should golden letters write,
It would but blot and blur, yea, jag and jar,
Unless Thou mak'st the pen and scribener.

I am this crumb of dust which is designed
To make my pen unto Thy praise alone,
And my dull fancy I would gladly grind
Unto an edge on Zion's precious stone;

And write in liquid gold upon Thy name
My letters till Thy glory forth doth flame.

Let not th' attempts break down my dust I pray,
Nor laugh Thou them to scorn, but pardon give.
Inspire this crumb of dust till it display
Thy glory though't: and then Thy dust shall live.
Its failings then Thou'lt overlook, I trust,
They being slips slipped from Thy crumb of dust.

Thy crumb of dust breathes two words from its breast,
That Thou wilt guide its pen to write aright
To prove Thou art and that Thou art the best
And shew Thy prosperities to shine most bright.
And then Thy works will shine as flowers on stems
Or as in jewelary shops do gems.

One of the most eloquent spiritual voices during the American colonial period was that of Reverend Edward Taylor, a physician and Congregational minister. Like most of the metaphysical prayers he wrote, this one was composed for his Sunday Eucharist services in Westfield, Massachusetts. When his collection of Eucharistic prayers was discovered in the archives at Yale University just before World War II, historians gained far greater insight into the sophisticated world of Puritan America.

Great God of Wonders

Great God of wonders! All Thy ways
Are worthy of thyself—divine;
But the bright glories of Thy grace
Among thine other wonders shine;
Who is pard'ning God like Thee?
Or who has grace so rich and free?

As the fourth president of Princeton (then known as the College of New Jersey) Samuel Davies worked arduously to deliver inspiring sermons to the student body. He always made sure that he accompanied his sermons with a prayer of some kind. While some conservative clergymen criticized him for composing invocations rather than turning exclusively to the Psalms he was undeterred and would write over a hundred such prayers. This particular prayer was later set to music and became his most famous.

Thoughts on the Work of Providence
(excerpt)

> Arise, my soul, on wings enraptur'd, rise
> To praise the monarch of the earth and skies,
> Whose goodness and beneficence appear
> As round its centre moves the rolling year . . .
>
> Almighty, in these wond'rous works of thine,
> What Pow'r, what Wisdom, and what Goodness shine!
> And are thy wonders, Lord, by men explor'd,
> And yet creating glory unador'd . . .
>
> Shall day to day, and night to night conspire
> To show the goodness of the Almighty Sire?
> This mental voice shall man regardless hear,
> And never, never raise the filial pray'r?
> To-day, O hearken, nor your folly mourn
> For time mispent, that never will return . . .
>
> Infinite Love where'er we turn our eyes
> Appears: this ev'ry creature's wants supplies;
> This most is heard in Nature's constant voice,
> This makes the morn, and this the eve rejoice;
> This bids the fost'ring rains and dews descend

To nourish all, to serve one gen'ral end,
The good of man: yet man ungrateful pays
But little homage, and but little praise.
To him, whose works arry'd with mercy shine,
What songs should rise, how constant, how divine!

Phillis Wheatley, born in Senegal around 1753 and sold to a Boston family at the age of seven, was as precocious as any young girl of her age. The family, recognizing her talents, soon began teaching her how to read and write English, Latin, and Greek. In turn, she took delight in writing her own poetry and personally poignant essays. Deeply religious, she composed several touching spiritual pieces, among them the prayer that is excerpted here.

I Love Thy Kingdom, Lord

I love Thy kingdom, Lord,
The house of Thine abode,
The church our blessed Redeemer saved
With His own precious blood.

I love Thy church, O God.
Her walls before Thee stand
Dear as the apple of Thine eye,
And written on Thy hand.

Should I wish coffers join
Her altars to abuse?
No! Better far my tongue were dumb,
My hand its skill should lose.

Believed to be the oldest American hymn still in common use, these lyrics were composed by the eminent president of Yale University Timothy Dwight. During his days as a young chaplain in the Revolutionary War, he forged enduring friendships with many of the Founding Fathers and became known in his later years for strongly advocating the need for prayer, particularly among families, in the early days of the new republic.

In Praise of Thee

Lord with glowing heart I'd praise Thee
For the bliss Thy love bestows,
For the pardoning grace that saves me,
And the peace that from it flows:

Help, O God, my weak endeavor;
This dull soul to rapture raise:
Thou must light the flame, or never
Can my love be warmed to praise.

Praise, my soul, the God who sought thee,
Wretched wand'rer far astray;
Found thee lost, and kindly brought thee
From the paths of death away:

Praise, with love's devoutest feeling,
Him who saw thy guilt-born fear,
And, the light of hope revealing,
Bade the bloodstained cross appear.

Praise thy Saviour God that drew thee
Top that cross, new life to give,
Held a blood-sealed pardon to Thee,
Bade Thee look to him and live:

Praise the grace whose threats alarmed Thee,
Roused Thee from thy fatal ease,
Praise the grace whose promise warm'd Thee,
Praise the grace that whispered peace.

Lord, this bosom's ardent feeling
Vainly would my lips express:
Low before Thy footstool kneeling,
Deign thy suppliant's pray'r to bless:

Let Thy love, my soul's chief treasure,
Love's pure flame within me raise;
And, since words can never measure,
Let my life show forth Thy praise.

Francis Scott Key, the composer of "The Star-Spangled Banner," was also one of America's first lawyers to argue cases before the Supreme Court, and strongly believed in the cause of justice and in the guiding hand of God in all things. This prayer of unconditional devotion was published in a compilation of his poetry, which was released eighteen years after his death.

Lord of All Worlds

Lord of all worlds, let thanks and praise
To Thee forever fill my soul;
With blessings Thou has crowned my days,
My heart, my head, my hand control:
O, let no vain presumptions rise,
No impious murmur in my heart,
To crave the boon Thy will denies,
Or shrink from ill Thy hands impart.

Thy child am I, and not an hour,
Revolving in the orbs above,
But brings some token of Thy power,
But brings some token of Thy love;
And shall this bosom dare repine,
In darkness dare deny the dawn,

Or spurn the treasures of the mine,
Because one diamond is withdrawn?

The fool denies, the fool alone,
Thy being, Lord and boundless might;
Denies the firmament, Thy throne,
Denies the sun's meridian light,
Denies the fashion of his frame.
The voice he hears, the breath he draws:
O idiot atheist! To proclaim
Effects unnumbered without cause!

Matter and mind, mysterious one,
Are man's for threesome years and ten;
Where, ere the thread of life was spun?
Where, when reduced to dust again?
All-seeing God, the doubt suppress;
The doubt then only canst relieve
My soul Thy Saviour-Son shall bless,
Fly to my gospel, and believe.

After leaving office as the sixth president of the United States, John Quincy Adams spent the last twenty years of his life serving as a member of the U.S. House of Representatives from Quincy, Massachusetts. In his spare time and during long-winded orations by his colleagues in the House Chamber, he immersed himself in writing, among other things, a series of intensely personal prayers. This piece was included in a collection of his works entitled *Poems of Religion and Society,* which was published after his death by Senators Thomas Hart Benton of Missouri and John Davis of Massachusetts.

My Soul Triumphant Wakes

Thou art the dawn to my blessed sight
That o'er the mountain breaks
Already by thy holy light
My soul triumphant wakes

We know thy growing light a sign
The sun himself is nigh;
The sun of Righteousness divine
Ascends the glorious sky . . .

Brighter and brighter grows the cross
The mountain-tops are gold
And o'er death's valley far across
The gorgeous light is rolled.

The nineteenth-century artists who belonged to the movement known as the Hudson River School believed that God had shown great favor to America, especially in endowing its land with such natural beauty. To give expression to that spiritual manifestation, these artists painted spectacular, idealized landscapes that captured lush vistas with thick forests, gushing streams, and imposing mountains. Thomas Cole, the founder of the school, would write a prayer to accompany "the divine visual language" contained in each of his paintings, of which this is one.

The Catholic Hymn

Sancta Maria! turn thine eyes—
Upon the sinner's sacrifice,
Of fervent prayer and humble love,
From thy holy throne above.

At morn—at noon—at twilight dim
Maria! thou hast heard my hymn!
In joy and woe—in good and ill—
Mother of God, be with me still!

When the Hours flew brightly by,
And not a cloud obscured the sky,
My soul, lest it should truant be,
Thy grace did guide to thine and thee;

Now, when storms of Fate o'ercast
Darkly my Present and my Past,
Let my Future radiant shine
With sweet hopes of thee and thine!

In his dark short story "Morella" written in 1835, Edgar Allan Poe included this prayer to convey the mysticism of his central character, Morella. In his original manuscript he referred to the prayer as "the Catholic Hymn," but when it was published again in 1845 in *The Raven and Other Poems,* he struck out the word "Catholic." Regardless of the change, he found Christ's Mother to be the perfect conduit to God.

Love and Hate

The sole thing I hate is Hate;
For hate is death; and Love is life,
A peace, a splendor from above;
And Hate, a never ending strife,
A smoke, a blackness from the abyss
Where unclean spirits coil and hiss!
Love is the Holy Ghost within;
Hate the unpardonable sin!
Who preaches otherwise than this
Betrays his Master with a kiss!

In this excerpt from Henry Wadsworth Longfellow's trilogy "The Christus: A Mystery," the great nineteenth-century poet reflects in old age on his spiritual life and beliefs by considering the life of Christ in the apostolic, Middle, and modern ages. This piece, which was both prayer and contemplation, puts love and its alternative in perspective.

Mutual Love

My Father: I now come to thee with a desire to thank thee for the continuance of our love, the one for the other. I feel that without thy love in me I should be alone here in the flesh. I cannot express my gratitude for what thou hast been and continuest to be to me. But thou knowest what my feelings are. When nought on earth seemeth pleasant to me, thou dost make thyself known to me, and teach that which is needful for me, and dost cheer my travels on. I know that thou hast not created me and placed me on earth, amidst its toils and troubles and the follies of those around me, and told me to be like thyself when I see so little of thee here to profit by; thou hast not done this, and then left me here to myself, a poor, weak man, scarcely able to earn my bread. No; thou art my Father and I will love thee, for thou didst first love me, and lovest me still. We will ever be parent and child. Wilt thou give me strength to persevere in this great work of redemption. Wilt thou show me the true means of accomplishing it.

The "father" of transcendentalism, Ralph Waldo Emerson, wrote this introspection as part of an overall treatise on the subject of prayer in 1843. Here he speaks of a mutual dependency of a father and a son as the bond of unconditional love that exists between him and God.

Our Father in Heaven

Our Father in Heaven,
We hallow Thy name!
May Thy kingdom so holy
On earth be the same—
O, give to us daily,
Our portion of bread!
It is from this bounty
That all must be fed.

Forgive our transgressions,
And teach us to know
That humble compassion
That pardons each foe—
Keep us from temptation,
From weakness and sin—
And Thine be the glory
Forever—Amen!

Sarah Josepha Hale, like Benjamin Franklin and other Americans, reflects in this piece on her own personal interpretation of the "Lord's Prayer." Intensely spiritual, Hale became America's first female editor, and was the prime motivator in convincing President Lincoln to adopt Thanksgiving as a national holiday.

Jesus Loves Me

Jesus loves me! This I know,
For the Bible tells me so;
Little ones to Him belong,
They are weak but He is strong.

Jesus loves me! He who died,
Heaven's gate to open wide;
He will wash away my sin,
Let His little child come in.

Jesus loves me! He will stay
Close beside me all the way;
Thou hast bled and died for me,
I will henceforth live for Thee.

Jesus loves me! loves me still,
When I'm very weak and ill;
From His shining throne on high,
Comes to watch me where I lie.

Jesus loves me! He will stay,
Close beside me all the way;
He's prepared a home for me,
And some day His face I'll see.

Yes, Jesus loves me!
Yes, Jesus loves me!
Yes, Jesus loves me!
The Bible tells me so.

Given its simple sentiment and easy melody, this is the first hymn millions of American children ever learn. Originally written in 1860 by Anna Warner as a poem for her sister Susan's novel *Say and Seal,* it became popular overnight for its reinforcement of Christ's steadfast love for everyone. Both sisters taught Sunday school not far from the gates of the U.S. Military Academy in West Point, New York. Many of their students were military cadets who would later be pitted against one another in the Civil War.

I Only Serve Thee

How dare I in thy courts appear,
Or raise to Thee my voice!
I only serve Thee, Lord, with fear,
With trembling I rejoice.

I have not all forgot Thy word,
Nor wholly gone astray;
I follow Thee, but oh, my Lord,
So faint, so far away!

That Thou wilt pardon and receive
Of sinners even the chief,
Lord, I believe,—Lord, I believe;
Help thou mine unbelief!

Along with her sister Alice, Phoebe Cary composed hundreds of
religious poems that conveyed both devotion to their faith of uni-
versalism as well as to their deep piety. Thanks in part to the
support of *New York Tribune* publisher Horace Greeley, their
works had become well known by the time of the Civil War. This
unusual prayer by Phoebe Cary conveys both adoration and the
need to ask for God's help for greater spiritual fortitude.

The Larger Love

At first I prayed for Light:
Could I but see the way,
How gladly, swiftly would I walk
To everlasting day.

And next I prayed for Strength:
That I might tread the road

With firm, unfaltering feet and win
The heaven's serene abode.

And then I asked for Faith:
Could I but trust my God,
I'd live infolded in His peace,
Though foes were all aboard.

But now I pray for Love:
Deep love to God and man,
A living love that will not fail,
However dark his plan.

And Light and Strength and Faith
Are opening everywhere;
God only waited for me, till
I prayed the larger prayer.

In this piece Edna Dow Cheney highlights how "love" had become the guiding force in her life. Little known to Americans today, she was one of the critical organizers of the suffragist movement after the Civil War and worked closely with Susan B. Anthony and Elizabeth Cady Stanton. Cheney drew on her Unitarian faith to fight discrimination against women.

Break Thou the Bread of Life

Break thou the bread of life, dear Lord, to me,
As thou didst break the loaves beside the sea.
Beyond the sacred pages, I seek Thee, Lord;
My spirit pants for Thee, O Living Word.

Bless thou the truth, dear Lord, to me, to me,
As thou didst bless the bread by Galilee;

Then shall all bondage cease, all fetters fall,
And I shall find my peace, my all in all.

The lyrics to this hymn, written by Mary A. Lathbury, became an
instant sensation when they were first published in 1877. Well
known for her compilation of children's stories and poems in
her popular *Ring-A-Round-A-Rosy,* she was also a leading figure in both the temperance and suffragist movements. In her
prayers she conveyed her never-ending desire to create a close,
personal union with God.

The Prayer of Swami Vivekananda

Lord, I do not want wealth, nor children, nor learning. If it be
thy will I will go to a hundred hells, but grant me this, that I may
love thee without hope of reward—unselfishly love for love's
sake.

The World's Parliament of Religions, held in conjunction with
the Chicago World's Fair in 1893, was one of the great milestones
in religious history. Representatives from the major religions of
the world gathered together for the first time to gain greater understanding of the faiths of one another. The individual who
made the most lasting impact was Swami Vivekananda, a Hindu
who traveled to the conference all the way from Calcutta, India.
To the seven thousand people gathered for his lecture, he offered
this prayer, showing that his belief in God was not unlike that of
those assembled in the hall.

Unconditional Love

I feel myself consuming with love for Thee, and this is a great torment to me, as a slow martyrdom at not being able to do something for Thee. From the moment I became acquainted with Thee I was so enchanted by Thy beauty that I followed Thee. The more I love Thee, it seems the less I love Thee, because I want to love Thee more. I can bear it no longer: expand, expand my heart! Convert me, Jesus, convert me completely to Thyself, for if Thou dost not make me a saint, I will not know how to work in Thy vineyard and will end by betraying Thy interests, instead of rendering them successful. O Jesus, Jesus Love, help always Thy poor miserable one. Thy miserable little bride, and carry her always in Thine arms. I love Thee, I love Thee very much, very much.

Mother Frances Cabrini, whose prayer life was legendary, was the first American citizen to be canonized a saint by the Roman Catholic Church. This Italian immigrant, who became a naturalized citizen in 1909, was best known for establishing schools, orphanages, and hospitals across the country. The imagery in this prayer has much in common with that of the prayers written by the founding Puritan fathers.

Take My Life

Take my life and let it be
consecrated, Lord to Thee;
Take my moments and my days,
Let them flow in ceaseless praise.

One of the most colorful personalities of the 1920s and 1930s was evangelist Aimee Semple McPherson. From her Foursquare Gospel Temple in Los Angeles, she mesmerized her followers with her stage presence and her ability to convey her personal vision of God. This prayer was the cornerstone of her ministry.

Thou Art the Pearl

I read of knights who laid their armor down,
And left the tourney's prize for other hands,
And clad them in a pilgrim's somber gown,
To seek a holy cup in desert lands.
For them no more the torch of victory;
For them lone vigils and the starlight pale,
So they in dreams the Blessed Cup may see—
Thou art the Grail!

An Eastern king once smelled a rose in sleep,
And on the morrow laid his scepter down.
His heir his titles and his lands might keep—
The rose was sweeter wearing than the crown.
Nor cared he that its life was but an hour,
A breath that from the crimson summer blows,
Who gladly paid a kingdom for a flower—
Thou art the Rose!

A merchant man, who knew the worth of things,
Beheld a pearl more priceless than a star;
And straight returning, all he hath he brings
And goes upon his way, Ah, richer far!
Laughter of merchants of the market place,
Nor taunting gibe nor scornful lips that curl,
Can ever cloud the rapture of his face—
Thou art the Pearl!

Raised and educated on the prairies of Nebraska, Willa Cather infused her writings with her love of wide-open spaces. This poem has become one of her best known, reflecting her wonderment at the precious nature of a Higher Being.

Prayer of Black Elk

Hey-a-a-hey! Hey-a-a-hey! Hey-a-a-hey! Hey-a-a-hey!

Grandfather, Great Mysterious One,
You have been always and before You nothing has been.
There is nothing to pray to but You.
The star nations all over the universe are Yours,
And Yours are the grasses of the earth.
Day in and day out You are the life of things.
You are older than all need,
Older than all pain and prayer.
Grandfather, all over the world the faces of the living ones
    are alike.
In tenderness they have come up out of the ground.
Look upon Your children with children in their arms,
That they may face the winds,
And walk the good road to the day of quiet.
Teach me to walk the soft earth,
A relative to all that live.
Sweeten my heart and fill me with light,
And give me the strength to understand and the eyes to
    see.
Help me, for without You I am nothing.

Hetchetu aloh!

A member of the Lakota tribe of the Midwest, Black Elk became highly renowned after the publication of his autobiography, *Black Elk Speaks,* in 1932. Although he converted to Roman Catholicism in later life he continued to use the language of his ancestors to relate to God, as this prayer of veneration, taken from his book, illustrates.

Joyful, Joyful, We Adore Thee

Joyful, joyful, we adore Thee,
God of glory, Lord of love;
Hearts unfold like flow'rs before Thee,
Op'ning to the sun above.
Melt the clouds of sin and sadness;
Drive the dark of doubt away;
Giver of immortal gladness,
Fill us with the light of day!

All Thy works with joy surround Thee,
Earth and heav'n reflect Thy rays,
Stars and angels sing around Thee,
Center of unbroken praise.
Field and forest, vale and mountain,
Flow'ry meadow, flashing sea,
Singing bird and flowing fountain
Call us to rejoice in Thee.

Thou art giving and forgiving,
Ever blessing, ever blest,
Wellspring of the joy of living,
Ocean depth of happy rest!
Thou our Father, Christ our Brother,
All who live in love are Thine;
Teach us how to love each other,
Lift us to the joy divine.

Mortals, join the happy chorus,
Which the morning stars began;

Father love is reigning o'er us,
Brother love binds man to man.
Ever singing, march we onward,
Victors in the midst of strife,
Joyful music leads us Sunward
In the triumph song of life.

Set to the music of Ludwig van Beethoven's "Ode to Joy," these words of Henry van Dyke, a Princeton educator, minister, and ambassador under President Woodrow Wilson, have been sung in every imaginable civic and spiritual setting since they were first published in 1908. One contemporary of van Dyke's referred to the work as "a standing ovation to God."

Prayer in the Stillness of the Night

I cannot teach you how to pray in words. God listens not to your words save when He Himself utters them through our lips. And I cannot teach you the prayer of the seas and the forests and the mountains. But you are born of the mountains and the forests and the seas can find their prayer in your heart, And if you but listen in the stillness of the night you shall hear them saying in silence,

Our God, who art our winged self, it is thy will in us that willeth.
It is thy desire that desireth.
It is thy urge in us that would turn our nights,
which are thine, into days, which are thine also.
We cannot ask thee for aught, for thou knowest our needs before they
Are born in us:
Thou art our need; and in giving us more of thyself thou givest us all.

This excerpt is taken from the chapter "On Prayer" from Khalil Gibran's 1923 masterpiece *The Prophet.* Gibran was a Maronite Catholic who emigrated from Lebanon to the United States as a young teenager. He was fascinated by the mystery of God and the evolving spiritual love between God and human beings, as this prayer underscores.

A Prayer in Spring

Oh, give us pleasure in the flowers to-day;
And give us not to think so far away
As the uncertain harvest; keep us here
All simply in the springing of the year.

Oh, give us pleasure in the orchard white,
Like nothing else by day, like ghosts by night;
And make us happy in the happy bees,
The swarm dilating round the perfect trees.

And make us happy in the darting bird
That suddenly above the bees is heard,
The meteor that thrusts in with needle bill,
And off a blossom in mind air stands still.

For this is love and nothing else is love,
The which it is reserved for God above
To sanctify to what far ends He will,
But which it only needs that we fulfil.

The product of a strong Unitarian Universalist family, Robert Frost often interwove in his poetry a pervasive spirituality and wonderment about the mysteries of the world. In reflecting on this "Prayer in Spring," written when he was a young man, Frost would later write that he had discovered that appreciating the greatness of God's love for the world did not lie simply in having "forward thinking thoughts."

O Light Invisible

O Light Invisible, we praise Thee!
Too bright for mortal vision.
O Greater Light, we praise Thee for the less;

The eastern light our spires touch at morning,
The light that slants upon our western doors at evening,
the twilight over stagnant pools at batflight,

Moon light and star light, owl and moth light,
Glow-worm glow light on a grassblade.
O Light Invisible, we worship Thee!

We thank Thee for the lights that we have kindled,
The light of altar and of sanctuary;
Small lights of those who meditate at midnight
And lights directed through the coloured panes of
    windows
And light reflected from the polished stone,
The gilded carven wood, the coloured fresco.
Our gaze is submarine, our eyes look upward
And see the light that fractures through unquiet water.
We see the light but see not whence it comes.
O Light Invisible, we glorify Thee!

Taken from his 1934 pageant play *The Rock*, this prayer by T. S. Eliot exudes his deep Anglo-Catholic faith. His metaphysical poetry, with its complexity, rich imagery, and depth of feeling, was a perfect means for him to express that spirituality. Born in St. Louis, the Nobel laureate would later move to London and compose some of the most exquisite works in the English language.

In the Garden of the Lord

The word of God came unto me,
Sitting alone among the multitudes;
And my blind eyes were touched with light.
And there was laid upon my lips a flame of fire.

I laugh and shout for life is good,
Though my feet are set in silent ways.

In merry mood I leave the crowd
To walk in my garden. Ever as I walk
I gather fruits and flowers in my hands.
And with joyful heart I bless the sun
That kindles all the place with radiant life.
I run with playful winds that blow after the scent.

Of rose and Jessamine in eddying whirls.
At last I come where tall lilies grow,
While the lilies pray, I kneel upon the ground;
I have strayed into the holy temple of the Lord.

This poem of exaltation, using the beauty of nature as a conduit
to God, was written by author and social activist Helen Keller.
Blind and deaf before the age of two, she advanced the special
needs of the disabled by printing Bibles and devotionals in braille
and by inspiring millions of people around the world to take
charge of their lives, no matter what their personal circumstances happened to be.

The Duke's Prayer

<pre>
        L
      GOD
        V
        E
</pre>

In the last years of his life, musician and composer Duke Ellington realized that his time was short and he regretted that he had not fully conveyed in his music his deeply held spirituality. In his quest to add to his legacy, he wrote a series of ecumenical pieces that became part of his Sacred Concerts. In his last Christmas card to his friends, he personally designed this prayer as a personal expression of God's inextricable love for mankind.

Day by Day

Day by day
Oh Dear Lord
Three things I pray
To see thee more clearly
Love thee more dearly
Follow thee more nearly
Day by day.

This simple devotion was written for the Broadway hit musical *Godspell* and was adapted by lyricist and composer Stephen Schwarz based on a prayer attributed to Saint Richard of Chichester, a thirteenth-century English bishop. The simplicity of the words and the lilting melody made this spiritual entreaty the most memorable song of the musical.

Father of Night

Father of night, Father of day,
Father, who taketh the darkness away,
Father, who teacheth the bird to fly,
Builder of rainbows up in the sky,
Father of loneliness and pain,
Father of love and Father of rain.

Father of day, Father of night,
Father of black, Father of white,
Father, who builds the mountain so high,
Who shapeth the cloud up in the sky,
Father of time, Father of dreams,
Father, who turneth the rivers and streams.

Father of grain, Father of wheat,
Father of cold and Father of heat,
Father of air and Father of trees,
Who dwells in our hearts and our memories,
Father of minutes, Father of days,
Father of whom we most solemnly praise.

These lyrics by Bob Dylan were written for his eleventh album, *New Morning,* released in 1970. His sentiments presage his religious conversion as a born-again Christian a decade later.

FAITH AND TRUST

Christic the Apple Tree

The tree of life my soul hath seen.
Laden with fruit, and always green:
The trees of nature fruitless be,
Compar'd with Christ the apple-tree.

His beauty doth all things excel:
By faith I know, but ne'er can tell,
The glory which I now can see,
In Jesus Christ the apple-tree.

For happiness long have sought
And pleasure dearly I have bought:
I miss'd of all; but now I see
'Tis found in Christ the apple-tree

I'm weary'd with my former toil,
Here I will sit and rest awhile:
Under the shadow I will be,
Of Jesus Christ the apple-tree.

With great delight I'll make my stay,
There's none shall frighten my soul away:

Among the sons of men I see
There's none like Christ the apple-tree.

I'll sit and eat this fruit divine,
It cheers my heart like spirit'al wine
And now this fruit is sweet to me,
That grows on Christ the apple-tree.

This fruit doth make my soul to thrive,
It keeps my dying faith alive;
Which makes my soul in haste to be
With Christ the apple-tree.

This mystical invocation, likening Christ to a bountiful apple tree, was written in 1761 by an unknown New England poet. Although beloved by generations of American children after it first appeared in a collection of hymns, it gained newfound popularity in 1967 after it was set to music as a Christmas carol by British composer Elizabeth Poston.

My Faith Looks Up to Thee

My faith looks up to thee,
thou Lamb of Calvary,
Savior divine!
Now hear me while I pray,
take all my guilt away,
O let me from this day
be wholly thine!

May thy rich grace impart
strength to my fainting heart,
my zeal inspire!
As thou hast died for me,

O may my love to thee
pure, warm, and changeless be,
a living fire!

While life's dark maze I tread,
and griefs around me spread,
be thou my guide;
bid darkness turn to day,
wipe sorrow's tears away,
nor let me ever stray
from thee aside.

When ends life's transient dream,
when death's cold, sullen stream
shall o'er me roll;
blest Savior, then in love,
fear and distrust remove;
O bear me safe above,
a ransomed soul!

Many prominent scholars consider this testament of faith to be the greatest hymn ever written by an American. Ray Palmer wrote the work in 1830, shortly after graduating from Yale University. Not long after he had completed the piece he showed it to Lowell Mason, the noted religious music composer. Mason was so taken with the hymn's inspirational message that he immediately wrote a tune for it. Ever since it has been a staple in religious services.

Simple Gifts

'Tis the gift to be simple, 'tis the gift to be free,
'Tis the gift to come down where we ought to be,
And when we find ourselves in the place just right,

'Twill be in the valley of love and delight.
When true simplicity is gain'd,
To bow and to bend we shan't be asham'd,
To turn, turn will be our delight
'Till by turning, turning we come round right.

One of America's most beloved melodies and spiritual lyrics is contained in this "quick prayer dance" of the Shakers. Written in 1848 by Joseph Bracket, an elder in the church in Alfred, Maine, "Simple Gifts" was most often sung and danced in synchronization by the Shakers during their Sunday evening worship services. This piece would be enshrined in American composer Aaron Copland's orchestral work *Appalachian Spring.*

Lord, I Believe

Lord, I believe. Help Thou mine unbelief. Philosophical argument, especially that drawn from the vastness of the universe in comparison with the apparent insignificance of this globe, has sometimes shaken my reason for the faith that is in me; but my heart has assured me that the gospel of Jesus Christ must be divine reality. The Sermon on the Mount cannot be a merely human production. The whole history of man proves it.

Upon his death in 1852, Massachusetts senator Daniel Webster, perhaps the greatest orator ever to have served in the U.S. Congress, asked that this prayer be chiseled on his gravestone in Marshfield, Massachusetts. Despite his political ambitions, he was a pious man. To the people who were caring for him at his deathbed, he cried out, "Hold me up; I do not wish to pray with a fainting voice," and with that he died.

Unconditional Affirmation

> I'm going to hold steady on You, an' You've got to see me
> through.

This ejaculation was recited regularly by Harriet Tubman when she led runaway slaves to freedom in the North. The nineteenth-century "Moses," herself having been enslaved, never lost a person along the Underground Railroad and attributed her success to her deep belief in God. She would say this prayer just as she began to engineer one of her daring escapes.

Hymn of Trust

> O Love Divine, that stooped to share
>> Our sharpest pang, our bitterest tear,
> On Thee we cast each earth-born care,
>> We smile at pain while Thou art near!
>
> Though long the weary way we tread,
>> And sorrow crown each lingering year,
> No path we shun, no darkness dread,
>> Our hearts still whispering, Thou art near!
>
> When drooping pleasure turns to grief,
>> And trembling faith is changed to fear,
> The murmuring wind, the quivering leaf,
>> Shall softly tell us, Thou art near!
>
> On Thee we fling our burdening woe,
>> O Love Divine, forever dear,
> Content to suffer while we know,
>> Living and Dying, Thou art near!

The renowned poet Oliver Wendell Holmes Sr. wrote these words in 1858, testifying to his deep religious beliefs. After its publication the poem became the subject of sermons on both sides of the Atlantic. Holmes explained that he wanted to convey a sense that God remained fast in his affection for the world and that all of creation should take comfort in that fact. The poem would later be set to a melody composed by Mozart.

I Am with Thee

Still, still with Thee, when purple morning breaketh,
When the bird waketh, and the shadows flee;
Fairer than morning, lovelier than daylight,
Dawns the sweet consciousness, I am with Thee.

Alone with Thee, amid the mystic shadows,
The solemn hush of nature newly born;
Alone with Thee in breathless adoration,
In the calm dew and freshness of the morn.

As in the dawning o'er the waveless ocean
The image of the morning star doth rest,
So in the stillness Thou beholdest only
Thine image in the waters of my breast.

Still, still with Thee, as to each newborn morning,
A fresh and solemn splendor still is given,
So does this blessed consciousness, awaking,
Breathe each day nearness unto Thee and Heaven.

When sinks the soul, subdued by toil, to slumber,
Its closing eye looks up to Thee in prayer;
Sweet the repose beneath the wings o'ershadowing,
But sweeter still to wake and find Thee there.

So shall it be at last, in that bright morning,
When the soul waketh, and life's shadows flee;
O in that hour, fairer than daylight dawning,
Shall rise the glorious thought, I am with Thee.

Harriet Beecher Stowe, the author of the historic and seminal novel *Uncle Tom's Cabin,* wrote hundreds of poems throughout her life, many of which attested to her deep piety, as this prayer shows. In old age she became an honored guest at the 1893 World's Parliament of Religions in Chicago, where representatives of the world's major religions met as a group for the first time. She came away with an even more profound faith in Divine Providence.

I Never Saw a Moor

I never saw a moor,
I never saw the sea;
Yet know I how the heather looks,
And what a wave must be.

I never spoke with God,
Nor visited in heaven;
Yet certain am I of the spot
As if the chart were given.

This two-stanza poem by Emily Dickinson has become one of her most loved and familiar pieces. Providing evidence of her succinct religious convictions, its simple logic affirms her belief in the existence of the Divine without the need for exacting, visible proof.

I Will Not Doubt

I will not doubt for evermore,
    Nor falter from a steadfast faith,
For though the system be turned o'er,
    God takes not back the word which once
    He saith.

I will not doubt the love untold
    Which not my worth nor want has bought,
Which wooed me young, and wooes me old,
    And to this evening hath me brought.

This excerpt is taken from Henry David Thoreau's essay "Inspiration." One of the great voices of the transcendental movement, Thoreau was anything but a traditionalist, but in this piece he expresses the need to trust in God's spiritual constancy in the world.

Jesus, Savior, Pilot Me

Jesus, Savior, pilot me
Over life's tempestuous sea;
Unknown waves before me roll,
Hiding rock and treach'rous shoal;
Chart and compass come from thee;
Jesus, Savior, pilot me!

As a mother stills her child,
Thou canst hush the ocean wild;
Boist'rous waves obey Thy will,
When Thou say'st to them, "Be still."
Wondrous Sov'reign of the sea,
Jesus, Savior, pilot me!

When at last I near the shore,
And the fearful breakers roar
'Twixt me and the peaceful rest,
Then, while leaning on Thy breast,
May I hear thee say to me,
"Fear not, I will pilot thee."

Presbyterian minister Edward Hopper originally wrote this testament of faith in 1871 for sailors, but over the years it has provided solace to people from all walks of life, both as a prayer and as a hymn. It was heralded as Hopper's lasting legacy and was sung at his funeral in 1888.

In the Sweet By and By

There's a land that is fairer than day,
And by faith we can see it afar,
For the Father waits over the way
To prepare us a dwelling place there.

We shall sing on that beautiful shore
The melodious songs of the blessed;
And our spirits shall sorrow no more,
Not a sigh for the blessing of rest.

To our bountiful Father above,
We will offer our tribute of praise
For the glorious gift of His love
And the blessings that hallow our days.

In the sweet by and by,
We shall meet on that beautiful shore;
In the sweet by and by,
We shall meet on that beautiful shore.

Written in 1868 by Sanford Bennett, the owner of a drugstore in Elkhorn, Wisconsin, these lines were put to music by his friend and customer Joseph Webster. It was Webster who provided Bennett with the inspiration when he walked into the drugstore one day, moping. When Bennett asked why he was so dejected, Webster responded, "It's no matter. It will be alright by and by." In a flash, Bennett began to write down the words and showed them to Webster, who then set them to music within thirty minutes. Over the next few years the hymn would become one of the most frequently sung hymns in churches across the country.

Soul Vision

Give no pity because my feet
Stumble along the dark, hard street,
And stub against the hostile stones,
Coldly deaf to the world's dumb moans.

The days move by on sullen wing
Like migrant birds that cannot sing,
Merging at last with a starless night,
Forever denied the gift of light.

Silent—I climb the anguished dark,
Still I can hear a heaven-bound lark.
Sightless—I see! And, seeing, find
Soul-vision though my eyes are blind!

This affirmation of faith and confidence in the Divine comes from one of the most prolific composers of religious music and lyrics in history, Fanny Crosby. Although she was blind from the time she was six weeks old due to a rare disease, she went on to work tirelessly on behalf of the poor and disabled, becoming one of the most renowned personalities of her day.

Nearer My God to Thee

Nearer, my God, to Thee,
Nearer to Thee!
E'en though it be a cross
That raiseth Thee!
Still all my song shall be,
Nearer, my God, to Thee,
Nearer to Thee!

Though like the wanderer,
The sun gone down,
Darkness be over me,
My rest a stone;
Yet in my dreams I'd be
Nearer, my God, to Thee,
Nearer to Thee!

There let my way appear
Steps unto heaven;
All that Thou sendest me
In mercy given;
Nearer, my God, to Thee,
Nearer to Thee!

Then, with my waking thoughts
Bright with Thy praise,
Out of my stony griefs,
Bethel I'll raise;
So by my woes to be
Nearer, my God, to Thee,
Nearer to Thee!

Or, if on joyful wing,
Cleaving the sky,
Sun, moon, and stars forgot,

Upward I fly,
Still all my song shall be
Nearer, my God, to Thee
Nearer to Thee!

The composer of this prayer, Sarah Flower Adams, was British,
but her lyrics, set to the music of renowned American musician
Lowell Mason, became part of American folklore. Legend has it
that this hymn was played by a group of ship musicians as the
Titanic sank. It was also performed at the funeral of President
James Garfield, and its verses reportedly were the last words of
President William McKinley, as he lay dying of an assassin's bullet.

It Is Well with My Soul

When peace, like a river,
attendeth my way,
When sorrows like sea billows roll;
Whatever my lot,
Thou hast taught me to say,
"It is well, it is well with my soul."

Though Satan should buffet,
though trials should come,
Let this blessed assurance control,
That Christ has regarded
my helpless estate,
And hath shed His own blood for my soul.

My sin, oh the bliss
of this glorious thought!
My sin, not in part but the whole,
Is nailed to the cross,
and I bear it no more,
Praise the Lord, praise the Lord, O my soul!

And Lord haste the day
when the faith shall be sight,
The clouds be rolled back as a scroll;
The trump shall resound,
and the Lord shall descend,
Even so, it is well with my soul.

It is well, with my soul.
It is well, with my soul.
It is well, it is well, with my soul.

Few American prayers have ever been composed under such dire circumstances as this piece. In 1871 Horatio Spafford, a successful lawyer and amateur hymnist, was mourning the death of his only son when a few months later, the historic and devastating Chicago fire wiped him out financially. Sending his family ahead to Europe in 1873, he learned that their ship had collided with another vessel. All four of his daughters drowned. His wife sent a two-word telegram that simply read "Survived Alone." As he set sail to meet his wife, he passed by the spot where his daughters had died and penned this extraordinary expression of trust in God.

His Eye Is on the Sparrow

Why should I feel discouraged,
Why should the shadows come,
Why should my heart be lonely
And long for Heav'n and home,
When Jesus is my portion?
My constant Friend is He:
His eye is on the sparrow,
And I know He watches me;
His eye is on the sparrow,
And I know he watches me.

"Let not your heart be troubled,"
His tender word I hear,
And resting on His goodness,
I lose my doubts and fears:
Tho' by the path He leadeth
But one step I may see:
His eye is on the sparrow,
And I know He watches me;
His eye is on the sparrow,
And I know He watches me.

Whenever I am tempted,
Whenever clouds arise,
When songs give place to sighing,
When hope within me dies,
I draw closer to Him,
From care He sets me free;
His eye is on the sparrow,
And I know He cares for me;
His eye is on the sparrow,
And I know He cares for me.

Civillia D. Martin was inspired to write this prayer in 1905 after she and her husband visited a severely disabled married couple in Elmira, New York. Amazed by their positive outlook, she could not help but ask how they managed to have such strong religious devotion. The wife responded, "His eye is on the sparrow, and I know He cares for me." Martin was so moved that she jotted down the woman's words and added some of her own. Later the poem was set to music by Iowa composer Charles Gabriel, and it reached its largest audiences after actress and gospel singer Ethel Waters made it her signature song.

Stand by Me

When the storms of life are raging,
Stand by me;
When the storms of life are raging,
Stand by me;
When the world is tossing me
Like a ship upon the sea
Thou Who rulest wind and water,
Stand by me.

In the midst of tribulation,
Stand by me;
In the midst of tribulation,
Stand by me.
When the hosts of hell assail,
And my strength begins to fail,
Thou Who never lost a battle,
Stand by me.

In the midst of faults and failures,
Stand by me;
In the midst of faults and failures,
Stand by me;
When I do the best I can,
and my friends misunderstand,
Thou who knowest all about me,
Stand by me.

When I'm growing old and feeble,
Stand by me;
When I'm growing old and feeble,
Stand by me;
When my life becomes a burden,
and I'm nearing chilly Jordan,
Oh thou Lily of the Valley,
Stand by me.

Charles Albert Tindley wrote this expression of reliance on Divine Providence and then set the words to music. Born into slavery, he went on to become a United Methodist minister and lead one of the largest African American congregations on the East Coast at his church in Philadelphia. Known as "the Prince of Preachers," Tindley became the first important gospel hymn writer and even launched his own publishing house to turn out copies of this new genre of American music. This hymn, one of the most recognizable of all gospel songs, reflected the difficult but resolute life of a remarkable man.

You Come to Me!

Out of need you come to me, O Father,
    Not as a spirit, gazing from on high,
Not as a wraith, gigantic in its outlines,
    Waiting against the tumult of the sky!
Father, you come to me in threads of music,
    And in the blessedness of whispered mirth,
And in the fragrance of frail garden flowers,
    When summer lies across the drowsy earth!

Out of my need you come to me, O Father,
    When I can scarcely see the path ahead—
It is your Hand that turns the sky, at evening,
    Into a sea of throbbing, pulsing red—
It is your call that sounds across the marshes,
    It is your smile that touches fields of grain,
Painting them with pale gold—it is your nearness
    That makes me see new beauty, after pain!

Out of my need you come to me, O Father—
    Not as a presence vast and great and still,
But as the purple mist that clings, each morning
    To the slim summit of a pine-crowned hill.

Not as a vague and awful power that urges,
  Urges and prods and hurries me along—
But as a hand that paints a lovely picture,
  But as a voice that sings a tender song!

In the earliest years of the twentieth century Margaret Sangster was ranked as America's favorite poet. She served as editor of *Harper's Bazaar, Hearth and Home,* and other magazines of the day, writing essays, short stories, and poems, many of which appealed directly to children. She gained her most lasting fame, however, for her lush, introspective spiritual reflections that transcended religious boundaries. As this prayer conveys, she believed that God appeared to her in every form and in every way to meet her daily needs.

O Lawd, I'm on My Way

I'm on my way to a Heav'nly Lan'
I'll ride dat long, long road.
If You are there to guide my han'.

Oh Lawd, I'm on my way.
I'm on my way to a Heav'nly Lan'—
. Oh Lawd. It's a long, long way, but
You'll be there to take my han'.

This piece, taken from George Gershwin's *Porgy and Bess,* is the last song of the opera and is sung into a crescendo by Porgy and the entire ensemble. While developing the opera over several months, Gershwin and novelist and lyricist DuBose Heyward explored the African American churches around Charleston, South Carolina, to observe their musical and religious heritage. Like the spirituals of the past, this finale communicates an unwavering belief in the promised land of Heaven.

Make Me Worthy of Thy Friendship

> Please, God, make me worthy of Thy friendship, for if I
> possess it, I know that no lasting harm can come to me. In
> Your friendship, I will grow to better manhood and be
> confident of eternal peace and happiness in Thy presence.

These simple words speak to heavyweight boxing champion
Gene Tunney's fundamental belief in God. Having mesmerized
the country in the 1920s with his bouts in the ring and by ultimately defeating world champion Jack Dempsey twice, he became one of the most admired figures in American sports of the
twentieth century. Few realized how deeply religious he was until his retirement from boxing.

Great Is Thy Faithfulness

> Great is Thy faithfulness, O God my Father;
> There is no shadow of turning with Thee;
> Thou changest not, Thy compassions, they fail not;
> As Thou hast been, Thou forever will be.
>
> Summer and winter and springtime and harvest,
> Sun, moon and stars in their courses above
> Join with all nature in manifold witness
> To Thy great faithfulness, mercy and love.
>
> Pardon for sin and a peace that endureth
> Thine own dear presence to cheer and to guide;
> Strength for today and bright hope for tomorrow,
> Blessings all mine, with ten thousand beside!
>
> Great is Thy faithfulness!
> Great is Thy faithfulness!
> Morning by morning new mercies I see.

All I have needed Thy hand hath provided;
Great is Thy faithfulness, Lord, unto me!

Born in a log cabin and without so much as a high school education, Thomas Obediah Chisholm wrote more than twelve hundred poems and became one of the most significant hymn writers of the twentieth century. This piece, written in 1923, was perhaps his most lasting legacy. Having led a difficult life, he firmly believed in God's covenant with humanity, to which this piece speaks so eloquently.

An Abiding Faith in Thee

To Thee, Oh God, Father of mankind, we come in deep humility, asking forgiveness for our sins. We have too often been selfish, unkind, and intolerant. May love for Thee and for our fellow men dominate and ennoble our lives! Give us to know the meaning of duty, the joy of service, the rewards of sacrifice. May even death have for us no fear so long as it be nobly met! And may we face the unknown, calm and unafraid, because of an abiding faith in Thee!

In the months before the end of World War II, John D. Rockefeller Jr. was asked to offer a prayer to be broadcast by radio across the country. Deeply religious, he believed that faith and prayer were indispensable to him in his everyday business life. In this piece the famous philanthropist asks for Divine insight and guidance.

Unconditional Trust

I turn to Thee as my partner and comrade. Stay close by and help me to be always near to Thee. With complete trust I put my loved ones and myself in Thy hands. I know that Thou wilt watch over them and me. Help me, to live, and if it be Thy will, to die as a Christian clean of soul and with love in my heart. Help me at all times to keep the faith.

Author of the wildly successful *The Power of Positive Thinking,* which was published in 1952, Dr. Norman Vincent Peale wrote this prayer long before he became one of the most recognizable personalities in the United States. As the longtime Reformed minister of the Marble Collegiate Church in New York City, he fervently espoused the need for people to lift their sights to God and to understand fully their enormous potential as God's instruments for good in the world.

America on Its Knees

Our Father in Heaven
We pray that You save us from ourselves.
The world that You have made for us, to live in peace,
we have made into an armed camp.
We live in fear of war to come.
We are afraid of "the terror that flies by night,
and the arrow that flies by day,
the pestilence that walks in darkness
and the destruction that wastes at noon-day."
We have turned from You to go our selfish way.
We have broken Your commandments and denied Your
truth.
We have left Your altars to serve the false gods of money
and
pleasure and power.

Forgive us and help us.
Now, darkness gathers around us and we are confused
in all our counsels.

Losing faith in You, we lose faith in ourselves.
Inspire us with wisdom, all of us of every color, race, and
    creed,
to use our wealth, our strength to help our brother,
instead of destroying him.
Help us to do Your will as it is done in heaven
and to be worthy of Your promise of peace on earth.
Fill us with new faith, new strength, and new courage,
that we may win the Battle for Peace.
Be swift to save us, dear God, before the darkness falls.

Hotel magnate Conrad Hilton wrote this prayer in 1951 as part of a speech he delivered in Chicago on the state of world affairs. Ominous in tone, it nonetheless conveys hope in the midst of the darkest days of the cold war based on a firm belief in the ultimate hand of Divine Providence. A few weeks later Hilton read the prayer live on NBC, and the response was overwhelming. It was estimated that over 200,000 Americans had the prayer framed in their homes. Given its popularity, Hilton made sure that copies of it were made for every room of his hotels around the world.

Elvis's Prayer

Send me some light—I need it.

Throughout his career the intensely spiritual Elvis Presley continuously asked for God's help, always searching for answers in his spiritual quest. Before each performance, he would find a quiet corner offstage, clear his mind, and offer this one-line prayer.

Master of Insight and Beauty

Master of beauty, craftsman of the snowflake,
inimitable contriver,
endower of Earth so gorgeous & different from the boring
    Moon,
thank you for such as it is my gift.

I have made up a morning prayer to you
containing with precision everything that most matters.
'According to Thy will' the thing begins.
It took me off & on two days. It does not aim at eloquence.

You have come to my rescue again & again
in my impassable, sometimes despairing years.
You have allowed my brilliant friends to destroy
    themselves
and I am still here, severely damaged, but functioning.

Unknowable, as I am unknown to my guinea pigs:
how can I 'love' you?
I only as far as gratitude & awe
confidently & absolutely go.

I have no idea whether we live again.
It doesn't seem likely
from either the scientific or the philosophical point of
    view
but certainly all things are possible to you,

and I believe as fixedly in the Resurrection-appearances to
    Peter and to Paul
as I believe I sit in this blue chair.
Only that may have been a special case
to establish their initiatory faith.

Whatever your end may be, accept my amazement.
May I stand until death forever at attention
for any your least instruction or enlightenment.
I even feel sure you will assist me again, Master of insight
    & beauty.

The first in his "Eleven Addresses to the Lord," this prayer by
Oklahoma-born poet John Berryman offers an unvarnished testament to faith that sets the tone for the rest of his "addresses."
When he was twelve years old his father committed suicide, and
the experience drove him to become highly introspective. It was
this quality that would be infused throughout his writings, and
lead to his receiving every literary award possible, from the
Pulitzer Prize to the National Book Award.

PETITION AND HOPE

Let Me Always Be the Same

Sun, my relative,
as you rise, be good to me.
Bring good things to us.
Give me strength to work,
so that I can be strong in the garden,
so that I can hoe, plant corn, and water my fields.
Sun, my relative,
as you go down, be good to me,
as we lay down to sleep,
give me peace.
As I sleep, may you come up again.
May you go on your course many times,
Making good things happen for people.
Let me be always the same as I am now.

This humble prayer is part of the eight-hundred-year heritage of
the nomadic Havasupai Indian tribe of the southern rim of the
Grand Canyon. It asks for nothing extraordinary, simply the
ability to lead a normal daily life.

Anticipating the New Day

> Earth our mother, breathe forth life
> all night sleeping
> now awaking
> in the east
> now see the dawn.
>
> Earth, our mother, breathe and waken
> leaves are stirring
> all things moving
> new day coming
> life renewing.

Anticipating the beginning of a new dawn, this prayer comes from the Pawnee tribe whose territory once spanned modern-day Nebraska and Kansas. Like other Native American peoples, the Pawnee would rise each morning from their lodges, face the east, and give praise and thanks, eagerly awaiting the day before them.

For Guidance

Dear Lord, Jesus! Thou that knowest my works! Help! Help! Help a poor creature, I earnestly beseech thee, so to improve his time as shall be most for thy glory, the good of thy people, and the rejoicing of his own soul, in that day when I shall see, my Lord, and speak with thee face to face! Amen! Amen! Amen!

My purpose, by thy help, O, Lord!, is to spend my time every day as followeth: . . .

Reverend Increase Mather, who was one of the most prominent colonial fathers, regularly spent hours in his study preparing his schedule for the week ahead, partly through prayer and meditation. In this piece, he laid out his petition to God for inspiration and support and then proceeded to write down his seven-day agenda.

Supplications

That I may be preserved from atheism and infidelity, impiety and profaneness, and in my addresses to Thee carefully avoid irreverence and ostentation, formality and odious hypocrisy,

Help me, O Father

That I may be loyal to my Prince, and faithful to my country, careful for its Good, valiant in its defense, and obedient to its laws, abhorring treason as much as tyranny,

Help me, O Father

That I may to those above me be dutiful, humble, and submissive, avoiding pride, disrespect, and contumacy,

Help me, O Father

That I may be sincere in friendship, faithful in Trust, and impartial in judgment, watchful against pride, and against anger (that momentary madness),

Help me, O Father

That I may possess integrity and evenness of mind, resolution in difficulties, and fortitude under affliction; that I may be punctual in performing my promises, peaceable and prudent in my behavior,

Help me, O Father

That I may have a constant regard to honor and probity; that I may possess a perfect innocence and a good conscience, and at length become truly virtuous and magnanimous,

Help me, Good God
Help me, O Father

As a young man Benjamin Franklin penned a number of prayers that not only represented his sense of the Almighty but collectively served as moral benchmarks by which he should chart his life. This particular invocation, written long before the Revolutionary War, became part of a published work he would call *Articles of Belief and Acts of Religion*.

Acts of Hope

O, my God! in all my dangers temporal and spiritual I will hope in thee who art Almighty power, and therefore able to relieve me; who art infinite goodness, and therefore ready and willing to assist me.

O precious blood of my dear Redeemer! O gaping wounds of my crucified Saviour! Who can contemplate the sufferings of God incarnate, and not raise his hope, and not put his trust in him. What though my body be crumbled into dust, and that dust blown over the face of the earth, yet I undoubtedly know my Redeemer lives, and shall raise me up at the last day; whether I am comforted or left desolate; whether I enjoy peace or am afflicted with temptations, whether I am healthful or sickly, succoured or abandoned by the good things of this life, I will always hope in thee, O my chiefest, infinite good.

Although the fig-tree shall not blossom, neither shall fruit be in the vines; although the labor of the olive shall fail, and the fields yield no meat; although the flock shall be cut off from the fold, and there shall be no herd in the stalls, yet I will rejoice in the Lord, I will joy in the God of my salvation.

What though I mourn and am afflicted here, and sigh under the miseries of this world for a time, I am sure that my tears shall one day be turned into joy, and that joy none shall take from me.

Whoever hopes for the great things in this world, takes pains to attain them; how can my hopes of everlasting life be well ground, if I do not strive and labor for that eternal inheritance? I will never refuse the meanest labors, while I look to receive such glorious wages; I will never repine at any temporal loss, while I expect to gain such eternal rewards. Blessed hope! be thou my chief delight in life, and then I shall be steadfast and immoveable, always abounding in the work of the Lord, be thou my comfort and support at the hour of death, and then I shall contentedly leave this world, as a captive that is released from his imprisonment.

Taken from the addendum to Reverend Richard Allen's posthumous 1833 autobiography, this prayer was one of three he wrote on the moral virtues of faith, hope, and love. It was intended to be part of "an address to the people of colour of the United States." Born into slavery, Allen bought his freedom by the time he reached twenty-five. He went on to become one of the most forceful voices for African Americans in the new republic, founding the African Methodist Episcopal Church.

Father of Love

Father of love, Father above,
Send down the blessing upon each head,
Shield us from pride while we here abide
Give us this day our daily bread.

Stephen Collins Foster, the composer of such American classics as "My Old Kentucky Home" and "Oh! Susanna," struggled throughout his adult life with finances and alcoholism. One source of quick income was writing lyrics and music for use in churches and Sunday schools. This song was one of his most popular religious pieces.

Swing Low, Sweet Chariot

Swing low, sweet chariot
Coming for to carry me home
Swing low, sweet chariot
Coming for to carry me home.

I looked over Jordan and what did I see
Coming for to carry me home
A band of angels coming after me
Coming for to carry me home

If you get there before I do
Coming for to carry me home
Tell all my friends I'm coming too
Coming for to carry me home

If I get there before you do
Coming for to carry me home
I'll cut a hole and pull you through
Coming for to carry me home.

Sometimes I'm up and sometimes I'm down
Coming for to carry me home
But still my soul feels heavenly bound
Coming for to carry me home.

This well-known spiritual, believed to have originated from one of the larger Southern plantations, radiates religious conviction in the midst of human bondage. Although the lyrics may seem to refer to the journey to freedom by means of the Underground Railroad, they most likely were intended to conjure the vision of the Old Testament prophet Elijah being taken up to Heaven in a fiery chariot by a band of angels.

Do for Me, God

Oh, God, you know I have no money, but you can make the people do for me, and you must make the people do for me. I will never give you peace till you do, God.

The indefatigable Sojourner Truth, the former slave who became outspoken in her defense of human dignity, often spoke to God in a no-nonsense way. She believed that if she was to do God's work on earth, Divine Providence should be with her each step of the way.

A Cowboy's Prayer

O Lord, I've never run where churches grow,
I've always loved Creation better as it stood
That day you finished it, so long ago,
And looked upon your work, and found it good.
I know that others might find You in the light
That's sifted down through tinted window panes,
And yet I seem to feel You near tonight.

Let me be easy on the man that's down
And make me square and generous with all;
I'm careless sometimes, Lord, when I'm in town
But never let them call me mean or small.
Make me as big and open as the plains,
As honest as the hoss between my knees,
Clean as the wind that blows behind the rains,
Free as the hawk that circles down the breeze!

I thank you, Lord, that I am placed so well,
That you made my freedom so complete;
That I'm no slave to whistle, clock, or bell,

Nor weak-eyed prisoner of wall and street.
Just let me live my life as I've begun
And give me work that is open to the sky;
Make me a pardner of the wind and sun,
And I won't ask for a life that's soft or high.

Forgive me, Lord, if sometimes I forget.
You know about the reasons that are hid.
You understand the things that gall and fret;
You know me better than my mother did.
Just keep an eye on all that's done and said
And right me, sometimes, when I turn aside,
And guide me on the long, dim trail ahead
That stretched upward toward the Great Divide.

Known as "A Cowboy's Prayer," this endearing piece was written by Badger Clark, who later in life would be named the first poet laureate of South Dakota. Clark's simple poem candidly lays out his spiritual retrospections to God while asking for understanding and guidance in his rugged life on the plains.

Pitching Prayer

O Lord,
give us some coaching
out at this tabernacle
so that people
can be brought home to You.
Some of them are dying, Lord,
and we don't want that.
Lord, have the people play the game of life
right up to the limit
so that home runs
may be scored.

One of the most colorful religious figures of the early twentieth century was the Reverend William Ashley "Billy" Sunday. Having pitched for the Chicago White Stockings and professional teams in Pittsburgh and Philadelphia early in his career, he underwent a religious conversion that would lead to his giving up baseball and launching his own ministry. Abhorring "stale" prayers, the charismatic Sunday enjoyed nothing more than to offer prayers in baseball metaphors, urging his followers to "shove in some shouts" when they addressed the Lord.

I Can!

> O God, I cried, no dark disguise
> Can e'er hereafter hide from me
> Thy radiant identity!
> Thou canst not move across the grass
> But my quick eyes will see Thee pass,
> Nor speak, however silently,
> But my hushed voice will answer Thee.
> I know the path that tells Thy way
> Through the cool eve of every day;
> God, I can push the grass apart
> And lay my finger on Thy heart!

The publication of *Renascence and Other Poems* in 1917 created a literary sensation for the young author Edna St. Vincent Millay, whose budding talent was heralded by critics everywhere. This prayer, taken from her major poem "Renascence," underscores her self-confidence in setting out to achieve her goals.

Prayer for Fair Weather

Almighty and merciful Father, we humbly beseech Thee, of Thy great goodness, to restrain these immoderate rains with which we have had to contend. Grant us fair weather for Battle. Graciously hearken to us as soldiers who call upon Thee that, armed with Thy power, we may advance from victory to victory, and crush the oppression and wickedness of our enemies, and establish Thy justice among men and nations. Amen.

Just before Christmas 1944 General George Patton's Third Army became bogged down by the merciless winter sleet and rain as the Allies made their final advance on Berlin toward the end of World War II. Facing uncertainty and growing morale problems, General Patton asked his chaplain, Brigadier General James O'Neil, to compose a prayer asking for better weather that could be printed on Christmas cards to be distributed to all of his soldiers. Within hours after the men received their card, the fog and foul weather broke, and more than 230,000 troops proceeded with the offensive.

Father, Save Us from Ourselves

Our Father, who has set a restlessness in our hearts and made us all seekers after that which we can never fully find, forbid us to be satisfied with what we make of life. Draw us from base content and set our eyes on far-off goals. Keep us at tasks too hard for us that we may be driven to Thee for strength. Deliver us from fretfulness and self-pitying; make us sure of the good we cannot see and of the hidden good in the world. Open our eyes to simple beauty all around us and our hearts to the loveliness men hide from us because we do not try to understand them. Save us from ourselves and show us a vision of the world made new.

This is the prayer that Eleanor Roosevelt wrote and recited before she went to bed each night. Her son Elliott would recall how his mother would go through the same rituals each evening from combing her hair to pulling on a certain nightgown and then getting on her knees to ask for God's blessing in her own very unique way.

Prayer at the End of a Rope

Dear Lord, observe this bended knee
This visage meek and humble,
And heed this confidential plea,
Voiced in a reverent mumble.

I ask no miracles nor stunts,
No heavenly radiogram;
I only beg for once, just once
To not be in a jam.

One little moment thy servant craves
Of being his own master;
One placid vale between the waves
Of duty and disaster.
Oh, when the postman's whistle shrills,
Just once, Lord, let me grin:
Let me have settled last month's bills
Before this month's come in.

Let me not bite more off this cob
Than I have teeth to chew;
Please let me finish just one job
Before the next is due.

Consider, too, my social life
Sporadic though it may be;

Why is it only mental strife
That pleasure brings to me?

For months, when people entertain,
Me they do not invite;
Then suddenly invitations rain,
All for the self-same night.

R.S.V.P.'s I pray thee send
Alone and not in bunches,
Or teach me I cannot attend
Two dinners or two lunches.

Let me my hostess not insult
Not call her diamonds topaz;
Else harden me to the result
Of my fantastic faux pas.

One little lull, Lord, that's my plea,
Then loose the storm again;
Just once, this once I begot be
Not in a jam.

The *Atlantic Monthly* once referred to the droll and urbane Ogden Nash as "God's gift to the United States." He filled his rich life by writing plays, television scripts, musical comedies, and hundreds of poems. In this prayer he good-humoredly asks Divine Providence to provide some calm in the midst of the frustrations of daily life.

To See My Shortcomings

I know that You alone have created me—created me spiritually in Your own image and likeness. I know that You guide and protect me every second. It is I who have wandered from Your love and care, and, at times, "forgetteth what manner of man I am"—seeing but dimly in the mirror.

I sincerely desire to see clearly my shortcomings, my faults, my sins. I earnestly pray to be humble, obedient and loving in order that I may inherit here and now and forever my divine sonship, to be worthy to walk with Thee.

Mary Pickford, one of the legends of the early film industry, composed this prayer after she retired as "America's Sweetheart" from silent movies and from her responsibilities as cofounder of United Artists. It was during her later years, after overcoming alcoholism, that she became particularly religious, sharing her spiritual reflections in her 1934 book *Why Not Try God?* from which this excerpt was taken.

Two Favorite Prayers

Please . . .

Please . . .

Please.

AND

Thank you . . .

Thank you . . .

Thank you.

These probably are the two most favorite prayers of Americans in some form or other. Often the second one is said for the opportunity to return to the first one at a later date.

Longing for More Time

I don't know what you want, but if you want me to go, well then I'm going to do just that. But if you can see your way clear to let me live, I've got some music to make and some children to raise here and I'd sure love to have the chance to do it.

After twenty years of alcohol and drug abuse, David Crosby, the rhythm guitarist for the Byrds and later a member of Crosby, Stills, Nash and Young, was on the verge of death, needing an emergency liver transplant. Awaiting his surgery and learning that his wife was pregnant with their child, he said this prayer and would become well again.

Supplication

O God, please help me
In my hour of awe.
Show me how to cease
The turbulent thoughts
In my tormented mind.
Please let me find
Peace and harmony.
Don't tear me apart
From the roots of love,
Leaving behind
Only my crushed, bleeding heart.

Almighty, upon You I call,
Please heal my suffering soul.
Let me accomplish my mission and goal
On this earth,
Assigned by You for me
At the time of my birth.
Send my way the Spirit of Creativity

And let me enter
The miraculous world of fantasy,
Where I can be free
Of worry and anxiety.

I am not young anymore,
I can't tell how many more years
Are for me in store.
Therefore, let me manifest
My innate true personality,
So I can become the person I was destined to be.
Help me to develop fully
The talents You bestowed upon me.
Open wide for me
The portals of imagination
So I can project the beauty
Of Your creation.
Let me teach the value of affection,
Kindness, and compassion.
Assist me to instill faith
And belief in Your Divine Power
In the heart of man
The best I can,
Through each waking hour.

Let me convey the strengths of prayer
And supplication
On my temporary earthly station.
You saved me so many times,
Ringing for me time and time again
Existence's chimes.
You helped me to keep up my strife
Through the most difficult episodes of my life,
Giving me endurance and persistence,
Increasing my resistance
To hardships, suffering, and emotional strain,

Reviving constantly my vitality.
Don't let me be caught in the trap
Of painful emotion.
Don't let pride and conceit
Cloud my reason.
Don't lock me into
Vanity's dark prison
Where the walls of reasoning break,
From where there is no escape
From the burning passions
Of revenge, intolerance, and cruelty.
Steer me away from the world of calamity,
Pettiness, and greed.

I look for a place
Where goodness dwells,
Where happiness and contentment reside.
My Creator, please be my Guide.
Let my human eyes behold
That heavenly blessed paradise
Where the spirit never dies.

As a young girl Magda Herzberger was forced from her home in Cluj, Romania, and was shipped off to the Nazi death camp of Auschwitz and then to the camps of Bremen and Bergen-Belsen. Unlike other members of her family, she somehow survived. With her husband, Eugene, a neurosurgeon, she settled in the new State of Israel, then immigrated to the United States in 1957. Having reached sixty years of marriage and a full life in Arizona, she shares with God here how she has overcome serious obstacles in the past, and how she looks forward to the challenges of the future.

THANKSGIVING AND APPRECIATION

We Return Thanks

We return thanks to our mother,
the earth, which sustains us.
We return thanks to the rivers and streams
which supply us with water.
We return thanks to all herbs, which furnish medicines
for the cure of our diseases.
We return thanks to the corn, and to her sisters,
the beans and squashes, which give us life.
We return thanks to the bushes and trees,
which provide us with fruit.
We return thanks to the wind,
which, moving the air, has banished diseases.
We return thanks to the moon and the stars,
which have given us their light when the sun was gone.
We return thanks to our grandfather He-no,
that he has protected his grandchildren from witches and
    reptiles,
and has given us his rain.
We return thanks to the sun,

that he has looked upon the earth with a beneficent eye.
Lastly, we return thanks to the Great Spirit,
in whom is embodied all goodness,
and who directs all things for the good of his children.

This Iroquois prayer of thanks has been invoked for generations. The tribes of the Iroquois confederation of Five Nations, located in what is now the northeastern United States, as well as Ontario and Quebec, have always been distinguished for their deep-seated spirituality. They believed that the Great Spirit guided them both in their daily lives and in their dreams.

In Gratitude

We thank you, God, for the moments of fulfillment;
The end of a day's work,
The harvest of sugarcane,
The birth of a child,
For in these pauses we feel the rhythm of the eternal.
    Amen

Long before Europeans and settlers from the American mainland arrived on the islands of Hawaii, in part to convert the natives to Christianity, the Hawaiian people had developed an extraordinarily deep spirituality. In creating their own rites of worship, they were particularly mindful of their blessings, as this simple prayer shows.

Deliverance from Another Sore Fit

In my distress I sought the Lord
When naught on earth could comfort give,
And when my soul these things abhorred,
Then, Lord, Thou said'st unto me, "Live."

Thou knowest the sorrows that I felt;
My plaints and groans were heard of Thee,
And how in sweat I seemed to melt
Thou help'st and Thou regardest me.

My wasted flesh Thou didst restore,
My feeble loins didst gird with strength,
Yea, when I was most low and poor,
I said I shall praise Thee at length.

What shall I render to my God
For all His bounty showed to me?
Even for His mercies in His rod,
Where pity most of all I see.

My heart I wholly give to Thee;
O make it fruitful, faithful Lord.
My life shall dedicated be
To praise in thought, in deed, in word.

Thou know'st no life I did require
Longer than still Thy name to praise,
Nor ought on earth worthy desire,
In drawing out these wretched days.

Thy name and praise to celebrate,
O Lord, for aye is my request.
O grant I do it in this state,
And then with Thee, which is the best.

Considered America's first true poet, Anne Bradstreet brought to life the experiences of colonial America through her prayers and poetry. Her eloquent spiritual musings in particular won her critical acclaim. Here she expresses her gratitude for having survived another serious fainting spell during one of two ill-fated pregnancies.

Thanks

> For Peace and Liberty, for Food and Raiment, for Corn and
> Wine, and Milk, and every kind of Healthful Nourishment,
>> *Good God, I thank Thee.*
> For the Common Benefits of Air and Light, for useful Fire
> and delicious water,
>> *Good, God, I thank Thee.*
> For Knowledge and Literature and every useful Art; for my
> Friends and their Prosperity, and for the fewness of my
> Enemies,
>> *Good God, I thank Thee.*
> For all Thy innumerable Benefits; for Life and Reason, and
> the Use of Speech, for Health and Joy and every Pleasant
> Hour,
>> *My Good God, I thank Thee.*

According to his *Articles of Belief,* which he wrote at the age of
twenty-two, Benjamin Franklin considered among his "first
principles" the need to "pay Divine Regards" to the "Author and
Owner of our System." Despite being labeled by some historians
as a hardcore deist, it is clear from the expanse of his writings
that he believed in the human need for prayer. In this particular
prayer he included a prelude noting that "ingratitude is one of
the most odious of vices" and that he wanted to avoid being "un-
mindful gratefully to acknowledge the favors I receive from
Heaven."

Quicken Our Gratitude

> Lord, for the erring thought
> Not unto evil wrought:
> Lord, for the wicked will
> Betrayed, and baffled still:

For the heart from itself kept,
Our thanksgiving accept.
For ignorant hopes that were
Broken to our blind prayer:
For pain, death, sorrow, sent
Unto our chastisement:
For all loss of seeming good,
Quicken our gratitude.

This prayer, taken from William Dean Howell's 1880 book *The Undiscovered Country,* helped to develop the novel's central theme of probing the country's spirituality, particularly through the Shaker religion. Arguably the most influential publisher and editor of the nineteenth century, he particularly was fascinated by the seemingly insatiable drive of Americans to relate to God.

Song of Gratitude

Dear Lord, I thank Thee, that I did not get
        An answer to my prayer of long ago.
In looking back, I see I asked amiss
        In praying for the things I longed for so.
I should have prayed to trust Thy wisdom more.
        To know Thy ways were better far than mine.
How blind we are, when stubborn human will
        Obscures the perfect plan of Love's design!

I thank Thee that in spite of my mistakes
        Thy hand was always there to bring me through,
And keep me steady, when my wayward feet
        Brought me in greater danger than I knew.
Oh keep me from our own undoing, Lord!
        So many times we might have slipped, and gone,
So many times we might have missed the way.
        Had not Thy tender mercy led us on.

I thank Thee that a prayer which is not right
    Love does not answer; for, if what seems best
To blind, misguided sense should have its way,
    One might be ruined at his own request!
That futile, selfish prayer of long ago
    Was never prayer at all, as now I see.
Today I have but one supreme desire,
    To go with joy wher'er God leadeth me.

For now each hour His purposes unfold
    Like flower petals smiling in the sun,
I can but lay the finger on the lip
    And count my blessings when the day is done.
Oh, well may those rejoice who, pressing on,
    Come to the milestone in the journey where
They lay at His dear throne their human will,
    And learn the reason for unanswered prayer.

One of the finest Christian Science writers in the earliest days of the church was Louise Wheatley Hovnanian. This prayer is a rather refreshing, unique offer of thanksgiving for prayers unanswered. She clearly understands that a loving God's infinite wisdom should always prevail.

Upon Seeing a Sunset

O God, I thank Thee for such direct manifestation of Thy goodness, majesty, and power!

Inventor, scientist, and social activist George Washington Carver believed that human knowledge and the hand of God were inextricably linked. While one could not test a personal relationship with God to the satisfaction of individuals through human quantification, he believed in the existence of an Almighty and that Divine Providence had a plan for everyone. In composing this simple expression of thanksgiving, Carver was recording his reactions in witnessing a spectacular sunset not far from his laboratory at Tuskegee University in Alabama.

Thank God for God

The roar of the world is in my ears,
Thank God for the roar of the world!
Thank God for the mighty tide of fears
Against me always hurled!
Thank God for the bitter and ceaseless strife.
And the sting of His chastening rod!
Thank God for the stress and pain of life,
And oh, thank God for God!

American poet Joyce Kilmer was a convert to Catholicism, and his faith came to permeate almost every aspect of his life. He and his wife, Aline, also a poet, became particularly devout after their daughter was diagnosed with infantile paralysis. Despite the problems they faced, the Kilmers continuously conveyed in their writings their gratitude to God for all that they had received in life, as this prayer shows.

i Thank You God

i thank You God for most this amazing
Day: for the leaping greenly spirits of trees
And a blue true dream of sky; and for everything
Which is natural which is infinite which is yes

(i who have died am alive again today,
and this is the sun's birthday; this is the birth
day of life and of love and wings: and of the gay
great happening illimitably earth)

how should tasting touching hearing seeing
breathing any—lifted from the no
of all nothing—human merely being
doubt unimaginable You?

(now the ears of my ears awake and
now the eyes of my eyes are opened)

The son of a Harvard professor and Unitarian minister, e. e. cummings was steeped in academia and liberal spirituality. With his trademark punctuation and mostly lowercase writing, this preeminent twentieth-century poet expressed gratitude for being awakened through all his senses to the reality of God.

Our Daily Bread

For all I have had this day I bless and thank Thee, O Lord. At no time has my need been left unsatisfied; only in those hours when I turned from Thee have I known want. I thank Thee, dear Lord and Master, for all that this day my brethren have shared with me. I thank Thee for sun and air, for house and food, for dear ones and friends, for every hour that has been mine. I thank Thee, also, for the hours of pain and stress that have widened my understanding. I thank Thee for the darkness that has made me see the light more clearly. I thank Thee for the enmity that has taught me to forgive.

How rich I am! How much hast Thou given me. Each day is added to all I already have. How generously hast Thou dealt with me! From the hour of my birth to this evening hour so much, so much hast Thou given me I cannot count it, I can but humbly thank Thee for Thyself: my daily bread.

Glory be to Thee, O Christ our God.

Mother Alexandra, who was born Princess Ileana to the royal house of Romania, immigrated to the United States after she and her family were forced into exile by the Communist government two decades earlier. Profoundly religious, she established her own order of nuns under the Orthodox Church of America. This prayer was one in a series of her reflections on the true meaning of the "Lord's Prayer."

This Day Is Yours

Dear God,

The sun is coming up, so I thank You for another beautiful day in my life.

Please reveal to me what You have planned this day. I am ready to serve and support You.

I usually am asking for my personal wishes, but this day is yours. Allow me to see where I may bring Your presence to people and to situations as my day unfolds. Open my eyes and my ears to Your message so I may share Your love with those in my life.

In all things You place before me, I know You are there helping me. And so as I proceed through this day, our day together, allow me to be your instrument in bringing comfort, courage, and hope to those in my path.

Thank you, God, for listening to my prayer. I will be in frequent touch this day. And thank You for all the blessings and miracles that I know will be revealed along the way.

I know this will be a wonderful day. How could it be otherwise for never am I alone . . . You are with me always.

This prayer of gratitude, written by Marie Gallo of the Ernest and Julio Gallo family in Modesto, California, combines words with action. Marie Gallo has dedicated much of her life to social and religious causes. For more than two decades she has held a popular annual religious retreat in Northern California for people of all religious faiths in which prayer has been a central focus.

On the Commuter Flight to Rochester

Content to be absorbed in my own distant thoughts, You
    upset me.
You turned my world upside down.

A little boy is carried aboard the plane in the arms of his
    father;
His eyes roll back, unaware of his surroundings, clutching
    a stuffed animal;
Visibly wearied, his father lovingly buckles him in;
They need your healing.

An elderly, natty woman easily makes her way to Seat 7A;
Her gait belies her condition, a strange green plastic cap,
    covering her bald head;
Alone but smiling, she remains confident before another
    round of chemotherapy;
She depends on your continued care.

A young man sits across the aisle in a baseball cap, light
    wool Michigan State pajamas;
His thin arms show skin abrasions, giving off an odor,
    holding up his head—barely;
A caring, overweight nurse steadies him in flight;
He stands at your doorstep.

These images swirl in my head as I stare at Your floor of clouds, listening to the quiet hum of propeller engines. Jarred, I do not focus my thoughts on my good fortune or try to deaden the images by turning away. No, I am fixed on him, on her, on them, and on You. When? Where? Why? How?

Landing in Rochester, the attendant clocks the local time, opens a front cabin door, and matches crutch to owner as she proceeds down the aisle. How had I missed the others? Have we arrived in Lourdes?

In the midst of Your great mystery, I cannot explain away Your plan for this human family of ours. All I know is that You have opened my eyes.

No longer will I be able to be disengaged or remain indifferent. You have changed me forever. Never to see my fellow passengers again, I instinctively know that they now are a part of me forever. Never can they be dislodged.

Thank you, God, for opening unknown gates to my compassion. Work needs to be done.

This prayer was composed after James P. Moore Jr., its author, flew to Rochester, Minnesota, to address the physicians, researchers, staff, and patients of the world-famous Mayo Clinic. The thoughts expressed here focus on gratitude to God for a rude awakening to human realities and the infirmities of others.

WISDOM, UNDERSTANDING, AND HUMILITY

Teach Me

Earth teach me stillness
As the grasses are stilled with light.
Earth teach me suffering
As old stones suffer with memory.
Earth teach me humility
As blossoms are humble with beginning.
Earth teach me caring
As the mother who secures her young.
Earth teach me courage
As the tree which stands all alone.
Earth teach me limitation
As the ant which crawls on the ground.
Earth teach me freedom
As the eagle which soars in the sky.
Earth teach me resignation
As the leaves which die in the fall.
Earth teach me regeneration
As the seed which rises in the spring.
Earth teach me to forget myself

As melted snow forgets its life.
Earth teach me to remember kindness
As dry fields weep with rain.

This ancient prayer from the Ute tribe, whose land encompassed what is today Utah and Colorado, speaks to the need for wisdom in all things. While people of the Native American nations and tribes had not developed a religious identity in the way European settlers had done, they nonetheless were deeply spiritual. Their prayers always appealed to a higher power as the major force in their lives and in nature.

Prayer for Appreciation

Oh Great Spirit, Whose voice I hear in the winds, and whose breath gives life to all the world, hear me. I am a man before You, one of Your many children—I am small and weak. I need your strength and wisdom. Let me walk in beauty and make my eyes ever behold the red and purple sunset. Make my hands respect the things You have made, my ears sharp to hear Your voice. Make me wise, so that I may know the things you have taught my people—the lesson you have hidden in every leaf and rock. I seek strength not to be superior to my brothers, but to be able to fight my greatest enemy—myself. Make me ever ready to come to You with clean hands and straight eyes, so when life fades as a fading sunset my spirit may come to You without shame.

This invocation for empathy for others and a greater respect for the wonders of the world was invoked by members of the Sioux Nation throughout the Dakotas. In 1887 Chief Yellow Lark of the Lakota, one of the seven tribes that make up the Sioux, translated it into English for the first time.

In Search of Empathy

> O, God, help us not to despise or oppose what we do not
> understand.

William Penn, the founder of the Pennsylvania Colony, was a convert to the Quaker faith and became passionate in his promotion of tolerance, opening Pennsylvania to individuals of all faiths and backgrounds. In this prayer he speaks of tolerance in the midst of human differences.

O Fountain of Wisdom

O Powerful Goodness! Bountiful Father! Merciful Guide!
Increase in me that Wisdom which discovers my truest Interests;

Strengthen my Resolutions to perform what that Wisdom
dictates.

Accept my kind Offices to Thy other Children, as the only Return
in my Power for Thy continual Favours to me.

In Benjamin Franklin's much heralded *Autobiography,* the Founding Father wrote, "Conceiving God to be the Fountain of Wisdom, I thought it right and necessary to solicit His assistance for obtaining it." This short prayer, taken from that work, was created by Franklin to recite as part of his regular daily regimen.

Live a Humble

Live a-humble, humble
Humble, yourselves, the bells done ring
Glory and honor!
Praise King Jesus!
Glory and honor!
Praise the Lord!
Watch the sun, how steady he runs
Don't let him catch you with your work undone

Live a-humble, humble
Humble, yourselves, the bells done ring
Glory and honor!
Praise King Jesus!
Glory and honor!
Praise the Lord!
Ever see such a man as God?
He gave up His Son for to come and die
Gave up His Son for to come and die
Just to save my soul from a burning fire

Live a-humble, humble
Humble, yourselves, the bells done ring
Glory and honor!
Praise King Jesus!
Glory and honor!
Praise the Lord!
See God and you see God in the morning
He'll come riding down the line of time
The fire'll be falling
He'll be calling, "Come to judgment, come."

Using the word "humble" as a noun, this African American spiritual combines devotion to God with total self-effacement. In order to serve God with true devotion, the prayer admonishes its listener to never forget that God is ever present, as the ringing bells remind the faithful. In the end a life of righteousness is the only true path to salvation.

Guide Us

> We thank Thee, O God, for a Prophet
> To guide us in these latter days.
> We thank Thee for sending the Gospel
> To lighten our mind with its rays.

Eliza Snow, one of the most celebrated Mormon leaders in history, was prolific in her spiritual writings, particularly in composing prayers and hymns. Known as "the poetess of Zion," she became an important voice for the Church of Jesus Christ of Latter Day Saints, and her influence continues to this day.

Holy Spirit, Truth Divine

> Holy Spirit, Truth divine,
> dawn upon this soul of mine;
> Breath of God and inward Light
> wake my spirit, clear my sight.
>
> Holy Spirit, Love divine,
> glow within this heart of mine;
> kindle every high desire;
> perish self in thy pure fire.
>
> Holy Spirit, Power divine
> fill and nerve this will of mine;
> by thee may I strongly live,
> bravely bear and nobly strive.

Holy Spirit, Right divine,
King within my conscience reign;
be my Lord, and I shall be
firmly bound, forever free.

Holy Spirit, Peace divine,
still this restless heart of mine;
speak to calm this tossing sea,
stayed in thy tranquility.

Holy Spirit, Joy divine,
gladden thou this heart of mine;
in the desert ways I sing,
"Spring, O Well, forever spring."

Samuel Longfellow, a Unitarian preacher, composed this classic prayer during the Civil War. In his continuous search for divine insight, the younger brother of American poet Henry Wadsworth Longfellow wrote dozens of hymns that were genuine reflections of his personal quest for spiritual truths.

O, My Savior!

Savior! I've no one else to tell—
And so I trouble thee.
I am the one forgot thee so—
Dost thou remember me?
Nor, for myself, I came so far—
That were the little load—
I brought thee the imperial Heart
I had not strength to hold.
The Heart I carried in my own—
Till mine too heavy grew—

Yet—strangest—heavier since it went—
Is it too large for you?

Emily Dickinson yearned to find answers in her search for a higher, spiritual truth. As she expresses in this prayer, she was saddened that she had not been more firmly anchored in her relationship with God.

To Him That Was Crucified

My spirit to yours dear brother,
Do not mind because many sounding your name do not
    understand you,
I do not sound your name, but I understand you,
I specify you with joy O my comrade to salute you, and to
    salute those who are with you, before and since, and
    those to come also,
That we all labour together transmitting the same charge
    and succession,
We few equals indifferent of lands, indifferent of times,
We, enclosers of all continents, all castes, allowers of all
    theologies,
Compassionaters, perceivers, rapport of men,
We walk silent among disputes and assertions, but reject
    not the disputes nor any thing that is asserted,
We hear the bawling and din, we are reach'd at by
    divisions, jealousies, recriminations on every side,
They close peremptorily upon us to surround us, my
    comrade,
Yet we walk unheld, free, the whole earth over, journeying
    up and down till we make our ineffaceable mark upon
    time and the diverse eras,
Till we saturate time and eras, that the men and women of

races, ages to come, may prove brethren and lovers as we are.

In his groundbreaking *Leaves of Grass,* a collection of twelve poems he published in 1855 at his own expense, Walt Whitman attempted to relate to the ordinary person as well as to the powerful. In this introspective prayer, he talks to Christ as though he were his brother, showing empathy, if not sympathy, for the cross that he bore as well as the burdens that are carried by all of humanity.

A Call to Prayer

Let us pray mightily to God that we may be replenished with heavenly grace according to our need, so that the law of kindness shall dwell in our hearts and on our tongues and charity, or love, which "vaunteth not itself, is not easily provoked, doth not behave itself unseemly," shall control our every action. Next to God's spirit dwelling in our own, nothing will so help us to be considerate and patient, as to pray for and speak gently of those who in our judgment have done injustice unto our motives, our record and our character. Let us be careful not to do them a parallel injustice but, by recalling their noble qualities and their kindness in the past, keep them hidden in the citadel of our generous regard and confidence until this storm be overpassed.

This prayer was delivered in 1887 by Frances E. Willard, president of the Women's Christian Temperance Union, at a rancorous annual conference in the midst of a divisive vote over the organization's efforts to battle "the scourge of alcoholism." Pious but forceful, Willard instilled in her followers that prayer was critical in fighting for their cause. She later would be introduced to a Senate hearing by Susan B. Anthony as a "general with an army of 250,000."

In Humbleness

O God our Father, deliver us from the foolishness of self-confidence, from all boasting and vanity from pride of energy and false notions of success. Teach us that our springs are not in ourselves but in Thee, that so far from being able to do what we will, we can neither will nor do any good except by Thy grace and with Thy help, that it is when we are weak in ourselves that we are strong in Thee, that Thy power is made perfect in our conscious lack of power that compels us to lay our helplessness on Thy strength. Here may we find our rest and feel, pouring through all our impotence, the tides of Thy mighty Spirit, for Thine is the kingdom, the power, and glory.

Born in the small town of Huntington, nestled in the Allegheny Mountains of western Pennsylvania, Robert Speer first came to prominence as an outspoken student at Princeton, where he led religious rallies calling for Christian unity. Later he became a senior executive and major voice with several national Protestant organizations. In this prayer calling for pious modesty, he echoes the sentiments of his famous adage "Prepare for the worst; expect the best; and take what comes."

Different Streams

As the different streams having their sources in different places all mingle their water in the same sea, Oh, Lord, so the different tendencies, various though they appear, crooked or straight, all lead to Thee.

The roots of the interest in Hindu religion in America often are traced back to the dynamic speech that Swami Vivekananda delivered at the Congress of World Religions in Chicago in 1893. In his closing comments to the thousands of attendees, which included some of the country's most prominent religious leaders, he delivered to thunderous applause this prayer, which is adapted from a Hindu prayer.

Feed My Sheep

> Shepherd, show me how to go
> O'er the hillside steep,
> How to gather, how to sow,—
> How to feed Thy sheep;
> I will listen for Thy voice,
> Lest my footsteps stray;
> I will follow and rejoice
> All the rugged way.
>
> Thou wilt bind the stubborn will,
> Wound the callous breast,
> Make self-righteousness be still,
> Break earth's stupid rest.
> Strangers on a barren shore,
> Lab'ring long and lone,
> We would enter by the door,
> And Thou know'st Thine own.
>
> So, when day grows dark and cold,
> Tear or triumph harms,
> Lead Thy lambkins to the fold,
> Take them in Thine arms;
> Feed the hungry, heal the heart,
> Till the morning's beam;
> White as wool, ere they depart,
> Shepherd, wash them clean.

Mary Baker Eddy, the founder of Christian Science, was dogged in her religious conviction that prayer, particularly silent prayer, was key to salvation and to a healthy physical and mental spirit.

By the time of her death in 1910 at the age of eighty-nine, she had established well over twelve hundred Christian Science congregations across the United States and a formidable publishing empire. This prayer to Christ the shepherd was one of seven hymns Mary Baker Eddy wrote that was integrated into the church's worship services.

A Mother's Knowing Prayer

Oh, God, keep him humble!

This is the one-line prayer that Nancy McKinley, the mother of William McKinley, was heard to say when she learned that her son had just been elected the twenty-fifth president of the United States.

Prayer of a Soldier in France

My shoulders ache beneath my pack
(Lie easier, Cross, upon His back).

I march with feet that burn and smart
(Tread, Holy Feet, upon my heart).

Men shout at me who may not speak
(They scourged Thy back and smote Thy cheek).

I may not lift a hand to clear
My eyes of salty drops that sear.

(Then shall my fickle soul forget
Thy Agony of Bloody Sweat?)

My rifle hand is stiff and numb
(From Thy pierced palm red rivers come).

Lord, Thou didst suffer more for me
Than all the hosts of land and sea.

So let me render back again
This millionth of Thy gift. Amen.

Joyce Kilmer, whose poem "Trees" was memorized by practically
all schoolchildren in the first half of the twentieth century, believed that it was his duty to enlist in World War I. In the last
poem he wrote before he was killed by enemy gunfire, one that
he enclosed in a letter to his wife, Aline, he drew a mystical parallel between his mortification on the battlefield and what Christ
endured on the road to Calvary.

The Essence of Prayer

Our God, who art our winged self, it is thy will in us that
    willeth.
It is thy desire that desireth.
It is thy urge in us that would turn our nights,
which are thine, into days, which are thine also.
We cannot ask thee for aught, for thou knowest our needs
    before they
Are born in us:
Thou art our need; and in giving us more of thyself thou
    givest us all.

Born in Lebanon to a Maronite Catholic family, Khalil Gibran immigrated to the United States at the age of twelve. The publication of *The Prophet* in 1923 gained him both fame and fortune.
In this passage from his chapter entitled "Prayer," he dons the
mantle of human submissiveness to an all-loving and all-
knowing God.

Help Me to Understand

Oh! Almighty and Everlasting God, Creator of Heaven,
Earth, and the Universe: Help me to be, to think. To act
what is right, because it is right; make me truthful,
honest, and honorable in all things; make me intellectually
honest for the sake of right and honor without thought of
reward to me. Give me the ability to be charitable,
forgiving, and patient with my fellowmen—help me to
understand their motives and their shortcomings—even as
Thou understandest mine!

When looking back on his long and very full life, President Harry
Truman recounted how he had recited this prayer every day of
his life since he was a high school student. He turned to it on the
World War I battlefield, taught it to his fiancée, Bess, and came
to rely upon it while serving in the White House. For the fa-
mously strong-headed thirty-third president of the United
States, this continuous reminder of the need for empathy belied
his reputation.

Holy Sonnet XIV: Batter My Heart

Batter my heart, three person'd God; for you
As yet but knock, breathe, shine and seek to mend;
That I may rise, and stand, o'erthrow me, and bend
Your force, to break, blow, burn and make me new.
I, like an usurpt towne, to another due,
Labour to admit you, but oh, to no end,
Reason, your viceroy in me, me should defend,
But is captiv'd, and proves weak or untrue.
Yet dearly' I love you, and would be loved fain,
But am betroth'd unto your enemy:
Divorce me, untie, or breake that knot again,
Take me to you, imprison me, for I,

Except you enthrall me, never shall be free,
Nor ever chaste, except you ravish me.

J. Robert Oppenheimer, director of the Manhattan Project, was enamored of the works of the early seventeenth-century poet John Donne. When it came time to name the first atomic bomb test in the desert of New Mexico during the summer of 1945, Oppenheimer chose to name it after the English poet's holy sonnet "Trinity." He saw in Donne's poem an expression of the destructive potential of the nuclear age, and the need to turn to God to protect the world from using the new technology for evil purposes.

On Balloon Tires of Conceit

O God Our Father, while we pride ourselves that we learn something every day, we seem to make little progress in spiritual things.

Nowhere is our ignorance more tragic. So long have we been riding on the balloon tires of conceit, for our own good we may have to be deflated, that on the rims of humility we may discover the spiritual laws that govern our growth in grace.

If our pride has to be punctured, Lord, make it soon, before we gain too much speed. For the salvation of our souls and the good of our country. In Jesus' name.

U.S. Senate Chaplain Peter Marshall, known to many as "the conscience of the Senate," delivered opening prayers to the chamber in the late 1940s that remain memorable to this day. Many of them, like this one, stirred apathetic and ego-driven personalities to understand their larger purpose in conducting the business of the country. Senators often would schedule their day around Marshall's daily invocations hoping not to miss a riveting invocation.

New Insights for Our Time

Almighty and ever living God, who art beyond the grasp of our highest thought but within the reach of our frailest trust: Come in the beauty of the morning's light and reveal Thyself to us. Enrich us out of the heritage of seers and scholars and saints into whose faith and labors we have entered, and quicken us to insights for our time; that we may be possessors of the truth of many yesterdays, partakers of Thy thought for today, and creators with Thee of a better tomorrow; through Jesus Christ, the Lord of ages.

Henry Sloane Coffin, moderator of the Presbyterian Church of the United States and president of Union Theological Seminary from 1926 to 1945, became one of the country's most influential religious voices. He believed that the teachings of Christ provided a base from which human beings could evolve, no matter what circumstances they might encounter. Here he asked for Divine guidance in comprehending the challenges of the modern day.

In Sublimation

> Lord, take me where You want me to go;
> Let me meet who You want me to meet;
> Tell me what You want me to say, and
> Keep me out of Your way.

Father Mychal Judge, a sixty-eight-year-old Franciscan priest who served as a firehouse chaplain in lower Manhattan, was the first official recorded victim of the World Trade Center attacks in New York City on September 11, 2001. He was killed by falling debris from Tower One as he was administering the last rites of the Catholic Church to a fireman. He carried this prayer with him always, as he did on that day, and often would give copies to friends and strangers alike.

Prayer for Moral Guidance

Bless this Great Body, O Lord, and Your servants who work within it.

Let them understand that they hold a special place among your people, representing and giving shape, as they do, to the best hopes and dreams of so many.

Allow them to realize, always, that even in the midst of partisanship, they serve a higher purpose in working together for the common good and in finding ways to do honor to the people of Texas and, in turn, to You.

Stir within them always the higher notion that when they invoke prayer together as a body, that by that very act alone, they bring down the walls that divide them,

they find common ground by which they become one,

they come to understand the greater perspective in their lives and in the lives of those they serve,

and most importantly, they acknowledge openly that they hold themselves accountable not only to their individual electorates but to You, who are all knowing, all loving, and all powerful.

Dear Lord, as this Special Session of the Legislature is launched, we also humbly ask that You grant the Members of this Senate tenacious courage to tackle and to persevere in the challenges that face them,

boundless creativity to find answers to the most confounding issues they confront,

farsighted wisdom to understand fully that their words and their actions in this chamber and beyond do count and do have consequences, and

relentless conviction to settle for nothing less than a personal code of uncompromising ethics, recognizing that in doing so they confer honor upon themselves, upon their families, upon their constituents, upon the future of Texas, and upon You.

We ask this in Your name.

This prayer was delivered by James P. Moore Jr. to open a special session of the Texas state senate. It came at a time of heightened concern in the state over a serious budget deadlock and rifts between parties and individual legislators. It asks for unity and for insight in working for the larger perspective.

PEACE AND JUSTICE

Peace of Mind

Oh Great Spirit of our
Ancestors, I raise
my pipe to you.
To your messengers the four winds, and
to Mother Earth who provides
for your children.
Give us the wisdom to teach our children
to love, to respect, and to be kind
to each other so that they may grow
with peace of mind.
Let us learn to share all good things that
you provide for us on this Earth.

This prayer by Chief Yellow Hawk, the great Sioux leader, was written in the late nineteenth century during difficult days when he and his people were being displaced from their lands. He wrote many prayers that spoke about the path toward peace through wisdom and understanding.

Liberty and Justice for All

And, O! thou father of the universe and disposer of events, thou that called from a dark and formless mass this fair system of nature, and created thy sons and daughters to bask in the golden streams and rivulets contained therein; this day we have convened under thy divine auspices, it's not to celebrate a political festivity, or the achievement of arms by which the blood of thousands were spilt, contaminating thy pure fields with human gore! but to commemorate a period brought to light by wise counsel, who stayed the hand of merciless power, and with hearts expanded with gratitude for the providences, inundated in the sea of thy mercies we further crave thy fostering care. O! wilt thou crush that power that still holds thousands of our brethren in bondage, and let the sea of thy wisdom wash its very dust from off the face of the earth; let LIBERTY unfurl her banners, FREEDOM and JUSTICE reign triumphant in the world, universally.

This prayer concluded a stirring speech delivered in New York City by George Lawrence, an African American, to commemorate the fifth anniversary of the abolition of the slave trade in the United States in 1808. While he praised the new law, Lawrence also bemoaned that slavery itself had not yet been eradicated.

O Judge Me, Lord, for Thou Art Just

O judge me, Lord, for thou art just;
Thou statutes are my pride
In thee alone I put my trust;
I therefore shall not slide;
O prove me, try my reins and heart;
Thy mercies, Lord, I know;

I never took the scorner's part,
Nor with the vain will go.

Of sinners I detest the bands,
Nor with them will offend;
In innocence will wash my hands,
And at thine altar bend;
There, with thanksgiving's grateful voice,
Thy wondrous works will tell,
I love the mansions of thy choice,
And where thine honors dwell.

No president of the United States ever engaged in more writing or intellectual pursuits than did John Quincy Adams. This invocation, published after his death, was one of the dozens of prayers he wrote after he had left the Oval Office and while serving in the U.S. House of Representatives.

Lead Us, O Father

Lead us, O Father, in the paths of peace;
without thy guiding hand we go astray,
and doubts appall, and sorrows still increase;
lead us through Christ, the true and living Way.

Lead us, O Father, in the paths of truth;
unhelped by thee, in error's maze we grope,
while passion strains, and folly dims our youth,
and age comes on, uncheered by faith and hope.

Lead us, O Father, in the paths of right;
blindly we stumble when we walk alone,
involved in shadows of a darksome night;
only with thee we journey safely on.

Lead us, O Father, to thy heavenly rest,
however rough and steep the pathway be;
through joy or sorrow, as thou deemest best,
until our lives are perfected in thee.

William Henry Burleigh, one of the great voices in both the anti-slavery and temperance movements of the nineteenth century, composed this prayer shortly after the close of the Mexican War. Physically imposing and mesmerizing as a speaker, he drew huge crowds wherever he appeared. Surprisingly, this hymn became instantly popular throughout Great Britain before it was embraced in America.

Give Us Peace!

Peace! Peace! God of our fathers, grant us Peace!
Unto our cry of anguish and despair give ear and pity!
From the lonely homes where widowed beggary and
    orphaned woe
        Fill their poor urns with tears;
From trampled plains, where the bright harvest Thou hast
    sent us rots—
The blood of them who should have garnered it calling to
    Thee—
        From fields of carnage, where the foul-beaked
           vultures, sated, flap their wings o'er crowded
           corpses, that but yesterday bore hearts of
           brother, beating high
        With love and common hopes and price, all blasted
        now—
Father of Mercies! Not alone from these our prayer and
    wail are lifted . . .

Peace! Peace! God of our fathers, grant us peace!
Peace to our hearts, and at Thine altars;

Peace on the red waters and their blighted shores;
Peace for the 'leagured cities, and the hosts that watch
    And bleed around them and within,
Peace for the homeless and the fatherless;
Peace for the captive on his weary way,
    And the mad crowds who jeer his helplessness;
For them that suffer, them that do the wrong
Sinning and sinned against. O God! For all;
For a distracted, torn, and bleeding land—
Speed the glad tidings! Give us peace, give us Peace!

This piece, taken from a much longer work, conveys the raw emotion that characterized so many prayers that were written during the difficult days of the Civil War. Severn Teackle Wallis, its author, was a prominent Baltimore lawyer and powerful member of the Maryland state legislature. Because of his opposition to the Civil War, he and several of his colleagues were arrested by federal authorities in 1861 and never given the exact reason for their incarceration. He was released unconditionally fourteen months later. Soon thereafter he published this prayer, which had come to him during his imprisonment.

The War Prayer

O Lord our Father, our young patriots, idols of our hearts go forth to battle—be Thou near them! With them—in spirit—we also go forth from the sweet peace of our beloved firesides to smite the foe.

O Lord our God, help us to tear their soldiers to bloody shreds with our shells; help us to cover their smiling fields with the pale forms of their patriot dead; help us to drown the thunder of the guns with the wounded writhing in pain; help us to lay waste their humble homes with a hurricane of fire; help us to wring

the hearts of their unoffending widows with unavailing grief;
help us to turn them out roofless with their little children
wandering and unfriended in the wastes of their desolated land
in rages and hunger and thirst, sport of the sun-flames of
summer and the icy winds of winter, broken in spirit, worn with
travail, imploring Thee for the refuge of the grave and denied
it—for our sakes, who adore Thee, Lord, blast their hopes,
blight their lives, protract their bitter pilgrimage, make heavy
their steps, water their way with tears, stain the white snow
with the blood of their wounded feet! We ask of one who is the
Spirit of love and who is the ever-faithful refuge and friend of
all that are sore beset, and seek His aid with humble and contrite
hearts. Amen

Outraged by what he saw as the country's political motives in
launching the Spanish-American War, Mark Twain vented his
frustrations by writing a short story he called "The War Prayer."
To make his point, he wrote about the congregation of a small-
town church gathered together to say good-bye to their anxious
young men about to take off for the war front the next day.
Suddenly, a strange old man appears in the sanctuary and recites
this prayer, dripping with sarcasm, and reminding everyone
about the human cost of war.

God of Nations

God of the nations, near and far,
Ruler of all mankind,
Bless thou thy peoples as they strive
The paths of peace to find.

The clash of arms still shakes the sky,
King battles still with king;
Wild through the frighted air of night
The bloody tocsins ring.

But clearer far the friendly speech
Of scientists and seers,
The wise debate of statesmen, and
The shouts of pioneers.

And stronger far the clasped hands
Of labor's teeming throngs
Who, in a hundred tongues, repeat
Their common creeds and songs.

From shore to shore the peoples call
In loud and sweet acclaim;
The gloom of land and sea is lit
With pentecostal flame.

O Father from the curse of war
We pray thee give release;
And speed, O speed thy blessed day
Of justice, love, and peace.

John Haynes Holmes, an ordained Unitarian minister and a co-founder of both the NAACP and the American Civil Liberties Union, wrote and delivered this prayer in New York City at an interfaith service on the eve of World War I. An ardent pacifist, he worked to keep the United States out of the war, and he was denounced vehemently for his stand. Nevertheless, his prayer would be added to the *New Hymn and Tune Book* of the Unitarian Church in 1914, and would become one of the church's most beloved hymns and prayers.

That Peace May Follow War

Our Father, who art in heaven, we lift our hearts to Thee, believing that Thou who hast been the help of Thy children in ages past will answer the cry of Thy children today.

We pray, O God, for strength and courage that we may not falter in these days that try the souls of men!

We pray that we may have vision to see what is the right way in which to walk.

We pray that in our effort to train for wise leadership we may not forget how to be humble and in our struggle to overcome evil we may not forget how to be merciful.

We pray that in the midst of deadly conflict we may have our eyes opened to the way of a just and durable peace.

We pray, O God, that we may so hunger and thirst after righteousness that we may help to realize Thy Kingdom among the children of men.

In the name of Christ, our Saviour.

Written as World War I was coming to a close, this invocation was composed by Mary E. Woolley, who was the first woman to graduate from Brown University and who served as president of Mount Holyoke College from 1900 to 1937. She was a biblical scholar and, as this prayer conveys, a strong personality who challenged political leaders to keep the peace.

For the Magistrate

Almighty God, you sit on the throne judging right: we humbly beseech you to bless the courts of justice and the magistrates in all this land; and give to them the spirit of wisdom and understanding, that they may discern the truth, and impartially administer the law in the fear of you alone; through him who shall come to be our Judge, your Son our Savior Jesus Christ. Amen.

Both a prominent lawyer and the chancellor of the New York Episcopal Diocese for twenty-five years in the early twentieth century, George Zabriskie became prominent for his unflagging commitment to a high standard of ethics and judicial impartiality throughout the U.S. court system. He composed this prayer as a reminder to lawyers and judges alike of their ultimate responsibility.

Opening Prayer at the Scopes Trial

We beseech Thee, our Heavenly Father, that Thou wilt grant unto every individual that share of wisdom that will enable them to go out from this session of the court, with the consciousness of having under God and grace done the very best thing possible, and the wisest thing possible.

Delivered by a local minister in the courtroom on the first day of the Scopes trial in Dayton, Tennessee, in 1925, this and subsequent daily prayers would provide legal fodder for attorney Clarence Darrow, who was defending John T. Scopes's right to teach Darwin's theory of evolution in a public school. The flamboyant civil rights lawyer argued unsuccessfully that the prayer prejudiced the case in favor of the plaintiff, the State of Tennessee.

We'll Understand It Better By and By

We are often tossed and driv'n on the restless sea of time,
Somber skies and howling tempest oft succeed a bright
    sunshine,
In the land of perfect day, when the mists have rolled
    away,
We will understand it better by and by.

Trials dark on every hand, and we cannot understand all
  the ways that God would lead us to that Blessed Promise
  Land.
But he guides us with his eye and we'll follow till we die.
For we'll understand it better by and by.

By and by, when the morning comes,
All the saints of God gathered home.
We'll tell the story how we've overcome.
For we'll understand it better by and by.

Charles Albert Tindley, the father of American gospel music,
wrote some of the most memorable Christian lyrics of any
American songwriter. In this piece, titled "We'll Understand It
Better By and By," he instills a sense of both justice and faith in
the ways of God. He reminds his listeners that all their trials and
uncertainties will be understood and revealed in their life in the
hereafter.

God's World

O world, I cannot hold thee close enough!
        Thy winds, thy wide grey skies!
        Thy mists that roll and rise!
Thy woods, this autumn day, that ache and sag
And all but cry with color! That giant crag
To crush! To lift the lean of that black bluff!
World, world, I cannot get thee close enough!

Long have I known a glory in it all,
        But never knew I this:
        Here such a passion is
As stretcheth me apart. Lord I do fear
Thou'rt made the world too beautiful this year.

My soul is all but out of me,—let fall
No burning leaf. Prithee, let no bird call.

Considered one of her finest works, this poetic cry for God's world conveys Edna St. Vincent Millay's passion for life. Written when she was a student at Vassar College, it was published upon her graduation in 1919 and helped establish her reputation as a first-rate poet.

Thou Art Nigh

The evening winds are saying
Sying o'er the plain
Moonbeams now are stirring
Like a silver rain
Stars are brightly shining
In the azure sky
I am fondly dreaming
Thou art nigh.

Hulda Hoover, the Quaker mother of future president Herbert Hoover, was working as a shepherdess at the age of seventeen when she felt unusual tranquility on a memorable, starlit night. Believing that she was experiencing the presence of God, she wrote down this prayer, much in keeping with the Quaker tenet of finding the "inner light" of one's spirituality.

To the Father of All Souls

Eternal God, Father of all souls, of the sin of war, such hearty hatred for the passions which create it and for the desolations which follow it that we may earnestly desire and tirelessly seek that cooperation between nations which alone can make war impossible.

As man by his inventions has made the whole world into one neighborhood, grant that he may not fail by his cooperation to make the whole world into one brotherhood. Break down all race prejudice, all ignoble narrowness in national loyalty; stay the greed of those who profit by war and the ambitions of those who profit by war and the ambitions of those who by imperialistic conquest seek a national greatness which, drenched in blood, cannot endure.

Guide all statesmen who seek a just basis for international action in the interests of peace; and arouse in the whole body of the people an adventurous willingness, as they sacrificed greatly for war, so also for international good will to dare bravely, to think wisely, to decide resolutely, and to achieve triumphantly.

Although a Baptist by ordination, Harry Emerson Fosdick, the author of this prayer, was the pastor of several Presbyterian churches during his ministry. Finding himself in the middle of the battle between liberal theologians and fundamentalists over the literal interpretation of the Bible, he walked a fine line that landed him on the cover of *Time* magazine in 1930. While he tried to find ways of bridging divides, he was incensed with those who favored war rather than seeking diplomatic solutions—as this prayer shows.

Our Prayer This Day

Our prayer, this day, O Lord, is for truth, right and freedom to come into its own. Give us faith and strength to do the task before us. Give us a future of peace and understanding between all peoples. Keep burning our love toward those of us less fortunate who have been subjected to the heel of the oppressor. This is our prayer.

As the first commanding officer of the Women's Army Corp during World War II, the first person to be appointed U.S. Secretary of Health, Education and Welfare, and later the chairman of the *Houston Post,* Oveta Culp Hobby was one of the most influential Americans of her day. She wrote this prayer during the darkest days of the war as she organized the country's women to support the war effort.

Misused Gifts

O God our Father, from whom all fatherhood in heaven and earth is named: Graciously behold us, Thy family. Thou art ever merciful, and makest Thy sun to rise on the just and on the unjust; but we have misused Thy gifts, marred Thy work, and robbed one another of our daily bread. Help us to see and feel our share of guilt in the world, and grant us Thy grace to bring forth fruits worthy of repentance; through Jesus Christ our Lord.

Barnard College professor and theologian Ursula Niebuhr, the wife of renowned theologian Reinhold Niebuhr, was outspoken in her condemnation of basic inequities around the world. She often articulated her concerns through prayer, as she does here in bemoaning mankind's sense of true justice.

Lord, Hold My Hand While I Run This Race

Lord, hold my hand
Lord, guide my feet
Lord, answer my prayer
While I run this race,
'Cause I don't want to run this race in vain.

These five lines have evolved in untold ways since they were first chanted as a spiritual in the early nineteenth century on Southern plantations. Later they became a staple among black Baptist congregations. Like other spirituals and African American hymns calling for strength in fighting for justice, this one took on new meaning during the civil rights movement of the 1960s. Sung by marchers as a way of bonding together and lifting their cause to a higher power, it became a rallying cry.

César's Prayer

Show me the suffering of the most miserable;
So I will know my people's plight.

Free me to pray for others;
For you are present in every person.

Help me to take responsibility for my own life;
So that I can be free at last.

Give me honesty and patience;
So that I can work with other workers.

Bring forth song and celebration;
So that the Spirit will be alive among us.

Let the Spirit flourish and grow;
So that we will never tire of the struggle.

Let us remember those who have died for justice;
For they have given us life.

Help us love even those who hate us;
So we can change the world.

In his quest for justice to improve the conditions and wages of farmworkers in California, Arizona, and elsewhere, César Chávez often prayed and fasted as a means to become spiritually cleansed and to bring purpose and focus to the task before him. He would say this prayer with his followers before any major decision or protest was about to take place.

In Search of Peace

Our Father, we marvel at three brave space pioneers as they prepare for a landing on the moon. From the depths of our hearts, we pray for a landing on the moon. From the depths of our hearts, we pray for the safe return of Neil Armstrong, Edwin Aldrin, and Michael Collins. Sustain their wives, their children, and families during these anxious days. We are grateful for the thousands of support personnel who literally are their brothers' keepers. Excite our imagination to transfer the genius of cooperation and spirit of teamwork to our many other needs, lest our success on the moon mock our failures on the earth. Even as our astronauts go to the moon in the name of peace, our world aches from the pain of wars. We perfect the means for destroying human life and then believe we have found security.

May the nations trust not in the power of their arms, but in the Prince of Peace, thy Son. O God, grant us deliverance from the rhetoric of peace when we personally are not willing to do things which make for peace: to love, to forgive, to use wisely all gifts and resources for the good of mankind; and to permit the invasion of the Holy Spirit into the lives of each of us—that it may be reflected in our homes between husbands and wives, between children and parents, and in commerce between management and labor, between citizen and government and among all races of men.

O Lord, keep us mindful that technical success does not
necessarily produce wisdom. We pray for wisdom for our
President and all who govern this nation. The true wisdom is
found in Scripture and is described by St. James as the wisdom
that comes from God, is utterly pure, then peace-loving,
considerate, open to reason, rich in mercy and kindly actions,
with no breath of favoritism or hint of hypocrisy. And the wise
are the peacemakers who go quietly sowing for a harvest of
righteousness in other people and in themselves. We pray for this
in the name of Thy Son, our Savior Jesus Christ. Amen.

Offered by U.S. Senator Mark Hatfield of Oregon at a White
House religious service on July 20, 1969, the day that *Apollo 11*
landed on the moon, this prayer acknowledges both the historic
milestone and the need for God's human family to live in harmony. Hatfield, who would become increasingly vocal in his opposition to the Vietnam War, delivered the invocation before a
small gathering that included President Richard Nixon, Vice
President Spiro Agnew, Chief Justice Warren Burger, and key
members of Congress.

To Keep Alive the Dream

O Lord our God,
help us pray, as our *ceremony* ends,
that our *service* might begin.
And keep us from forgetting the difference.

Keep us from feeling too good
about what we say and do today,
for words are not enough,
and it is far too easy to recall
gigantic evil done by others,
yet miss the link to seeds of future horror

in our own lives:
in apathy, in the careless racial slur,
in blindness to a neighbor's wound,
or deafness to his cry . . .

And yet,
let us take some pride—and hope—
in what we do today,
for sometimes, words can pave the way:
songs and prayers
can bear witness to the good within us still,
can give dreams a voice—
a call which might be, must be, heard,
to give direction to our lives.

So, *from* the Holocaust, we learn:
when we deny humanity in others,
we destroy humanity within ourselves.
When we reject the human, and the holy,
in any neighbor's soul,
then we unleash the beast, and the barbaric,
in our own heart.

And, *since* the Holocaust, we pray:
if the time has not yet dawned
when we can all proclaim our faith in God,
then let us say at least
that we admit we are not gods ourselves.
If we cannot yet see the face of God in others,
then let us see, at least,
a face as human as our own.

So long ago
the Bible taught that life might be
a blessing or a curse:
the choice is in our hands.

Today we vow:
the curse will be remembered.
But our prayer must also be
to fight despair;
to find the strength, the courage,
and the faith,
to keep alive the dream
that—through us and through our children—
the *blessing* might still be.

Rabbi Arnold E. Resnicoff, a retired U.S. Navy chaplain and one of the country's foremost advocates for interfaith dialogue, delivered this invocation in 1987 at a memorial in the rotunda of the U.S. Capitol for the victims of the Holocaust. Focusing more on the living than on the dead, he reminded future generations of the evil that can be unleashed in the absence of moral vigilance.

FORGIVENESS AND COMPASSION

Until I Have Walked in His Moccasins . . .

> Great Spirit, help me never to judge another until I have
> walked in his moccasins.

This inspirational prayer of the Sioux Nation is among the most
regularly quoted invocations from early Native America. Its lesson on empathy remains timeless.

Tened Piedad, Dios Mío

> Tened piedad, Dios mío,
> suma bondad eterna, eterna,
> de mí según la grande
> misericordia vuestra, vuestra.
>
> Según la muchedumbre
> de tus piedades tiernas, tiernas,
> borra, Señor, mis culpas
> del libro de la cuenta, cuenta.
>
> Líbrame aun más el alma
> de mi iniquidad fea, fea . . .

Have Pity, My God
(English Translation)

> Have pity, my God,
> total goodness eternal, eternal,
> mine through the great
> mercy of yours, of yours.
>
> Through the multitude
> of your tender pities, tender, tender,
> erase, Lord, my guilt
> from the book of accounts, accounts.
>
> Free my soul even more
> from my iniquity, unsightly, unsightly.

In the 1930s, Stanford University professor Juan Rael set out to record the hymns of early Hispanic America, which blend the music and words of Native Americans of the Southwest with those of the Franciscan priests from Spain who settled there. Passed down orally from generation to generation, these *alabados,* or hymns, were finally written down for posterity and are cataloged at the Library of Congress. This particular hymn, crying out for forgiveness, is a synthesis of four very similar penitential prayers from New Mexico. It would have been sung mainly at funerals without musical accompaniment.

In Consideration of Others

Upon the Sight of	*Ejaculations*
A *tall* man.	*Lord,* give that Man, *High Attainments* in Christianity: Let him fear God, *above many.*

A lame *Man.*	*Lord,* help that Man, to *walk uprightly.*
A *Merchant*	*Lord,* make that man a *wise Merchant.*
Children at *Play.*	*Lord,* let not these Children always forget the *Work,* which they came into the World upon.
Young Gentlewomen.	*Lord,* make 'em *wise Virgins,* as the *polish'd Stones of Thy Temple.*
A Man, who going by me took *no Notice* of me.	*Lord,* help that Man, to take a *due Notice* of the Lord Jesus Christ I pray thee.
One whom I *know not:* (and no other singular Circumstance about him, to shape any Thoughts upon).	*Lord,* let this Person be so known to, as to be *sav'd* by the Lord.
One who (as I heard) had spoken very *reproachfully* and *injuriously* of me.	*Lord,* bless and spare and save that person, even as *my own Soul.* May *that Person* share with me, in all the *Salvations* of the Lord.
One that was reckon'd a very *wicked* Man.	*Lord,* rescue that poor Man, from Satan, who *leads him captive.*

Wherefore all that I now add is, that I have unspeakable Cause, to bless my Lord Jesus Christ for teaching me, by His Holy Spirit, before I was *twenty years of Age,* these methods of living unto His glory.

The son of the formidable Reverend Increase Mather, Cotton Mather became a great influence throughout colonial America. His writings about life and spirituality in New England would reverberate among future American novelists and essayists for generations to come. In this unusual collection of short prayers, which he wrote as a young man, he tried to emulate the thoughts of a true Christian in the diversity of the people he encountered in daily life.

An Evening Thought: Salvation by Christ, with Penitential Cries

Salvation comes by Christ alone,
The only Son of God;
Redemption now to every one,
That love his holy Word.

Dear Jesus, we would fly to Thee,
And leave off every Sin,
Thy tender Mercy well agree;
Salvation from our King;

Salvation comes now from the Lord,
Our victorious King.
His holy Name be well ador'ed,
Salvation surely bring.

Dear Jesus, let the Nations cry,
And all the People say,
Salvation comes from Christ on high,
Haste on Tribunal Day.

Ten Thousand Angels cry to Thee,
Yea, louder than the Ocean.

Thou art the Lord, we plainly see;
Thou art the true Salvation.

Come Holy Spirit, Heavenly Dove,
The Object of our Care;
Salvation doth increase our Love;
Our hearts hath felt thy fear.

Now Glory be to God on High,
Salvation high and low;
And thus the Soul on Christ rely,
To heaven surely go.

Come, Blessed Jesus, Heavenly Dove,
Accept repentance here;
Salvation give, with tender Love;
Let us with Angels share.

This excerpt from a much longer poem was written in 1760 by
Jupiter Hammon, a slave from Lloyd's Neck, New York. The
complete prayer, which focuses solely on the need for penitence
and salvation, was the first work of an African American ever to
be published. Hammon's consecutive slave owners recognized
his talent, supported his education, and helped promote his literary endeavors.

A Prayer for a Public Fast

Thou, O God, hast been a constant witness of all the follies of
our youth, and the sins of our riper years. How great has been
the pride, the unbelief, and the obstinacy of our hearts? We have
been walking in the way of our own hearts, and in the sight of
our own eyes, while we have been practically saying to God,
depart from us, for we desire not the knowledge of our ways.

May things ever go well with us; dispose Thy people to the practice of all those duties on which the welfare of society depends; restrain a spirit of faction and division; subdue that selfishness which produces perilous times; and may that righteousness which exalteth a nation, be promoted.

May we lie down this night, pardoned and accepted. Amen

Up to the twentieth century presidents of the United States rarely issued public declarations to pray without a call to fast as well. Only through fasting, it was believed, could Americans properly ask God for forgiveness for their failings before expressing their thanksgiving and presenting their petitions for Divine Providence. This piece from a much longer prayer, published just after the end of the War of 1812, was meant to be recited in the evening during public fasts.

Softly Now the Light of Day

Softly now the light of day
fades upon my sight away;
free from care, from labor free,
Lord, I would commune with thee.

Thou, whose all pervading eye
naught escapes, without, within,
pardon each infirmity,
open fault and secret sin.

Soon for me the light of day
shall for ever pass away;
then, from sin and sorrow free,
take me, Lord, to dwell with thee.

Thou who, sinless, yet hast known
all of man's infirmity;
then, from thine eternal throne,
Jesus, look with pitying eye.

George Washington Doane was born in 1799, the year that George Washington died. He served as a bishop in the Episcopal Church in New Jersey and became one of the most influential clergymen and educators in the country, establishing churches and schools throughout the state and offering some of the most riveting sermons of his day. This prayer, anticipating his death, became his most lasting literary legacy.

Let Us Break Bread Together

Let us break bread together on our knees, yes, on our
    knees
Let us break bread together on our knees, yes, on our
    knees
When I fall on my knees with my face to the rising sun,
O Lord, have mercy on me.

Let us drink wine together on our knees, yes, on our knees
Let us drink wine together on our knees, yes, on our knees
When I fall on my knees with my face to the rising sun,
O Lord, have mercy on me.

Let us praise God together on our knees, yes, on our knees
Let us praise God together on our knees, yes, on our knees
When I fall on my knees with my face to the rising sun,
O Lord, have mercy on me.

This African American spiritual has been integrated into the Eucharistic liturgy of churches of all denominations to ask for

God's forgiveness before receiving Communion. Musicologists have long conjectured that the song's line "When I fall on my knees with my face to the rising sun" may well have had its origins among enslaved Africans born into Muslim families.

A Balm in Gilead

> There is a balm in Gilead
> To make the wounded whole
> There is a balm in Gilead
> To heal the sin-sick soul
>
> Sometimes I feel discouraged
> And think my work's in vain
> But then the Holy Spirit
> Revives my soul again
>
> Don't ever feel discouraged
> For Jesus is your friend
> And if you lack of knowledge
> He'll ne'er refuse to lend
>
> If you cannot preach like Peter
> If you cannot pray like Paul
> You can tell the love of Jesus
> And say, "He died for all."

This much-loved spiritual long has been sung in churches of different faith traditions as a way to reaffirm God's continual forgiveness. The "balm of Gilead" is most likely a metaphor for the healing properties of a balsam tree found in a mountainous region east of the Jordan River.

From "The Vision of Sir Launfal"

And the voice that was softer than silence said,
"Lo it is I, be not afraid!
In many climes, without avail,
Thou hast spent thy life for the Holy Grail;
Behold, it is here,—this cup which thou
Didst fill at the streamlet for Me but now;
This crust is My body broken for thee;
This water His blood that died on the tree;
The Holy Supper is kept, indeed,
In whatso we share with another's need;
Not what we give, but what we share,
For the gift without the giver is bare;
Who gives himself with his alms feeds three, Himself, his
hungering neighbor, and Me."

Poet, essayist, editor of the *Atlantic Monthly*, and U.S. diplomat
to Portugal and Great Britain, James Russell Lowell was one of
the great names in American letters in the nineteenth century.
The 1848 poem "The Vision of Sir Launfal," from which this
prayer is taken, explores the journey of a British knight in search
of the Holy Grail. In this poem Lowell constructed a clever and
prayerful running dialogue between Sir Launfal and God.

The Drummer Boy of Shiloh

On Shiloh's dark and bloody ground
The dead and wounded lay,
Amongst them was a drummer boy
Who beat the drums that day.
A wounded soldier held him up
His drum was by his side;
He clasped his hands, then raised his eyes

And prayed before he died.
He clasped his hands, then raised his eyes
And prayed before he died.

Look down upon the battle field,
Oh, Thou our Heavenly Friend!
Have mercy on our sinful souls!
The soldiers cried, "Amen!"
For gathered 'round a little group,
Each brave man knelt and cried.
They listened to the drummer boy
Who prayed before he died.
They listened to the drummer boy
Who prayed before he died.

"Oh, mother," said the dying boy,
"Look down from Heaven on me,
Receive me to thy fond embrace—
Oh, take me home to thee.
I've loved my country as my God;
To serve them both I've tried."
He smiled, shook hands—death seized the boy
Who prayed before he died;
He smiled, shook hands—death seized the boy
Who prayed before he died.

Each soldier wept, then, like a child,
Stout hearts were they, and brave;
The flag his winding sheet, God's Book
The key unto his grave.
They wrote upon a simple board
These words: "This is a guide
To those who'd mourn the drummer boy
Who prayed before he died;
To those who'd mourn the drummer boy
Who prayed before he died."

Ye angels 'round the Throne of Grace,
Look down upon the braves
Who fought and died on Shiloh's plain,
Now slumb'ring in their graves!
How many homes made desolate?
How many hearts have sighed?
How many, like that drummer boy,
Who prayed before they died;
How many, like that drummer boy,
Who prayed before they died!

Arguably the most famous prayer ballad of the Civil War was written by Will "Shakespeare" Hays. His inspiration came in the aftermath of the bloody Battle of Shiloh, Tennessee, April 6–7, 1862. Of the 23,741 deaths that were recorded, none had greater resonance than that of a young, innocent drummer boy. The melancholy of the piece speaks to the waste and sinfulness of war.

Prayer of the South

And for my dead, My Father, may I pray?
Ah! Sighs may soothe, but prayer shall soothe me more!
I keep eternal watch above their clay;
Oh! Rest their souls, my Father, I implore;
Forgive my foes—they know not what they do—
Forgive them all the tears they made me shed;
Forgive them, though my noblest sons they slew,
And bless them. Though they curse poor, dear dead.

O may my woes be each a carrier dove,
With swift, white wings, that, bathing in my tears,
Will bear thee, Father, all my prayers of love,

And bring me peace, in all my doubts and fears.
Father, I kneel, 'mid ruin, wreck, and grave—
A desert waste where all was erst so fair—
And, for my children and my foes, I crave
Pity and pardon: Father, hear my prayer.

Reverend Abram Ryan, a Roman Catholic priest, was one of the more colorful and prominent voices of the South during the Civil War era. Despite the prevalence of anti-Catholicism in those days, his writings were read in homes of every faith. These verses are the last two in a much longer prayer written within hours of the North's defeat of the South. Within days of General Lee's surrender at Appomattox, it was read in Catholic and Protestant churches alike.

Jesus Is Calling

Softly and tenderly Jesus is calling,
Calling for you and me;
See, on the portals, He's waiting and watching,
Watching for you and me.
Come home, come home,
Ye who are weary, come home,
Earnestly, tenderly, Jesus is calling—
Calling, "O sinner, come home!"

This hymn, written by composer and music publisher Will L. Thompson in the days following the Civil War, was particularly popular at prayer meetings and revivals well into the twentieth century. Its lyrics convey Christ's unconditional love for all sinners.

Dear Lord and Father of Mankind

Dear Lord and Father of mankind,
forgive our foolish ways!
Re-clothe us in our rightful mind,
in purer lives thy service find,
in deeper reverence, praise.

In simple trust like theirs who heard,
beside the Syrian sea,
the gracious calling of the Lord,
let us, like them, without a word,
rise up and follow thee.

O Sabbath rest by Galilee!
O calm of hills above,
where Jesus knelt to share with thee
the silence of eternity
interpreted by love!

Drop thy still dews of quietness,
till all our strivings cease;
take from our souls the strain and stress,
and let our ordered lives confess
the beauty of thy peace.

Breathe through the heats of our desire
thy coolness and thy balm;
let sense be dumb, let flesh retire;
speak through the earthquake, wind, fire,
O still, small voice of calm!

This prayer is an excerpt from John Greenleaf Whittier's poem "The Brewing of Soma," published in 1872. No more than a decade later these lines were set to a tune composed by Sir Hubert Parry. Consistently, the piece has been voted as one of the favorite hymns of the British people with its plea to God for forgiveness of humanity's foolish ways. Whittier, true to his Quaker heritage, believed that experiencing the true reality of God and understanding human transgressions could only be done in the tranquility of a person's inner soul, and not by unnecessary worldly distractions.

A Last Prayer

> Father, I scarcely dare to pray,
> So clear I see, now it is done,
> How I have wasted half my day,
> And left my work just begun.
>
> So clear I see that things I thought
> Were right or harmless were a sin
> So clear I see that I have sought
> Unconscious, selfish aims to win;
> So clear I see that I have hurt
> The soul I might have helped to save,
> That I have slothful been inert,
> Deaf to the calls thy leaders gave.
>
> In outskirts of the kingdom vast,
> Father, the humblest spot give me;
> Set me the lowliest task thou hast:
> Let me repentant work for thee!

Helen Hunt Jackson, a longtime friend and neighbor of Emily Dickinson, was a prominent writer in her own right. One work that has stood the test of time is one she wrote in the last months of her life. In it she lamented having wasted too much of her life on meaningless ventures, and asks that God forgive her.

O! Kou Aloha No

O! kou aloha no
Aiaika lani,
Ao kou oiaia
He hemolele hoi.

Kou noho mihi ana
A paahoao ia
Ooe kuu lama
Kou nani kou koo.

Mai nana ino ino.
Na hewa o kanaka
A ka e huikala
A maemae no.

Nolaila kou eheu
Malalo koy eheu
Ko makou malubia
A mau loa aku no. Amen

The Queen's Prayer
(English Translation)

Oh! Lord thy loving mercy,
Is high as the heavens,
It tells us of thy truth,
And 'tis filled with holiness.

Whilst humbly meditating
Within these walls imprisoned
Thou art my light my haven
Thy glory my support.

Oh! Look not on their failings
Nor on the sins of men
Forgive with loving kindness
That we might be made pure.

For thy grace I beseech thee
Bring us 'neath thy protection
And peace will be our portion
Now and forever more. Amen

One of the great figures in Hawaii's history was its last monarch, Queen Liliuokalani. For eight months in 1895 she was held under house arrest by American settlers who declared the islands a republic. During her incarceration she wrote this prayer, which expressed sorrow and forgiveness for her captors. It is a testament to her selflessness, which endeared her to her people and created a legacy that lasts to this day.

Brighten the Corner Where You Are

Do not wait until some deed of greatness you may do,
Do not wait to shed your light afar;
To the many duties ever near you now be true,
Brighten the corner where you are.

Just above are clouded skies that you may help to clear,
Let not narrow self your way debar;
Though into one heart alone may fall your song of cheer,
Brighten the corner where you are.

Here for all your talent you may surely find a need,
Here reflect the bright and Morning Star;
Even from your humble hand the Bread of Life may feed,
Brighten the corner where you are.

Brighten the corner where you are!
Brighten the corner where you are!
Someone far from harbor you may guide across the bar;
Brighten the corner where you are!

These lyrics, admonishing people to turn their small part of the world into a better place, were written by Ina Ogden in 1912. Receiving an invitation to speak in Chautauqua, New York, at a Sunday school training camp, an annual event where both William Jennings Bryan and Theodore Roosevelt had once spoken, was a dream come true for Ogden. As she was about to leave for the lake resort, she learned that her father had been seriously injured in a car accident. After unpacking her bags, she took both the tragedy and her great disappointment in stride by writing this prayer. Upon its publication it became wildly popular at evangelical revivals, including those held in Chautauqua.

Sunday Plea

Oh Lord, Thou hast told us how to pray. Help us to shut the door, shutting out the world, and the enemy and any fear or doubt, which spoils prayer. May there be no distance between our souls and Thee.

Our Father, we have come to sit down together to rest, after a busy week, and to think. We are not satisfied with ourselves for we all, like sheep, have gone astray. What we have done is what we ought not to have done. We are stung to the quick with disappointment, sorrow, and desolation. It seems as though there were a cankerworm eating at the core of our hearts, and there is no rest for our souls day or night. Have pity on us, Lord, and cut us down in Thy displeasure. We confess our sin and bring it to Thee. Let our prayer prevail in Heaven and do Thou heal and help us to a new life in Christ Jesus. Amen.

One of the most successful merchants in U.S. history, Philadelphia's John Wanamaker was a very devout individual. He served as the Sunday school superintendent at his beloved Bethany Presbyterian Church for sixty-five years and often spoke from the church's pulpit. In this prayer he reminds his fellow parishioners of the need to sit back from the roar of their busy lives to reflect on their sins of both omission and commission.

In Appreciation of Immigrants

O Thou great Champion of the outcast and the weak, we remember before Thee the people of other nations who are coming to our land, seeking bread, a home and a future. May we look with Thy compassion upon those who have been drained and stunted by the poverty and oppression of centuries, and whose minds have been warped by superstition or seared by the dumb agony of revolt. We bless thee for all that America has meant to the alien folk that have crossed the sea in the past, and for all the patient strength and God-fearing courage with which they have enriched our nation. We rejoice in the millions whose life has expanded in the wealth and liberty of our country, and whose children have grown to fairer stature and larger thoughts; for we, too, are the children of immigrants, who came with anxious hearts and halting feet on the westward path of hope.

In early-twentieth-century America, Baptist clergyman Walter Rauschenbusch emerged as the major voice of the "social gospel." Like others in the movement, he believed that prayer should be joined to action, and that collectively people needed to take responsibility for healing the social ills of the day. This was particularly true in welcoming the newly arrived immigrants to America's shores.

A Plea

God grant me these: the strength to do
Some needed service here;
The wisdom to be brave and true;
The gift of vision clear,
That in each task that comes to me
Some purpose I may plainly see.

God teach me to believe that I
Am stationed at a post,
Although the humblest 'neath the sky,
Where I am needed most.
And that, at last, if I do well
My humble services will tell.

God grant me faith to stand on guard,
Uncheered, unspoke, alone,
And see behind such duty hard
My service to the throne.
Whate'er my task, this be my creed:
I am on earth to fill a need.

This is perhaps the most famous of the eleven thousand poems that Edgar Guest, known in his day as "the people's poet," published over his lifetime. It was included in a compilation of poems he called *War Time Rhymes.* The collection, published just as America was entering World War I, spoke to the anxious soul of the country. This particular prayer encourages people to serve God by serving others.

At the End of Life's Journey

Dear Lord, I am a living witness to the fact that she was a mother to the motherless, father to the fatherless, a home for the homeless for thousands of Thy dark-skinned children here in Thy vineyard; working night and day to convert them to love Thee, to follow Thee and to serve Thee, and to educate them that they too have a God to serve and a soul to save; and please dear Lord spare her to look over the fruits of her labor for a few more years. Thou will send down a legion of angels to bear her loving soul to the foot of Thy throne, and grant I pray that when she arrives she may find her dear mother and father and my mother and father waiting her arrival to present her to the throne.

Katherine Drexel was born into a wealthy banking family in Philadelphia. Choosing to devote her life to the less fortunate after taking her vows as a nun, she founded her own religious order, the Sisters of the Blessed Sacrament, and used her vast fortune to invest in schools, orphanages, and hospitals. She was particularly concerned over the plight of Native Americans, African Americans, and Hispanic Americans. This prayer, which was composed by the son of a former servant of the Drexel estate, attests to her altruism. In 2000 Mother Drexel was canonized a saint by the Roman Catholic Church.

Revelation

I knelt to pray when day was done,
And prayed, "O Lord bless everyone;
Lift from each saddened heart the pain
And let the sick be well again."
And then I woke another day
And carelessly went on my way.

The whole day long I did not try
To wipe a tear from any eye;
I did not try to share the load
Of any brother on my road;

I did not even go to see
The sick man just next door to me.

Yet once again when day was done
I prayed, "O Lord, bless everyone."
But as I prayed, into my ear
There came a voice that whispered clear:
"Pause, hypocrite, before you pray,
Whom have you tried to bless today?

"God's sweetest blessing always go
By hands that serve him here below."
And then I hid my face, and cried,
"Forgive me, God, for I have lied;
Let me but see another day
And I will live the way I pray."

With nothing but a seventh-grade education, Whitney Mont-gomery became one of the most prominent and beloved literary voices of his native Texas in the early twentieth century. In this piece and in his other prayers and writings he revealed the high bar he set for himself throughout his life.

For True Understanding

Teach us, dear God, to have compassion enough to realize that all men are created in Thine image.

Teach us to understand that man's ultimate happiness depends upon his concern and desire to seek wisdom and comprehension for living and for sharing with all mankind.

Contralto Marian Anderson was deeply religious, once remark-ing that "prayer begins where human capacity ends." She was unexpectedly thrust into the middle of the civil rights debate when she was barred from singing at Washington's Constitution Hall in 1939 because of her race. She came to believe that in order to overcome their deepest prejudices, people needed to ask God to teach them compassion, wisdom, and understanding.

Babe's Prayer

My Jesus, mercy.

Babe Ruth helped redefine the game of baseball with his athletic prowess and his showmanship both on and off the field. When he learned that he had cancer, he feared death was near. Feeling remorse over the course that his personal life had taken, he said this prayer repeatedly. They would be the last words he would utter.

A Litany for All Workers

O God, who hast made us a royal priesthood, that we might offer unto thee prayer and intercession for all sorts and conditions of men, hear us as we pray.

For all who toil in the burden and the heat of the day, that they may enjoy the rewards of their industry, that they may not be defrauded of their due, and that we may never cease to be mindful of our debt to them, remembering with gratitude the multitude of services which must be performed to make our life tolerable:

We pray Thy grace and pledge our concern, O God.

For those who have authority and power over their fellow men, that they may not use it for selfish advantage, but be guided to do justice and to love mercy:

We pray Thy grace and pledge our concern, O God.

For those who have been worsted in the battles of life, whether by the inhumanity of their fellows, their own limitations, or the fickleness of fortune, that they may contend against injustice without bitterness, overcome their own weakness with diligence, and learn how to accept with patience what cannot be altered:

We pray Thy grace and pledge our concern, O God.

For the rulers of the nations, that they may act wisely and without pride, may seek to promote peace among the peoples and establish justice in our common life:

We pray Thy grace and pledge our concern, O God.

For teachers and ministers of the word, for artists and interpreters of our spiritual life, that they may rightly divide the word of truth, and not be tempted by pride or greed or any ignoble passion to corrupt the truth to which they are committed:

We pray Thy grace and pledge our concern, O God.

For prophets and seers and saints, who awaken us from our sloth, that they may continue to hold their torches high in a world darkened by prejudice and sin, and ever be obedient to the heavenly vision:

We pray Thy grace and pledge our concern, O God.

O Lord, who hast bound us together in this bundle of life, give us grace to understand how our lives depend upon the courage, the industry, the honesty and integrity of our fellow men; that we may be mindful of their needs, grateful for their faithfulness, and faithful in our responsibilities to them.

In this series of invocations, written just after World War II, Reinhold Neibuhr, one of the most influential theologians in U.S. history, eloquently tailors the major tenets of the Christian faith to the concerns of all workers everywhere. This prayer only reinforced his reputation as a strong proponent of social ethics.

For the Casualties of War

O Lord, we pray thee to have mercy upon all who are this day wounded and suffering. Though kindred and friends be far away, let thy grace be their comfort. Raise them to health again, if it be thy good pleasure; but chiefly give them patience and faith in thee; through Jesus Christ our Lord. Amen

During each of the country's wars, the Episcopal Church of the United States has issued devotionals for its members and others serving in the U.S. armed services. This prayer for those wounded on the battlefield is taken from a hand-sized book that was distributed among the troops during the Korean War.

If Your Brother Stumbles

Father, I love my brother and I love You. I want to offer You a sacrifice, and beg you in return to send Arthur or Louis the grace to overcome the most dangerous failing they suffer from. Give us this day our daily bread of strength to suffer for each other these little ways of sacrifice, as well as daily pinpricks of daily living which can become a martyrdom in a family and grow into hate and violence.

Dorothy Day was one of the most prominent social activists and journalists of the twentieth century. Having founded the Catholic Worker movement in 1933, she focused her life's work on the lot of American society as a whole and the individuals within it. Her cause for sainthood was initiated by the Catholic Church in 2000. In this plea she speaks to God about two separate tragedies involving two men consumed by alcohol and drugs.

Praying for Each Other

Our God and Father, we need not beg you to be present here, for you have promised that where two or three are gathered in your name, you are in their midst. So we gratefully acknowledge your presence with us. You have wanted us to have fullness of life, and so you have told us to love you with all our heart, soul, strength, and mind, and then to love others in the same way in which we love ourselves.

Forgive us, therefore, O Father, when we have rejected you by not thanking you for the creation you have made or for the leadership you offer. Forgive us when we have degraded or belittled ourselves or hurt others around us. We desire to make these things right. So help us to walk in the assurance that once we have honestly admitted these things and given them to you, we *are* forgiven. We also pray for each other in these days of heavy responsibilities of leadership. May we do these jobs—no matter how important or lowly the task may be—without a sense of superiority or inferiority, realizing that each has his place, that the team would not be complete without any one of us. May we do our tasks with the joy of knowing that we are needed, that others are about us to fill in where we cannot and thus we complement one another.

Above all, O Father, give us love. A love that can be expressed for you, for ourselves, and for one another.

Six weeks after President Richard Nixon took office, this invocation was delivered by the Reverend Louis H. Evans Jr. at a White

House Sunday service. Against the backdrop of the continuing war in Vietnam and the fresh scars from America's race riots just months earlier, the Presbyterian minister from Bel Air, California, called for human kindness through understanding, forgiveness, and resolve.

Public Forgiveness

In this I ask for your prayers and for your help in healing our nation. . . . It is very important that our nation move forward. . . .

Lord, help us to turn from callousness to sensitivity, from hostility to love, from pettiness to purpose, from envy to contentment, from carelessness to discipline, from fear to faith.

Turn us around, Lord, and bring us back toward you. Revive our lives as at the beginning. And turn us toward each other, Lord, for in isolation, there is no life.

I ask you to share my prayer that God will search me and know my heart, try me, and know my anxious thoughts, see if there is any hurtfulness in me and lead me toward a life everlasting. I ask that God give me a clean heart, let me walk by faith and not sight.

At the height of the Monica Lewinsky scandal, President Bill Clinton attempted unsuccessfully to put the matter behind him in a nationwide address from the White House. Realizing that the sincerity of his explanation had not come across to the American people as he had hoped, he decided to use the occasion of his appearance before the National Prayer Breakfast on September 11, 1998, to offer public contrition. He adapted this prayer from the Yom Kippur liturgy.

The Millennium Prayer

Dear Lord, as we awaken to this second morning of a new millennium, help us to remember that all we are and all we do begins with you, for whom a thousand years are but as yesterday when it is passed, and as a watch in the night.

So we begin this jubilee year in humility, with profound thanks for the divine light first revealed 2,000 years ago that has brought us now to this sacred place today. Each in our own way, we thank you for the blessings of this life. For me and my family, I give you thanks for good health, good fortune, and the opportunity to serve the American people.

We thank you for the amazing grace you have shown in getting us through and beyond our individual and collective sins and trials. Through the darkest hours of the 20th century, the shameful trauma of racial oppression, the pain and sacrifice of war, the fear and deprivation of depression, when all we could do was walk by faith, it was your guiding light that saw us through.

We thank you for the promise of the new century, and ask your guidance and grace in helping us to make the most of it; to free our children of hunger, neglect and war; to ease the burdens of the less fortunate; to strengthen the bonds of family; to preserve and protect our earthly home; to use new advances in science and technology to lift all the human family and draw us all closer together.

Finally, we thank you for the rich and wonderful diversity of human life with which you have graced this planet, and ask you to give us the strength and wisdom to give up our fear, distrust and hatred of those who are different. Teach us instead to learn from each other, and celebrate our differences, secure in the knowledge that we are all your children.

Our Constitution tells us you created us all equal. Jesus told us to love our neighbors as ourselves. The Koran says we must do unto all men as you wished to have done to you, and reject for others what you would reject for yourself. The Talmud instructs us, should anyone turn aside the right of the stranger, it is as though he were to turn aside the right of the most high God.

By your grace, we have survived in spite of our blindness to this, your truth. Help us now to accept, at long last, the enduring truth that the most important fact of life is not wealth, or power, or beauty, or scientific advance, but our kinship as brothers and sisters, and our oneness as children of God.

This, Holy Father, is our prayer for the new millennium.

This millennium prayer was delivered by President Bill Clinton on the morning of January 2, 2000, before an overflowing congregation at Washington National Cathedral. It thanks God for sustaining the American people in the past and asks for help from Divine Providence in charting a course for the future.

The Prayer of a Hindu

Let us pray.

We meditate on the transcendental Glory of the Deity Supreme, who is inside the heart of the Earth, inside the life of the sky, and inside the soul of the Heaven. May He stimulate and illuminate our minds.

Lead us from the unreal to the real, from darkness to light, and from death to immortality. May we be protected together. May we be nourished together. May we work together with great vigor. May our study be enlightening. May no obstacle arise between us.

May the Senators strive constantly to serve the welfare of the world, performing their duties with the welfare of others always in mind, because by devotion to selfless work one attains the supreme goal of life. May they work carefully and wisely, guided by compassion and without thought for themselves.

United your resolve, united your hearts, may your spirits be as one, that you may long dwell in unity and concord.

Peace, peace, peace be unto all.

On July 12, 2007, the U.S. Senate opened its daily session with a prayer delivered by a guest chaplain of the Hindu faith. As Mr. Rajan Zed of the Indian Association of Northern Nevada began to speak, he was shouted down by protesters who believed that a non-Christian prayer was unacceptable. He continued his invocation after the protesters were escorted out of the Senate gallery by Capitol police.

PURPOSE AND PERSPECTIVE

Understanding My Existence

With your feet I walk
I walk with your limbs
I carry forth your body
For me your mind thinks
Your voice speaks for me
Beauty is before me
And beauty is behind me
Above and below me hovers the beautiful
I am surrounded by it
I am immersed in it
In my youth I am aware of it
And in old age I shall walk quietly
The beautiful trail.

This old Navajo prayer discerns the life and beauty of God's earth. It provides a moral compass point, making clear that all of creation has been lovingly provided by a higher power.

Whether Life Be Short or Long

> Lord it belongs not to my care,
> Whether I die or live;
> To love and serve Thee is my share,
> And this Thy grace must give.
> If life be long, I will be glad,
> That I may long obey;
> If short, yet why should I be sad,
> That shall have the same pay!

This eulogy was delivered at the funeral of William Brewster, who was well into his eighties when he died in 1644. The most famous of the original Pilgrims, Brewster represented the qualities idealized by most of America's early settlers—determination, persistence, and deep faith in God. More than simply a prayerful oration, these words expressed the core philosophy of life of the Pilgrims.

On the Gallows

I pray God that I may be a warning to you all, and that I may be the last that ever shall suffer after this manner: in the fear of God I warn you to have a care of taking the Lord's Name in vain; mind and have a care of that Sin of drunkenness, for that is a sin that leads to all manner of sins and wickedness: mind, and have a care of breaking the sixth Commandment, where it is said, *Thou shalt do no Murder,* for when a Man is in Drink he is ready to commit all manner of sin till he fill up the cup of the wrath of God, as I have done by committing that Sin of Murder . . .

But here I am, and know not what will become of my poor Soul which is within a few moments of Eternity; I, that have Murdered a poor Man, who had but a little time to Repent, and I

know not what's become of his poor Soul; O that I may make use
of this opportunity that I have; O that I may make improvement
of this little time before I go hence and be no more: O let all
mind what I am saying now, I am going out of this World; O take
warning by me, and beg of God to keep you from this Sin which
hath been my ruin.

O Lord receive my Spirit, I come unto thee O Lord, I come unto
thee O Lord; I Come, I Come, I Come.

One of the more dramatic episodes in early colonial America
was the hanging of convicted murderer James Morgan in 1686.
Reverend Increase Mather, who had just been named president
of Harvard a year earlier, counseled the man to confess his sins
publicly as a means of finding redemption. Given the eloquence
of the prayer, Increase Mather undoubtedly had a hand in writing the prayer that was delivered that morning.

Nurturing a Proper Attitude

O God animate us to cheerfulness. May we have a joyful sense of
our blessings, learn to look on the bright circumstances of our
lot, and maintain a perpetual contentedness under thy
allotments. Fortify our minds against disappointment and
calamity. Preserve us from despondency, from yielding to
dejection. Teach us that no evil is intolerable but a guilty
conscience, and that nothing can hurt us, if, with true loyalty of
affection, we keep thy commandments and take refuge in thee;
through Jesus Christ our Lord. Amen.

The most prominent Unitarian minister in U.S. history, William
Ellery Channing preached the universality of the human family
throughout his ministry. In this prayer he asks God to help people put their lives into proper perspective and to find joy in their
daily existence.

A Psalm of Life

Tell me not, in mournful numbers,
Life is but an empty dream!
For the soul is dead that slumbers,
And things are not what they seem.

Life is real! Life is earnest!
And the grave is not its goal;
Dust thou art, to dust returnest,
Was not spoken of the soul.

Not enjoyment, and not sorrow,
Is our destined end or way;
But to act, that each to-morrow
Find us farther than to-day.

Art is long, and Time is fleeting,
And our hearts, though stout and brave,
Still, like muffled drums, are beating
Funeral marches to the grave.

In the world's broad field of battle,
In the bivouac of Life,
Be not like dumb, driven cattle!
Be a hero in the strife!

Trust no Future, howe'er pleasant!
Let the dead Past bury its dead!
Act,—act in the living Present!
Heart within, and God o'erhead!

Lives of great men all remind us
We can make our lives sublime,
And, departing, leave behind us
Footprints on the sands of time;

Footprints, that perhaps another,
Sailing o'er life's solemn main,
A forlorn and shipwrecked brother,
Seeing, shall take heart again.

Let us, then, be up and doing,
With a heart for any fate;
Still achieving, still pursuing,
Learn to labor and to wait.

Henry Wadsworth Longfellow wrote this piece in the 1830s during a bout of severe depression. At first he showed it to no one, believing it was too personal, but after many months he reluctantly decided to share it with his students at Harvard. Like the Psalms of King David it is deeply introspective and has been considered one of the greatest short poems ever written in the English language.

Most Richly Blessed

I asked You, God, for strength that I might achieve,
I was made weak that I might learn humbly to obey;
I asked for health that I might do greater things,
I was given infirmity that I might do better things;
I asked for riches that I might be happy,
I was given poverty that I might be wise;
I asked for power that I might have the praise of men,
I was given weakness that I might feel the need of God;
I got nothing that I asked for,
But everything I hoped for;
I am among all men most richly blessed.

In the hours following the Battle of Gettysburg, which registered the largest number of casualties during the Civil War, both the

North and South collected their dead. The body of a Confederate soldier was found in Devil's Den, the bloodiest site of the battle, with this prayer in his pocket. Although his name remains unknown to this day, his prayer stands as one of the most compelling introspections ever written.

Then I Am Ready to Go

Tie the Strings to my Life, My Lord,
Then, I am ready to go!
Just a look at the Horses—
Rapid! That will do!

Put me in on the firmest side—
So I shall never fall—
For we must ride to the Judgment—
And it's partly, down Hill—

But never I mind the steeper—
And never I mind the Sea—
Held fast in Everlasting Race—
By my own Choice, and Thee—

Goodbye to the Life I used to live—
And the World I used to know—
And kiss the Hills, for me, just once—
Then—I am ready to go!

Emily Dickinson became celebrated for her simple and witty poems, and this one is no exception. Although reclusive in real life, she nonetheless showed intense spiritual restlessness. Here she shares her unvarnished and matter-of-fact approach to death.

Consecration

Behold thy sons and daughters, Lord,
On whom we lay our hands;
They have fulfilled the Gospel word,
And bowed at thy commands.

Seal them by thine own Spirit's power,
Which purifies from sin;
And may they find from this blest hour,
Thy Spirit rules within.

Strengthen their faith, confirm their hope
And guide them in the way;
With comfort bear their spirits up
Until the perfect day.

Parley Pratt, a direct ancestor of former Massachusetts governor Mitt Romney, was one of the most popular figures of the early Mormon Church. Not only did he serve as a Mormon apostle, but he was elected to the Utah Territorial Legislature in 1854. This prayer, one of dozens he composed, was written for new members of the church, to be used on the occasion of their confirmation.

Before the March

Kind Heavenly Father, we are about to march into the unknown. We don't know what lies up the road in New Market, but we expect it isn't going to be good. We ask your protection for these fine boys. We ask that You also watch over their homes, their mothers and fathers, until they are all reunited with their families. Bless our young country, Father, whether we are on our way to victory or defeat. And if any of our number should die in the coming battle, we ask that You take us into eternity with You.

May we all be safe in the coming battle, and may we show mercy to our enemy. Amen

One of the more moving prayers written in time of war was composed on May 15, 1864, by Captain Frank Preston, an instructor of English, Latin, and Tactics at the Virginia Military Institute. With little notice Confederate general John C. Breckinridge ordered the cadets to begin a twenty-six-mile march to New Market, Virginia, to face off against Union forces. Realizing that many of the young men would soon be killed in battle, Preston composed this prayer on the spot and led the young soldiers in reciting it. Seven of the boys would be dead within hours.

Two Prayers in Pursuit of Personal Duty

APRIL 14
Lord, thy teaching grace impart,
That we may not read in vain;
Write thy precepts on our heart,
Make thy truths and doctrine plain;
Let the message of Thy love
Guide us to Thy rest above.

APRIL 15
Far from the paths of men, to Thee
I solemnly retire;
See Thou, who dost in secret see,
And grant my heart's desire.

These two prayers were part of a collection of daily invocations entitled *Believers Daily Treasure* and published in London in 1852. A copy of the book was found among the personal possessions of Abraham Lincoln. Pulitzer Prize winner and Lincoln biographer Carl Sandburg believed that in all likelihood Mary Todd

Lincoln, the president's wife, had given it to him on a special occasion and that he turned to it regularly. The first entry on April 14, Good Friday, would have been the day Lincoln was shot. The second one was the devotional offered on the day he died.

Rest, Noble Martyr

Rest, noble Martyr! Rest in peace:
Rest with the true and brave,
Who like thee, fell in Freedom's cause,
The nation's life to save.

Thy name shall live while time endures,
And men shall say of thee,
"He saved his country from its foes,
And bade the slave be free."

These deeds shall be thy monument,
Better than brass or stone;
They leave thy fame in glory's light,
Unrival'd and alone.

This consecrated spot shall be
To Freedom ever dear;
And Freedom's sons of every race
Shall weep and worship here,

O God! Before whom we, in tears,
Our fallen Chief deplore;
Grant that the cause, for which he died,
May live forevermore.

In the last days of Abraham Lincoln's life, there was no spiritual mentor to whom he was closer than Reverend Phineas Gurley.

On many Wednesday evenings Lincoln would attend the minister's prayer services at the New York Avenue Presbyterian Church in Washington, sitting in a room just off from the congregation with the door ajar so as not to distract anyone. Upon the president's death, Gurley accompanied the body on the long, circuitous train route to Springfield, Illinois. During the trip, Gurley wrote this prayer, which was sung by a choir as Lincoln's body was being interred.

Prayer at the Golden Spike Ceremony

Our Father and God, and our fathers' God, God of Creation and God of Providence, thou hast created the heavens and the earth, the valleys and the hills; Thou art also the God of mercies and blessings. We rejoice that thou hast created the human mind with its power of invention, its capacity of expansion, and its guardian of success. We have assembled here this day, upon the height of the continent, from varied sections of our country, to do homage to thy wonderful name, in that thou hast brought this mighty enterprise, combining the commerce of the east with the gold of the west to so glorious a completion. And now we ask thee that this great work, so auspiciously begun and so magnificently completed, may remain a monument to our faith and good works. We here consecrate this great highway for the good of thy people. O God, we implore thy blessings upon it and upon those that may direct its operations. O Father, God of our fathers, we desire to acknowledge thy handiwork in this great work, and ask thy blessing upon us here assembled, upon the rulers of our government and upon thy people everywhere; that peace may flow unto them as a gentle stream, and that this mighty enterprise may be unto us as the Atlantic of thy strength, and the Pacific of thy love. Through Jesus, the Redeemed.

One of the great technological and human achievements in history, the construction of the transcontinental railroad captured the imagination of Americans and symbolized the country's enormous potential. When the Central Pacific and Union Pacific Railroads were joined at Promontory Point in Utah, an elaborate ceremony was held to celebrate the final "golden spike" being driven into the ground. Congregational minister John Todd of Pittsfield, Massachusetts, offered this opening prayer.

Roll On, Thou Bright Evangel

> O God of grace, this Chapel speed,
> Wherever sin is found
> Display thy light, thy love, thy life,
> Till grace much more abound.
> Go forth, go forth to all mankind;
> Go preach my gospel true.
> All pow'r is mine; go forth, go forth!
> I am with you, I am with you!

With the launch of the transcontinental railroad, distant regions of the country became interconnected as never before. The Baptist, Catholic, and Episcopalian churches decided to meet the religious needs of their rural followers by building "chapel cars" that could be attached to trains. Each car, set up with pews, a sanctuary, stained-glass windows, and a sleeping compartment for the clergy, was commissioned with a prayer that was engraved on a prominent plaque. This particular invocation was part of the "Amazing Grace" chapel car sponsored by the Baptist Church in Los Angeles.

The Old Rugged Cross

On a hill far away stood an old rugged cross.
The emblem of suffering and shame;
And I love that old cross where the dearest and best
For a world of lost sinners was slain.

So I'll cherish the old rugged cross
Till my trophies at last I lay down;
I will cling to the old rugged cross
And exchange it some day for a crown.

Written by George Bennard in 1913 after his religious conversion at a Salvation Army meeting, this hymn came to symbolize the social gospel movement that began in the early twentieth century. With its blend of Christian imagery, sense of duty, and a memorable melody, it became instantly popular and remains one of the most frequently recorded hymns of all time.

The Gifts I Ask

These are the gifts I ask
Of thee, Spirit serene:
Strength for the daily task,
Courage to face the road,
Good cheer to help me bear the traveler's load,
And, for the hours of rest that come between,
An inward joy in all things heard and seen.
These are the sins I fain
Would have thee take away:
Malice, and cold disdain,
Hot anger, sullen hate,
Scorn of the lowly, envy of the great,
And discontent that casts a shadow gray
On all the brightness of the common day.

These are the things I prize
And hold of dearest worth:
Light of the sapphire skies,
Peace of the silent hills,
Shelter of forests, comfort of the grass,
Music of birds, murmur of little rills,
Shadow of clouds that swiftly pass,
And, after showers,
The smell of flowers
And of the good brown earth,—
And best of all, along the way, friendship and mirth.

So let me keep
These treasures of the humble heart
In true possession, owning them by love;
And when at last I can no longer move
Among them freely, but must part
From the green fields and from the waters clear,
Let me not creep
Into some darkened room and hide
From all that makes the world so bright and dear;
But throw the windows wide
To welcome in the light;
And while I clasp a well-beloved hand,
Let me once more have sight
Of the deep sky and the far-smiling land,—
Then gently fall on sleep,
And breathe my body back to Nature's care,
My spirit out to thee, God of the open air.

This prayer, full of rich, human insight, seeks to put life in mean-ingful balance. Its author, Henry van Dyke, was a Presbyterian minister, a professor of English literature at Princeton, and am-bassador to the Netherlands and Luxembourg during President Woodrow Wilson's administration. He was eventually elected to the American Academy of Arts and Letters. His broad and rich career provided him with an extraordinary foundation for producing hundreds of prayers over his lifetime.

In Joy or Pain

O Lord by all Thy dealings with us, whether of joy or pain, of light or darkness, let us be brought to Thee. May we value no treatment of us simply because it makes us happy or because it makes us sad, because it gives or denies what we want, but may all that Thou sendest us draw us to Thee; that knowing Thy loving wisdom, we may be sure in every disappointment that Thou art still caring for us, in every darkness that Thou art enlightening us, and in every enforced idleness that Thou art still using us: yea, in every death giving us life, as in his death Thou didst give life to Thy Son, our Savior Jesus Christ.

Phillips Brooks, a graduate of the Virginia Theological Seminary and one of the most prominent Episcopal bishops in history, could trace his ancestry back to the renowned Reverend John Cotton of the Massachusetts Bay Colony. His intellectual and spiritual influence on Americans was enormous at the turn of the twentieth century. Helen Keller, the deaf-blind author, activist, and lecturer, considered Brooks to be a great mentor and was particularly inspired by this prayer.

The Virgin of Chartres

Gracious Lady:—
Simple as when I asked your aid before;
Humble as when I prayed for grace in vain
Seven hundred years ago; weak, weary, sore
In heart and hope, I ask your help again . . .

So I too wandered off among the host
That racked the earth to find the father's clue.
I did not find the Father, but I lost
What now I value more, the Mother,—You! . . .

But when we must, we pray, as in the past
Before the Cross on which your Son was nailed.
Listen, dear Lady! You shall hear the last
Of the strange prayers Humanity has wailed.

Henry Adams, the grandson of John Quincy Adams and great-grandson of John Adams, evolved into one of the great intellectuals of the early twentieth century. One of the most pivotal periods in his life came during an extended trip to Europe when he became absorbed in history, architecture, art, religion, and much more. After a visit to France's Chartres Cathedral, dedicated to Mary, the Mother of God, he wrote an open letter to Mary of which these three verses were a part.

Use Me

Use me then, my Saviour, for whatever purpose,
and in whatever way, you may require.
Here is my poor heart, an empty vessel;
fill it with your grace.
Here is my sinful and troubled soul;
quicken it and refresh it with your love.
Take my heart for your abode;
my mouth to spread abroad the glory of your name;
my love and all my powers,
for the advancement of your believing people;
and never suffer the steadfastness and
confidence of my faith to abate;
so that at all times I may be enabled from the heart to say,
"Jesus needs me, and I Him."

Dwight Lyman Moody, one of the great evangelical preachers in U.S. history, was driven to spread Christ's Gospel around the world and to leave a foundation in place, including the Moody Bible Institute, that would continue his work long after his death. Thousands would throng to his crusades to hear his message of God's salvation. This particular prayer, composed and often recited by Moody, both publicly and privately, was the cornerstone of his ministry.

Ready

Lord, I am ready to do your work.

Thomas Dorsey, the author of such famous works as "Precious Lord, Take My Hand" and "Peace in the Valley," wrote well over eight hundred gospel songs. Early in his career he suffered from serious depression, losing considerable weight and withdrawing from all public contact. After his parson intervened and told him to snap out of it, Dorsey experienced what he would later describe as a personal epiphany. He knelt down and said these words.

Teach Me to Pray

Lord, teach me to pray
Not for myself alone, but for all who need You
Not with my lips alone, but with Your Mind in me
Seeking not only Your gifts but, above all, You.
Not my will, but Yours,
Not my feverish pursuit of things, but Your Grace
Make the mind a channel for the Divine Mind—and let the
spirit of truth speak through my lips,

Whether I work or play or eat or sleep or read or talk or
   whatever I do
Even when I forget You
Abide in me.
Use me
Always
Not for myself alone, but for all who need You.
Increase my faith.
Dear God—I thank You for Your Wonder and Your Glory.
I thank You that You hear our prayers.
So be it—always.

Cecil B. DeMille, one of Hollywood's legendary directors, was a religiously complex individual. After producing such blockbusters as *The King of Kings* and *The Ten Commandments*, he found that the depth of his spirituality had only increased. This prayer conveys both his recognition of the hand of God in his life and the need for commitment to others.

In the Passage of Time

Master of the Universe, let us make up. It's time. How long can we go on being angry? . . . What about my faith in you, Master of the Universe? I now realize I never lost it, not even over there, during the darkest hours of my life. I don't know why I kept on whispering my daily prayers, and those one reserves for the Sabbath and for the holidays, but I did recite them, often with my father and, on Rosh ha-Shana eve, with hundreds of inmates at Auschwitz. Was it because the prayers remained a link to the vanished world of my childhood? . .˙. questions have been haunting me for five decades. . . . Yes, in spite of it all, let us make up: for the child in me, it is unbearable to be divorced from you so long.

Nobel Peace Prize winner, Holocaust survivor, and naturalized
U.S. citizen Elie Wiesel composed this meditation a half century
after suffering the gross indignities of Hitler's "Final Solution."
Only with the passage of time was he able to address the rift that
had developed in his mind between him and God.

Prayer for an Invading Army

Let them come home! Oh let the battle, Lord, be brief,
and let our boys come home!
So cries the heart, sick for relief
from its anxiety, and seeking to forestall
a greater grief.

So cries the heart aloud. But the thoughtful mind
has something of its own to say:
On that day
when they come home from very far away
and further than you think
(for each of them has stood upon the very brink
or sat and waited in the anteroom
of Death, expecting every moment to be called by name)

Now look to this matter well: that they
upon returning shall not find
seated at their own tables,—at the head,
perhaps, of the long festive board prinked out in prodigal
    array,
the very monster which they sallied forth to conquer and
    to quell;
and left behind for dead.

Let us forget such words, and all they mean,
as Hatred, Bitterness and Rancor, Greed,

Intolerance, Bigotry; let us renew
our faith and pledge to Man, his right to be
Himself, and free.

Say that the Victory is ours—then say
and each man search his heart in true humility
Lord! Father! Who are we,
that we should wield so great a weapon for the rights
and rehabilitation of Thy creature Man?

Lo, from all corners of the Earth we ask
all great and noble to come forth—converge
upon this errand and this task with generous and gigantic
    plan:
Hold high this Torch, who will.
Lift up this Sword, who can!

A lifelong pacifist, Edna St. Vincent Millay had a change of heart toward the end of World War II when the atrocities of Hitler and others became well known. On the dawn of the D-day invasion she was asked to write an appropriate poem to be read on NBC radio by actor Ronald Colman. This was the piece she composed, and one that is relevant to any war.

Looking to the Future

Lord, for these simple things I plead:
That my mind may be a quiet harbor where ships of
    thought may dock;
That my heart may be a temple of love;
That my soul be a flourishing vine that reaches steadily
    upward toward heaven and God;
That my religion be as a loaf of bread that gives
    nourishment to me and my hungering neighbor;

That my life may be a light kept aglow by the fuel of kindly
deeds done

For others;
That my friendship be a cool, bubbling brook where all
races may drink its water;
Lastly, that I be dedicated to the truth and clothed in
the fire of righteousness.

Written by seventeen-year-old Wilma Curtis of Abilene, Texas,
this prayer demonstrates unusual maturity and eloquence for
someone so young. She decided to publish the piece for the ben-
efit of her classmates and other young people just after World
War II.

The Prayer of the Game Guy

Dear God, help me to be a sport in this little game of life.
I don't ask for any easy place in this lineup.
Play me anywhere you need me.
I only ask you for the stuff to give you
one hundred percent of what I have got.
If all the hard drives seem to come my way, I thank you for
the compliment.
Help me to remember that you won't ever let anything
come my way that you and I together can't handle.

And help me to take the bad break as part of the game.
Help me to understand that the game is full of knots and
knocks and trouble, and make me thankful for them.
Help me to be brave, so that the harder they come, the
better I like it.
And, oh God, help me to always play on the square.

No matter what the other players do, help me to come
  clean.

Help me to study the book, so that I'll know the rules, to
  study and think a lot about the greatest player that ever
  lived and other players that are portrayed in the book.
If they ever found out the best part of the game was
  helping other guys who are out of luck, help me to find
  it out, too.
Help me to be regular, and also an inspiration with the
  other players. Finally, oh God, if fate seems to uppercut
  me with both hands, and I am laid on the shelf in
  sickness or old age or something, help me to take that as
  part of the game, too.
Help me not to whimper or squeal that the game was a
  frame up or that I had a raw deal.
When, in the falling dusk, I get the final bell, I ask for no
  lying, complimentary tombstones.
I'd only like to know that you feel that I have been a good
  guy, a good game guy, a saint in the game of life.

This anonymous prayer took on a life of its own after journalist
Edward R. Murrow read it during a segment of his legendary
CBS program *Person to Person.* No sooner had it been aired than
CBS telephone lines were jammed with people wanting a copy.
By 1989 the piece returned to public prominence when the
U.S. Supreme Court was ruling on a sentencing matter in a murder case that took place in South Carolina. The defendant,
Demetrius Gathers, claimed to be a preacher and was found to
have a copy of the prayer among his belongings when he was arrested. He was convicted of the crime, and the South Carolina
prosecutor successfully argued that Gathers should receive the
death sentence on the grounds that possession of the tract
clearly showed the man understood the consequences of his
actions. In a decision written by Associate Justice William
Brennan, the U.S. Supreme Court overruled the lower court, de-

claring that mere possession of "The Prayer of the Game Guy" should have no bearing on the man's sentence.

A Public Prayer for Divine Perspective

Eternal and everlasting God, who art the Father of all mankind, as we turn aside from the hurly-burly of everyday living, may our hearts and souls, yea our very spirits, be lifted upward to Thee, for it is from Thee that all blessing cometh. Keep us ever mindful of our dependence upon Thee, for without Thee our efforts are but naught. We pray for Thy divine guidance as we travel the highways of life. We pray for more courage. We pray for more faith and above all we pray for more love.

May we somehow come to understand the true meaning of Thy love as revealed to us in the life, death and resurrection of Thy son and our Lord and Master, Jesus Christ. May the Cross ever remind us of Thy great love, for greater love no man hath given. This is our supreme example, O God. May we be constrained to follow in the name and spirit of Jesus, we pray.

Coretta Scott King, the wife of the Reverend Martin Luther King Jr., wrote her own spiritual essays and prayers attesting to her abiding faith in God. Her spiritual horizons expanded dramatically during her marriage and throughout her life-changing experiences in the civil rights movement in the 1950s and early 1960s, when she composed this piece.

Prayer of a Breton Fisherman

O God, thy sea is so great, and my boat is so small.

Admiral Hyman Rickover, the father of the nuclear navy, presented a copy of this prayer, which he had engraved on a small desk plaque, to each new submarine commander assigned to the Polaris nuclear submarine program. After the election of John F. Kennedy to the presidency, Rickover presented the former U.S. Navy lieutenant and World War II hero with a copy of the same plaque. The prayer would occupy a special place on his desk in the Oval Office, and after the president's assassination in 1963, the plaque was put on display at the Kennedy Library in Boston.

Prayer to Allah

I submit to no one but Thee, O Allah, I submit to no one but Thee. I submit to Thee because Thou hast no partner. All praise and blessings come from Thee, and Thou art alone in Thy kingdom.

This prayer, which stems from the teachings of the Koran, has had some significance in recent U.S. history. To Malcolm X, who was an avowed racist for a good portion of his adult life, it became the catalyst for his personal conversion. On a pilgrimage to Mecca in 1964, he witnessed tens of thousands of Muslims, including "blond-haired, blue-eyed men I could call my brothers," reciting these words, and he realized that he could no longer adhere to his prejudices.

The Kitchen Conversion

Lord, I'm down here trying to do what's right. . . . Lord, I must confess that I'm weak now. . . . I am at the end of my powers. I have nothing left. I can't face it alone.

When Rosa Parks was arrested on December 1, 1955, in Montgomery, Alabama, for not giving up her seat on a bus to a white person, Dr. Martin Luther King Jr. led the ensuing 382-day bus boycott in Montgomery, and became a prime target of racial hatred. After retiring to bed early on New Year's Eve in 1955, Reverend King received a call in the middle of the night from a white racist who threatened his life and those of his wife and six-week-old daughter. At his wit's end, he quietly went to the kitchen and prayed for guidance, prepared to give up his leadership role in the civil rights movement. Within minutes he experienced what he would call his "kitchen epiphany," realizing that he had no choice but to go forward.

My Daily Journey

Almighty God, our loving heavenly Father, through faith and the Holy Ghost I am totally one unity with Thee. I am completely whole in mind and body.

Thou art all of me and I am a little part of Thee. Every little cell, every little vibration which is me is only an outward expression of Thy divine will in perfect health and harmony.

Thou art always guiding me, inspiring me to make the right decisions in family matters, in business matters, in health matters, and especially in spiritual matters.

And dear God, I am deeply, deeply grateful for Thy millions of blessings and millions of miracles with which you surround each of us.

Today and every day, I am especially grateful for the miracle of prayers answered and for the joy of being a humble servant of Thine on earth.

Help me to see more clearly how to use these marvelously increasing assets and talents to accomplish the very most for Thy purposes on earth.

Dear God, help me to open my mind and heart more fully to receive Thy unlimited love and wisdom, and to radiate these to Thy other children on earth especially today and every day this year.

Thank Thee for my redemption and salvation and for Thy gift of the Holy Ghost by grace, which fills me to overflowing, and increasingly dominates my every thought and word and deed.

To Thee we pray in the name of Thy beloved son whom I adore and seek to imitate, my savior and my God, Christ Jesus.

Few individuals have helped to shape the message of God and universal truth in today's world more than Sir John Templeton. Having become a billionaire by pioneering the use of globally diversified mutual funds in the years after World War II, he later set up a foundation dedicated to engaging the world in a dialogue about God, nature, and the universe. For the past two decades he has recited this series of prayers each day as a reminder to remain disciplined and committed to God.

A Prayer for Morning

I am so weary, Father, of using myself as the measure of everything and everybody. Just for one day, I beg you, help me to find release from the old pattern of seeing the different-from-me as either less-than or more-than-me. Grant instead that, for just this one day at least, I may see everything and everybody I meet in terms of how I want you to see me this day's end.

Phyllis Tickle was the founding editor of the religion department of *Publishers Weekly* and has written more than two dozen books on spirituality. In this prayer she strikes to the heart of self-involvement and asks God to help his children see others as they would like to be seen by Him.

Lord, You Give the Great Commission

Lord, you give the great commission:
"Heal the sick and preach the word."
Lest the Church neglect its mission
and the Gospel go unheard,
help us witness to your purpose
with renewed integrity;
with the Spirit's gifts empower us
for the work of ministry.

Lord, you call us to your service:
"In my name baptize and teach."
That the world may trust your promise,
life abundant meant for each,
give us all new fervor,
draw us closer in community;
with the Spirit's gifts empower us
for the work of ministry.

Lord, you make the common holy:
"This my body, this my blood."
Let your priests, for earth's true glory,
daily lift life heavenward,
asking that world around us
share your children's liberty;
with the Spirit's gifts empower us
for the work of ministry.

Lord, you show us love's true measure:
"Father, what they do, forgive."
Yet we hoard as private treasure
all that you so freely give.
May your care and mercy lead us
to a just society;
with the Spirit's gifts empower us
for the work of ministry.

Lord, you bless with words assuring:
"I am with you to the end."
Faith and hope and love restoring,
may we serve as you intend,
and, amid the cares that claim us,
hold in mind eternity;
with the Spirit's gifts empower us
for the work of ministry.

This hymn was composed by Jeffrey Rowthorn in 1978 when he was chapel minister at Yale Divinity School. Born in Wales, he immigrated to the United States after being ordained an Anglican priest and serving in several English parishes. In addition to his service at Yale, he would become the chaplain of Union Theological Seminary in New York City and would later be named Suffragan Bishop of Connecticut. This work, charging all Christians to carry out the message of the Gospels, was sung by 47,000 congregants at the Mass celebrated by Pope Benedict XVI at Washington, D.C.'s Nationals Park in April 2008.

COURAGE AND STRENGTH

The Prayer of a Lenape Warrior

O poor me!
Who am going out to fight the enemy
And know not whether I shall return again,
To enjoy the embraces of my children
And my wife
O poor creature!
Whose life is not in his own hands,
Who has no power over his own body,
But tries to do his duty
For the welfare of his nation.
O! thou Great Spirit above!
Take pity on my children
And on my wife!
Prevent their mourning on my account!
Grant that I may be successful in this attempt—
That I may slay my enemy,
And bring home the trophies of war
To my dear family and friends,
That we may rejoice together.
O! Take pity on me!
Give me strength and courage to meet my enemy,

Suffer me strength and courage to meet my enemy,
Suffer me to return again to my children,
To my wife
And to my relations!
Take pity on me and preserve my life
And I will make to thee a sacrifice.

Written by an early Lenape Indian warrior, this prayer chronicles the anxiety felt universally by anyone setting off to face his enemy. John Heckewelder, a prominent Moravian missionary from eastern Pennsylvania in the late eighteenth century, was moved by the man's unvarnished sentiments and set out to translate the prayer and have it published along with notes from his diary. This work has become one of the most poignant and beloved prayers passed down from early Native America.

Overcoming My Fears

O Great Father,
I think over again my small adventures.
My fears,
Those small ones that seemed so big,
For all the vital things
I had to get and reach.
And yet there is only one great thing,
The only thing,
To live to see the great day that dawns
And the light that fills the world.

This anonymous prayer from the Inuit, the indigenous peoples of Alaska and the Arctic regions of North America, was written in the nineteenth century. It has gained renewed interest in recent years, particularly among those addressing the effects of global warming.

On the Eve of Battle

> God, give me guts.

An officer in the Revolutionary War and later a member of the Connecticut State Assembly, Eli Mygatt saw some of the worst fighting of the war, including his home and most of the town of Danbury being burned to the ground by the British in April 1777. Days after being commissioned a lieutenant colonel, he led his men in battle and wrote these words down in his diary. This four-word prayer would not only become an inspiration for future U.S. soldiers, but it would be echoed by generations of competitive athletes as well.

O Heal Me, Lord, for I Am Weak

> O heal me, Lord, for I am weak;
> My bones are vexed with pain;
> Let not thy hot displeasure speak;
> Thy burning wrath restrain.
> My soul what sore vexations try!
> How long shall they assail?
> Return, and listen to my cry;
> Let mercy, Lord, prevail.
>
> Of thee no memory remains
> In death's relentless cave;
> To thee ascend no grateful strains
> Of glory from the grave;
> With ceaseless pain I groan and weep,
> So cruel are my foes;
> My very couch in tears I steep,
> My bed with grief overflows.

Depart from me, all who rejoice
Iniquity to share;
The Lord hath heard my moaning voice,
And listened to my prayer;

What though my foes despise the Lord,
And my destruction plot?
Vexation shall be their reward
And sudden shame their lot.

Throughout his long political career John Quincy Adams gained a reputation for being distant, an effete intellectual, and a bit of a curmudgeon. He also made his share of political enemies who at times were the bane of his existence. In this prayer he lays his enormous frustrations before God, asking for God's mercy and justice.

O God, Where Art Thou?

O God, where art thou? And where is the pavilion that covereth thy hiding place?

How long shall thy hand be stayed, and thine eye, yea thy pure eye, behold from the eternal heavens the wrongs of thy people and of thy servants, and thine ear be penetrated with their cries?

Yea, O Lord, how long shall they suffer these wrongs and unlawful oppressions, before thine heart shall be softened toward them, and thy bowels be moved with compassion toward them?

Let thine anger be kindled against our enemies; and, in the fury of thine heart, with thy sword avenge us of our wrongs.

Remember thy suffering saints, O our God; and thy servants will rejoice in thy name forever.

Joseph Smith, the founder of the Church of Jesus Christ of Latter-day Saints (better known as the Mormon Church) recorded this series of ejaculations while he and his companions were incarcerated for espousing their religious beliefs. Never in his life had he experienced such anguish, as this prayer attests. A few months later he would be killed by an unruly mob in Carthage, Illinois.

Life's Railway to Heaven

Life is like a mountain railway,
With an engineer that's brave;
We must make the run successful,
From the cradle to the grave;
Watch the curves, the fills, the tunnels;
Never falter, never fail;
Keep your hands upon the throttle,
And your eyes upon the rail.

You will roll up grades of trial;
You will cross the bridge of strife;
See that Christ is your conductor
On this lightning train of life;
Always mindful of obstruction,
Do your duty, never fail;
Keep your hands upon the throttle,
And your eyes upon the rail.

You will often find obstructions,
Look for storms and wind and rain;
On a fill, or curve, or trestle

They will almost ditch your train;
Put your trust alone in Jesus,
Never falter, never fail;
Keep your hands upon the throttle,
And your eyes upon the rail.

As you roll across the trestle,
Spanning Jordan's swelling tide,
You behold the Union Depot
Into which your train will glide;
There you'll meet the Sup'rintendent,
God, the Father, God the Son,
With the hearty, joyous plaudit,
"Weary Pilgrim, welcome home."

Blessed Savior, Thou wilt guide us,
Till we reach that blissful shore,
When the angels wait to join us
In Thy praise forevermore.

Eliza Snow was one of the most famous hymn writers of the early Mormon Church. She was married first to Mormon founder Joseph Smith and later to Brigham Young after Smith's death. Known as the "poetess of Zion," she wrote prayers that largely spoke to the virtue of possessing fealty in God. In this piece, perhaps her most famous, she likens traveling life's journey to guiding a train along a mountainous course that requires unwavering determination, skill, and bravery.

In Black Distress

In black distress, I called my God,
When I could scarce believe Him mine,
He bowed his ear to my complaints—
No more the whale did me confine.

Taken from Herman Melville's *Moby-Dick*, this verse was adapted from an old Dutch Reformed Church hymn and tailored to the needs of the novel. The obsessed Ahab and his men sing these haunting words during a worship service held by the mesmerizing Father Mapple. They then file out of the church and begin their quest for the great whale.

In Search of Freedom

You are loosed from your moorings, and are free; I am fast in my chains and am a slave! You move merrily before the gentle gale and I sadly before the bloody whip! You are freedom's swift-winged angels that fly round the world; I am confined in bands of iron! O that I were free! O, that I were on one of your gallant decks, and under your protecting wing! Alas! Betwixt me and you, the turbid waters roll. Go on, go on. O that I could also go! Could I but swim! If I could fly! O, why was I born a man, of whom to make a brute! The glad ship is gone; she hides in the dim distance. I am left in the hottest hell of unending slavery. O God, save me! God deliver me! Let me be free! Is there any God? Why am I a slave? I will run away. I will not stand it. Get caught, or get clear. I'll try it. I had as well die with ague as the fever. I have only one life to lose. I had as well be killed running as die standing. Only think of it; one hundred miles straight north, and I am free! Yes! God helping me, I will.

Through prayer and introspection, Frederick Douglass tried to make sense of his enslavement on a Maryland plantation. This piece, calling out to God for deliverance, was taken from his riveting autobiography published seven years after his escape to freedom.

Standin' in the Need of Prayer

It's me, it's me
It's me, O Lord,
Standin' in the need of prayer.
'Taint my mother or my father,
But it's me, O Lord,
Standin' in the need of prayer.

Although the author of this spiritual is unknown, like so many of the spirituals of early African Americans, this one came most probably from the Deep South. With its message of personal desolation mixed with hope, it gained great popularity during the civil rights movement.

I Wish I Was Never Born

Lord, how come me here?
I wish I never was born.

There ain't no freedom here, Lord.
I wish I never was born.

They treat me so mean here, Lord.
I wish I never was born.

They sold my children away, Lord.
I wish I never was born.

Lord, how come me here?
I wish I never was born.

This is arguably the most gut-wrenching of all the spirituals. The sheer anguish of these simple, impassioned protestations evokes the cruel injustices of slavery and the people who were captured within it.

John Brown's Prayer

Omnipotent and steadfast God,
Who, in Thy mercy, hath
Upheaved in me Jehovah's rod
and his chastising wrath,

For fifty-nine unsparing years
Thy Grace hath worked apart
To mould a man of iron tears
With a bullet for a heart.

Yet, since this body may be weak
With all it has to bear,
Once more, before Thy thunders speak,
Almighty, hear my prayer.

I saw Thee when Thou did display
The black man and his lord
To bid me free the one, and slay
The other with the sword.
I heard Thee when Thou bade me spurn
Destruction from my hand
And, though all Kansas bleed and burn,
It was at Thy command.

I hear the rolling of the wheels,
The chariots of war!
I hear the breaking of the seals
And the opening of the door!

The glorious beasts with many eyes
Exult before the Crowned.
The buried saints arise, arise
Like incense from the ground!

Before them march the martyr-kings,
In bloody sunsets drest,
O, Kansas, bleeding Kansas,
You will not let me rest!

I hear your sighing corn again,
I smell your prairie-sky,
And I remember five dead men
By Pottawattamie.

Lord God it was a work of Thine,
And how might I refrain?
But Kansas, bleeding Kansas,
I hear her in her pain.

Her corn is rustling in the ground,
An arrow in my flesh.
And all night long I staunch a wound
That ever bleeds afresh.

Get up, get up, my hardy sons,
From this time forth we are
No longer men, but pikes and guns
In God's advancing war.

And if we live, we free the slave,
And if we die, we die.
But God has digged His saints a grave
Beyond the western sky.

Oh, fairer than the bugle-call
Its walls of jasper shine!
And Joshua's sword is on the wall
With space beside for mine.

And should the Philistine defend
His strength against our blows,
The God who doth not spare His friend,
Will not forget His foes.

Few figures in American history have become the stuff of legends and controversy more than abolitionist John Brown. His decision to lead an armed insurrection in 1859 to fight the institution of slavery riveted both North and South. Stephen Vincent Benet, the much-acclaimed early-twentieth-century writer, composed this prayer in 1928 as part of his Pulitzer Prize–winning narrative *John Brown's Body*.

In Distress

Oh, God, you know how much I am distressed, for I have told you again and again. Now, God, help me get my son. If you were in trouble, as I am, and I could help you, as you can me, think I wouldn't do it? Yes, God, you *know* I would do it.

A freed slave, Sojourner Truth became one of the country's most recognized and outspoken abolitionists. Known for her straightforward manner of speaking, she often spoke to God lovingly but bluntly. In this prayer, which she dictated to her chronicler, Olive Gilbert, Sojourner turned to God when she learned that her son had been sold illegally to an Alabaman slave trader.

Prayer of Columbus

I am too full of woe!
Haply I may not live another day;
I cannot rest, O God—I cannot eat or drink or sleep,
Till I put forth myself, my prayer, once more to Thee,
Breathe, bathe myself once more in thee—commune with
    Thee,
Report myself once more to Thee.

Thou knowest my years entire, my life,
(My long and crowded life of active work, not adoration
    merely);
Thou knowest the prayers and vigils of my youth,
Thou knowest my manhood's solemn and visionary
    meditations,
Thou knowest how before I commenced I devoted all to
    come to Thee,
Thou knowest I have in age ratified all those vows and
    strictly kept them,
Thou knowest I have not once lost nor faith nor ecstasy in
    Thee,
(In shackles, prison'd, in disgrace, repining not,
Accepting all from Thee, as duly come from Thee.)

All my emprises have been fill'd with Thee,
My speculations, plans, begun and carried on in thoughts
    of Thee,
Sailing the deep or journeying the land for Thee;
Intentions, purports, aspirations mine, leaving results to
    Thee.

O I am sure they really came from Thee,
The urge, the ardor, the unconquerable will,
The potent, felt, interior command, stronger than words,

A message from the Heavens whispering to me even in
    sleep,
These sped me on.

By me and these the work so far accomplish'd,
By me earth's elder cloy'd and stifled lands uncloy'd,
    unloos'd,
By me the hemispheres rounded and tied, the unknown to
    the known.

The end I know not, it is all in Thee,
Or small or great I know not—haply what broad fields,
    what lands,
Haply the brutish measureless human undergrowth I
    know,
Transplanted there may rise to stature, knowledge worthy
    Thee,
Haply the swords I know may there indeed be turn'd to
    reaping-tools,
Haply the lifeless cross I know, Europe's dead cross, may
    bud and blossom there.

One effort more, my altar this bleak sand;
That Thou O God my life hast lighted,
With ray of light, steady, ineffable, vouchsafed of Thee,
Light rare untellable, lighting the very light,
Beyond all signs, descriptions, languages;
For that O God, be it my latest word, here on my knees,
Old, poor, and paralyzed, I thank Thee.

My terminus near,
The clouds already closing in upon me,
The voyage balk'd, the course disputed, lost,
I yield my ships to Thee.

In this section of *Leaves of Grass,* among the most compelling poems of this seminal work, Walt Whitman imagines what it must have been like for Christopher Columbus to share his last earthly thoughts with God. Whitman was so concerned about setting the correct tone that he rewrote the prayer more than twenty times.

Courage and Patience, These I Ask

Courage and patience, these I ask
Dear Lord, in this my latest strait;
For hard I find my ten years' task,
Learning to suffer and to wait.

Life seems so rich and grand a thing
So full of work for heart and brain,
It is a cross that I can bring,
No Help, no offering, but pain.

The hard-earned harvest of these years
I long to generously share;
The lessons learned with bitter tears
To teach again with tender care;

To smooth the rough and thorny way
Where other feet begin to tread;
To feed some hungry soul each day
With sympathy's sustaining bread.

So beautiful such pleasures show,
I long to make them mine;
To love and labor and to know
The joy such living makes divine.

But if I may not, I will only ask
Courage and patience for my fate,
And learn, dear Lord, Thy latest task,—
To suffer patiently and wait.

Louisa May Alcott, the author of *Little Women,* was steeped in the burgeoning ideals of transcendentalism in nineteenth-century America. She contracted typhoid fever while working as a nurse during the Civil War, and was administered a mercury compound, the standard treatment at the time. Her health was never the same, and over time the aftereffects of mercury poisoning took their toll, eventually leading to her premature death in 1888 at the age of fifty-six.

Stand Up, Stand Up for Jesus

Stand up, stand up for Jesus, ye soldiers of the cross;
Lift high His royal banner, it must not suffer loss.
From victory unto victory His army shall He lead,
Till every foe is vanquished, and Christ is Lord indeed.

Stand up, stand up for Jesus, the solemn watchword hear;
If while ye sleep He suffers, away with shame and fear;
Where'er ye meet with evil, within you or without,
Charge for the God of battles, and put the foe to rout.

Stand up, stand up for Jesus, the trumpet call obey;
Forth to the mighty conflict, in this His glorious day.
Ye that are brave now serve Him against unnumbered
    foes;
Let courage rise with danger, and strength to strength
    oppose.

Stand up, stand up for Jesus, stand in His strength alone;
The arm of flesh will fail you, ye dare not trust your own.

Put on the Gospel armor, each piece put on with prayer;
Where duty calls or danger, be never wanting there.

Stand up, stand up for Jesus, each soldier to his post,
Close up the broken column, and shout through all the
    host:
Make good the loss so heavy, in those that still remain,
And prove to all around you that death itself is gain.

Stand up, stand up for Jesus, the strife will not be long;
This day the noise of battle, the next the victor's song.
To those who vanquish evil a crown of life shall be;
They with the King of Glory shall reign eternally.

The inspiration for this rousing prayer came to George Duffield, a Presbyterian minister from Philadelphia, in the midst of a tragedy that befell his friend Dudley Tyng in 1858. Tyng, a prominent clergyman of the day with dazzling rhetorical skills, had launched a mass movement of businessmen, encouraging them to turn their daily lives over to God. After one Sunday church service, the twenty-nine-year-old Tyng was involved in a bizarre fatal accident on a farm near his home. With his evangelical ministry foremost in his mind, he lay dying, and whispered his last words to his friend: "Tell them to stand up for Jesus!" Deeply moved, Duffield took those words, added lyrics, and set them to the music of George Webb, the organist of Boston's famed Old South Church. The hymn he wrote is one of the most recognizable hymns to this day.

Savior, Do Not Pass Me By

Pass me not, O Gentle Savior,
Hear my humble cry;
While on others Thou art smiling,
Do not pass me by.

Let me at a throne of mercy
Find a sweet relief;
Kneeling there in deep contrition
Help my unbelief.

Trusting only in thy merit,
would I seek thy face;
heal my wounded, broken spirit,
save me by Thy grace.

Thou the spring of all my comfort,
more than life to me,
whom have I on earth beside Thee?
Whom in heaven but Thee?

Savior, Savior, hear my humble cry;
while on others Thou art calling,
do not pass me by.

One of the most prolific hymn writers in American history was Frances Jane Crosby, better known as Fanny. Blinded from infancy, she was inspired to write this piece in 1868 after she heard a fellow parishioner cry out from a nearby pew, "Savior, don't pass me by." The hymn was so popular that it became a standard addition to most revival meetings at the turn of the century.

When Will I Behold My God?

When, oh when shall it be given to me
To behold my God?
When,
Oh, when shall the captivity of my wretched soul
Cease in this strange land night and day

Weeping,
Weeping alone is my portion;
When, oh when shall I leave this valley of sorrow,
Where the only bread I eat is my continual tears?
When, oh when shall I see my well-beloved Lord?
Prince of the Heavens is He,
Guardian of my soul, my Hope, my Saviour,
My all.

In the nineteenth century and early twentieth century the island of Molokai, Hawaii, became the last refuge for people suffering from Hansen's disease, better known as leprosy. Since there was no cure for the disease, lepers were banished to the island, where a few stalwart individuals gave up their lives to serve them in their remaining days. Father Damien de Veuster, a Dutch immigrant priest, chose to live his ministry among them. To prepare them for death as well as to buoy their spirits, he helped them compose prayers that were combined with lilting Hawaiian tunes accompanied by native musical instruments. This was one of them.

For Just Dealing

O God, who hast taught us to do unto others as we would have them do unto us; Give us grace to keep our hands from fraud and wrong, that we may hurt nobody by word or deed, but be true and just in all our dealings; so that, keeping innocence and taking heed unto the thing that is right, we may have peace at last; through Jesus Christ our Lord. Amen

Up through the mid-twentieth century U.S. schools at every level held regular prayer services. Some even required their students to own devotionals for their personal use. This prayer, taken from *Prayers for Schools and Colleges,* published in 1933, admonishes young people that the only way to achieve true peace in their lives is to strive to do "the thing that is right."

War Is Kind

In the night
Gray, heavy clouds muffled the valleys
And the peaks looked toward God alone;
"O Master, that moveth the wind with a finger,
Humble, idle, futile peaks are we.
Grant that we may run swiftly across the world
To huddle in worship at Thy feet."

In the morning
A noise of men at work came through the clear blue miles,
And the little black cities were apparent.
"O Master, that knowest the meaning of raindrops,
Humble, idle, futile peaks are we.
Give voice to us, we pray, Lord,
That we may sing Thy goodness to the sun."

In the evening
The far valleys were sprinkled with tiny lights.
"O Master,
Thou that knowest the value of kings and birds,
Thou hast made us humble, idle, futile peaks.
Thou only needest eternal patience;
We bow to Thy wisdom, O Lord—
Humble, idle, futile peaks."

In the night
Gray, heavy clouds muffled the valleys,
And the peaks looked toward God alone.

Stephen Crane, author of *The Red Badge of Courage,* was consumed by the horrors of war, which he had experienced first-
hand as a journalist for Joseph Pulitzer's *New York World.* In the
last year of his life, before tuberculosis took him at the age of
twenty-eight, he wrote a series of poems under the title *War Is
Kind.* This excerpted poem depicts the realities of the battlefield
against the backdrop of God's sustaining presence.

A New Year's Plea

Lord, let me stand in the thick of the fight,
Let me bear what I must without whining;
Grant me the wisdom to do what is right,
Though a thousand false beacons are shining.

Let me be true as the steel of a blade,
Make me bigger than skillful or clever;
Teach me to cling to my best, unafraid,
And harken to false gospels, never.

Let me be brave when the burden is great,
Faithful when wounded by sorrow;
Teach me, when troubled, with patience to wait
The better and brighter to-morrow.

Spare me from hatred and envy and shame,
Open my eyes to life's beauty;
Let not the glitter of fortune or fame
Blind me to what is my duty.

Let me be true to myself to the end,
Let me stand to my task without whining;
Let me be right as a man, as a friend,
Though a thousand false beacons are shining.

Having immigrated to the United States from England at the age of nine, Edgar Guest became one of America's favorite poets in the first half of the twentieth century, writing works that audiences from all walks of life could relate to and understand. Reciting this reflection would become an annual New Year's Day tradition in churches and civic settings alike after the poem was published in 1918.

O Courage, My Soul!

O courage, my soul, and let us journey on,
For tho' the night is dark, it won't be very long.
O thanks be to God, the morning light appears,
And the storm is passing over, Hallelujah!

O billows rolling high, and thunder shakes the ground,
The lightning's flash, and tempest all around,
But Jesus walks the sea and calms the angry waves,
And the storm is passing over, Hallelujah!

The stars have disappeared, and distant lights are dim,
My soul is filled with fears, the seas are breaking in.
I hear the Master cry, "Be not afraid, 'tis I,"
And the storm is passing over, Hallelujah!

Now soon we shall reach the distant shining shore,
Then free from all the storms, we'll rest forevermore.
And safe within the veil, we'll furl the riven sail,
And the storm will all be over, Hallelujah!

The name Charles Albert Tindley is practically synonymous with gospel music. Starting out as the janitor of the Calvary Methodist Episcopal Church, Tindley became its illustrious pastor. In composing his hymns, he tried always to relate his lyrics to the needs of a person's soul. In this work he counsels for courage and faith in the midst of life's difficulties, reinforcing the ultimate promise of Heaven.

Give Us Grace

Give us grace, O God, to dare to do the deed which we well know cries to be done. Let us not hesitate because of ease, or the words of men's mouths, or our own lives. Mighty causes are calling us—the freeing of women, the training of children, the putting down of hate and murder and poverty—all these and more. But they call with voices that mean work and sacrifices and death. Mercifully grant us, O God, the spirit of Esther, that we say: I will go unto the King and if I perish, I perish.

Educator and civil rights activist W. E. B. Du Bois became the first African American to receive a doctorate from Harvard. An agnostic for much of his life, he nonetheless wrote dozens of exquisite spiritual entreaties. In this prayer he recalls the Old Testament figure of Esther, who daringly confronts her husband, King Xerxes, and demands that he overturn his court's order to kill all the Jews of the Persian Empire.

God Grant Me This

God grant me this: the right to come at night
Back to my loved ones, head erect and true;
Beaten and bruised and from a losing fight,
Let me be proud in what I have tried to do.

Let me come home defeated if I must,
But clean of hands, and honor unimpaired.

Still holding firmly to my children's trust,
Still worthy of the faith which they have shared.

God grant me this: what e'er the fates decree,
Or do I win or lose life's little game,
I still would keep my children proud of me,
Nor once regret that they must bear my name.

This plea for ethical and moral courage was written in the early
half of the twentieth century by Edgar Guest, known to millions
of Americans as "the people's poet." He believed that a person's
integrity could best be gauged through the eyes of his or her
children.

Father of My Soul

Father of my soul,
Where shall I find you?

Defiler!
Look at your work—
A black body striped bloody,
Eyes rolled back white in the black face,
And gleaming teeth trying to eat
The swollen red tongue.

"Father of my soul,
And Lord of all bodies,
Where shall I find you?"

Profanity!
He who shudders
In the blue webs
Of your holy twilight,

He who sways in your lament at night
And your song by day.
He who trembles in the corners
Of your unborn desires,
He who calls you, craves you, tears at you—
Has become black meat
With thick lips and strange hair.

And you dug you
Dug nails into his ribs,
Knives into the heart.

Spitting on his agony,
You left him dangling
On the tree.

As a young man Yehoash Solomon Bloomgarden, a Polish Jew who would become one of the greatest Yiddish poets in history, immigrated to New York City in 1890. Horrified by press accounts of lynchings in the South, and sensitive to the historic and spiritual parallels of the Jews and African Americans, he wrote this excruciating cry to God.

Prayer Before the Democratic Convention of 1932

Dear crucified Lord, in the shadow of Thy cross may we receive that moral strength, that divine courage which will enable us to combat the evils of selfishness, greed, indulgence and all unworthiness that would prevent our deliberations leading us to decisions for the highest good of the little village as well as of the great city; for the poor and nearly poor as well as for those who have plenty; for the places of hard toil as well as for the places of affluence; for those who are weak in the face of temptation as well as for those who can stand strong. Help us to remember, dear Savior, to remember that in this great throng, this morning we appear before Thee as individuals, separate and alone. Be Thou the captain of our souls! Then if poverty comes we shall not be so poor and if sorrow comes we shall not be so sad, and if death comes we shall not be afraid. O Thou God of all nations, Jesus Christ the world's Redeemer, hear us as we pray, and have mercy upon us, for Jesus' sake.

Evangeline Cory Booth, whose father founded the Salvation Army in London in 1878, moved to the United States believing that her soon to be adopted country would provide fertile ground for her work within the organization. Serving as the territorial commander for the Salvation Army in North America, she delivered this prayer at the 1932 Democratic National Convention that nominated Franklin Roosevelt to be the next president of the United States.

Stand Forth, My Soul

> Stand forth, my soul, and grip thy woe,
> Buckle thy sword and face thy foe.
> What right hast thou to be afraid
> When all the universe will aid?
> Ten thousand rally to thy name,
> Horses and chariots of flame.
> Do others fear? Do others fail?
> My soul must grapple and prevail.
> My soul must scale the mountain side
> And with the conquering army ride—
> Stand forth, my soul!
>
> Stand forth, my soul, and take command.
> 'Tis I, thy master, bit thee stand.

Claim thou thy ground and thrust thy foe,
Plead not thine enemy should go.
Let others cringe! My soul is free,
No hostile host can conquer me.
There lives no circumstance so great
Can make me yield, or doubt my fate.
My soul must know what kings have known,
Must reach and claim its rightful throne—
Stand forth, my soul!

I ask no truce, I have no qualms,
I seek no quarter and no alms.
Let those who will, obey the sod;
'Tis I, the king, who bid thee stand;
Grasp with thy hand my royal hand—
Stand forth!

Angela Morgan wrote this tribute as both prayer and testament to the courage of President Franklin Roosevelt's personal battle with infantile paralysis. She became one of the earliest American converts to the Baha'i faith and found purpose in her life by combining cosmic spirituality with social activism.

The Perspective of War

Almighty God, we are about to be committed to a task from which some of us will not return. We go willingly to this hazardous adventure because we believe that those concepts of human dignity, rights and justice that Your Son expounded to the world, and which are respected in the government of our beloved country, are in peril of extinction from the earth. We are ready to sacrifice ourselves for our country and our God. We do not ask, individually, for our safe return. But we earnestly pray that You will help each of us to do his full duty. Permit none of us to fail a comrade in the fight. Above all, sustain us in our conviction in the justice and righteousness of our cause so that we may rise above all terror of the enemy and come to You, if called, in the humble pride of the good soldier and in the certainty of Your infinite mercy.

In the last months of World War II General Dwight Eisenhower, then serving as Supreme Commander of the Allied Forces in Europe, was asked to recall a prayer that held special significance for him. He recounted the moving words of a company commander who had addressed his men on a damp, dreary night just as they were about to march to the front line.

I Have Seen Too Much

Lord, I have seen too much for one who sat
In quiet at his window's luminous eye
And puzzled over house and street and sky,
Safe only in the narrowest habitat;
Who studied peace as if the world were flat,
The edge of nature linear and dry,
But faltered at each brilliant entity
Drawn like a prize from some magician's hat.

Too suddenly this lightning is disclosed:
Lord, in a day the vacuum of Hell.
The mouth of blood, the ocean's ragged jaw,
More than embittered Adam ever saw
When driven from Eden to the East to dwell,
The lust of godhead hideously exposed!

This prayer, taken from Karl Shapiro's Pulitzer Prize–winning *V-Letter and Other Poems,* was written while Shapiro served in New Guinea during World War II as a clerk with the U.S. medical corps. From his vantage point he experienced up close the hell of war.

Prayer of the 15th Field Artillery Regiment

Our Father, we pray for the personal courage and strength of spirit to continue to serve our regiment, our army, and our nation. . . . Guide us through the dark tunnel of fear as we seek to establish our own heritage of courage and honor through our daily duties. Give us the wisdom to accept our responsibility to our fellow soldiers and earn the right to shout "Let's Go!" as we endeavor to fulfill our duty. . . . Teach us not to mourn those who have died in the service of the regiment, but rather help us to gain strength from the contagion of their courage. Teach us to stand together in Your Name so that we may remain strong and vibrant. . . . Amen

During the most difficult days of the Vietnam War, individual units would gather together to pray for fallen comrades and for the courage to confront the unknown. This particular prayer was invoked regularly by one of the most heralded field regiments. Reciting the words together had the effect of binding the men to one another, particularly when the 15th Field Artillery was engaged in the bloody Tet Offensive.

Restore Our Faith

O God, Our Heavenly Father, restore our faith in the ultimate triumph of Thy plan for the world Thou has made. In spite of present difficulties, our disappointments, and our fears. Reassure us that Thou art still in control. When we become frustrated and give up, remind us that Thou art still holding things together, waiting and working and watching. When we make mistakes, help us to remember that Thou does not give up on us.

After arriving penniless at Ellis Island as a young émigré from Scotland, Peter Marshall quickly found his calling as a Presbyterian minister. After serving as pastor of the New York Avenue Presbyterian Church, where Abraham Lincoln had often attended services, he went on to serve the U.S. Senate as chaplain, his most influential role. He captivated the chamber with his daily invocations during challenging times, and became known as the "conscience of the Senate." He delivered this prayer before the U.S. Senate the morning after Hungary fell to the Communists in 1948.

On the Eve of Battle

On this eve of battle we ask Thee, our Heavenly Father, for strength and courage. We fight, not only for our country, but for our God as well, because we battle for continuance of Christian principles among all men. Give us the strength and the courage to fight well. Help us, in our hour of need, to follow the words of the Bible: "Be of good courage, and let us behave ourselves for our people, and for the cities of our God."

Give us Thy guidance, Dear Lord, in the hours of crisis that lie ahead. Grant us the power to face our enemies and Thine enemies without fear. And bless, we pray Thee, our families and loved ones at home. Give them comfort and courage and grant them Thy divine protection. These things we ask in your name. Amen

General Mark Clark, a hero from World War II who would go on to command UN forces during the Korean War, wrote several prayers on the eve of battle as a means to reinforce his resolve and to provide greater perspective. This reflection was a particular favorite of his that he composed while serving in Europe.

Lift Us Up

Eternal Spirit, from whom we come and to whom we belong, and in whose service is our peace, we worship Thee.

Lift us up, we beseech Thee, from cowardice to courage. Save us from self-pity. Recover us from our whimpering complaints. Lo, we are the sons and daughters of soldiers who fought a good fight before they fell on sleep, and were not afraid. Build into us also stout hearts, that we in our generation may stand undaunted by fear, unconquered by adversity, unstained by cowardice.

Lift us up, we pray Thee, from vindictiveness to goodwill. If we are harboring grudges, if hatefulness has taken hold of our spirits, save us, we pray Thee, from such a desecration of this holy hour. Bring sympathy back to us, and understanding and the fair grace to put ourselves in others' places before we judge them.

Lift us up above malice and evil-speaking and unkindness of heart. Arouse in us the spirit of Christ, who could pray upon the cross for those who put him there. O God, help us to be more Christian in our hearts because love is there.

Lift, us, we pray Thee, from selfishness to service. Remind us of downcast stricken lives. Let our imaginations run out into our prisons, the houses where the poor lie down in cold and penury, the asylums where disordered minds beat themselves out against their vain imaginings, the unprivileged areas of our city's life, and of the world where blessings that we take for granted are little known, and hunger stalks and fear haunts and tomorrow is full of terror. Wake up within us, we beseech Thee, our forgotten kindliness.

And with all this, Spirit of the eternal Christ, lift us up from doubt to faith. Lift us out of our cynicism, our skepticism, our unwillingness to believe that the good may be true, into a courageous faith and certitude concerning God and divine purposes. Illumine us, thou Sun of the morning, until not only shall our mountain peaks shine with a new confidence, but the very valleys shall feel thy noontime's splendor and we have faith again in ourselves, in others, and in Thee.

We pray in the Spirit of Christ.

Prominent Baptist minister Harry Emerson Fosdick served as pastor of the historic Riverside Church in New York City, taking head-on the social concerns of his day. He was a critical force in the launching of Alcoholics Anonymous, serving as its spiritual counselor and editing its first members manual. In this invocation he asks God to lift all of mankind from their all-too-human weaknesses so that they can serve others with love and understanding.

Finding Courage in Life

How will I leave this world, Lord?
Will I find that I frittered away my days without proper
    service to others?
Will I regret that I did not cross that mountain?
Will I look back and ask myself those unimaginable
    questions—
"Why didn't I?" or "If only I had . . ."

Grant me the courage each day, Lord, to look in the
   mirror
and take stock of myself.
Remind me that these days on earth are precious ones
that deserve no less than my personal best.

Reinforce within me that I can make a difference
again and again in the life I choose to lead.
Let me never cower in adversity, bend in the compromise
   of principle,
or turn my back on those who need me most.

If You are there to guide me, Lord, I know I will avoid the
   easier path
and make my mark with the tools You have given me.

And when my time does come, know that with Your help,
   Lord,
I intend to look back on a life that was more courageous,
more fulfilled, and more loving
than any one I dare could have imagined.

This prayer, written by James P. Moore Jr., stands as a reminder
that it takes courage and spiritual toughness to choose the prudent course in life. Only by forging such a path from moment to
moment, even in the seemingly small things in life, can a person
truly make a mark.

Pain Incomprehensible

There is too much pain
I cannot understand
I cannot pray

I cannot pray for all the little ones with bellies bloated
by starvation in India;
for all the angry Africans striving to be separate in a
    world
struggling for wholeness;
for all the young Chinese men and women taught that
hatred and killing are good and compassion evil;
or even all the frightened people in my own city looking
for truth in pot or aid.

Here I am
and the ugly man with beery breath beside me reminds me
that it is not my prayers that waken your concern, my
    Lord;
my prayers, my intercessions are not to ask for your love
for all your lost and lonely ones,
your sick and sinning souls,
but mine, my love, my acceptance of your love.
Your love for the woman sticking her umbrella and
her expensive parcels into my ribs and snarling,
"Why don't you watch where you're going?"
Your love for the long-haired, gum-chewing boy who
    shoves
The old lady aside to grab a seat,
Your love for me, too, too tired to look with love,
too tired to look at Love, at you, in every person on the
    bus.
Expand my love, Lord, so I can help to bear the pain,
help your love move my love into the tired prostitute with
    false eyelashes and bunioned feet,
the corrupt policeman with his hand open for graft,
the addict, the derelict, the woman in the mink coat and
    discontented mouth,
the high school girl with heavy books and frightened eyes.

Help me through these scandalous particulars
to understand
Your love.

Madeleine L'Engle, best known as a writer of children's books, particularly *A Wrinkle in Time* and its sequels, jotted down this "spontaneous" prayer on the back of an envelope while riding the 104 Broadway bus in New York City. She focuses on the people she encounters in an urban setting as an occasion to reflect on what she owes God and her fellow man.

Prayer After a Suicide

Crucified Savior, there is no place for me to go but to the foot of Your Cross. I feel desolation, defeat, betrayal, rejection. I tried to stop the flood, to calm the earthquake, to put out the raging fire. I did not even know how desperate it all was. There is absolutely no consolation, no answer, no softening of my grief. It is complete darkness. I grieve for my dear friend for what was and would have been. Is life so awful that all that struggle has to end, that defeat was inevitable? There is nothing but silence outside and screaming inside. I know that the wound will heal, but now I don't even want it to. I know that there will be a huge scar in its place. That scar will be all that I have left. . . . We have no place to go in the world, in the whole universe but here to You, to Your cross—it is our only hope.

The senseless loss of life has always been hard to fathom, whether in war, in the killing rampages of Columbine High School and Virginia Tech, or by suicide. Father Benedict Groeschel, one of the country's best-known Catholic authors and lecturers, wrote this prayer after reflecting on the suicide of a disturbed young man who shot himself after being rejected by a girlfriend. Father Benedict would later write that the memory "still echoes through my mind."

ENDURANCE AND RESOLVE

In Pursuit of the Goal

Ho! Sun, Moon, Stars, all that move in the heavens
I bid you hear me!
Into your midst has come a new life.
Consent, I implore you!
Make its path smooth, that it may reach the brow of the
    first hill!

Ho! You Winds, Clouds, Rain, Mist, all you that move in the
    air,
I bid you hear me!
Into your midst has come a new life.
Consent, I implore you!
Make its path smooth, that it may reach
the brow of the second hill!

Ho! You Hills, Valleys, Rivers, Lakes, Trees, Grasses, all
    you of the earth.
I bid you hear me!
Into your midst has come a new life.
Consent, I implore you.
Make its path smooth, that it may reach
The brow of the third hill!

Each stanza of this prayer, invoked by the early Omaha tribe of the Great Plains, progressively projects one more goal that needs to be achieved in pursuit of "the goal." Given that their daily survival depended on the elements of nature, they directed their appeals to the heavens, the air, and the earth.

In Pursuit of Fortitude

> O Lord God, when Thou givest to Thy servants any great
>   matter,
> grant us to know that it is not the beginning,
> but the continuing of the same unto the end,
> until it be thoroughly finished, which yieldeth the true
>   glory:
> through Him who for the finishing of Thy work laid down
>   His life,
> our Redeemer Jesus Christ.

Sir Francis Drake, one of the most heralded explorers of the New World, was a devout Anglican. This prayer, which he wrote early in his career, was one of the favorite prayers of the early colonists and is included in the Episcopal Church's *Book of Common Prayer.*

By Night When Others Soundly Slept

> By night when others soundly slept,
> And had at once both case and rest,
> My waking eyes were open kept
> And so to lie I found it best.
>
> I sought Him whom my soul did love,
> With tears I sought Him earnestly;

He bowed His ear down from above.
In vain I did not seek or cry.

My hungry soul He filled with good,
He in His bottle put my tears,
My smarting wounds washed in His blood,
And banished thence my doubts and fears.

What to my Savior shall I give,
Who freely hath done this for me?
I'll serve Him here whilst I shall live
And love Him to eternity.

This meditation in spiritual restlessness was composed by early Puritan pioneer Anne Bradstreet. As the mother of eight children and the wife of the governor of the Massachusetts Bay Colony, she continuously faced personal setbacks. It was through her poetry and prayers, however, that she found the solace and the strength to endure the rigors of the New World.

Words into Deeds

Lord, strengthen our souls, so that many firm resolutions may be more than mere words.

This "ejaculation" was composed by Mother Elizabeth Seton, who founded the Sisters of Charity of Saint Joseph's and effectively launched the parochial school system in the United States. She was the first American-born citizen to be canonized a saint by the Roman Catholic Church, and would become an inspiration to Catholics and non-Catholics alike for her struggles and accomplishments in the early days of the republic.

Keep Me from Sinking Down

O Lord, O My Lord
O my Lord, keep me from sinking down

I shall tell you what I mean to do
Keep me from sinking down
I mean to get to heaven too
Keep me from sinking down

Sometimes I'm up, sometimes I'm down
Keep me from sinking down
Sometimes I'm almost on the ground
Keep me from sinking down

I bless the Lord I'm going to die
Keep me from sinking down
I'm going to Judgment by and by
Keep me from sinking down.

This spiritual expresses the anguish of enslaved African Americans in their daily struggle to persevere. At the same time it holds up an abiding hope and trust in the promise of heaven. It would become part of the early repertory of the Fisk Jubilee Singers, who first introduced spirituals to the world.

My Prayer

Great God, I ask thee for no meaner pelf
Than that I may not disappoint myself,
That in my action I may soar as high,
As I can now discern with this clear eye.
And next in value, which thy kindness lends,
That I may greatly disappoint my friends,

Howe'er they think or hope that it may be,
They may not dream how thou'st distinguished me.
That my weak hand may equal my firm faith,
And my life practise more than my tongue saith;
That my low conduct may not show,
Nor my relenting lines,
That I thy purpose did not know,
Or overrated thy designs.

Henry David Thoreau felt a genuine sense of moral urgency about addressing a world he felt had gone awry. In this introspective piece, which he wrote early in his career in 1842, he calls out to the God whom he perceives as existing in every living organism, and asks for help to focus on what is truly important in his life.

The Higher Good

Father, I will not ask for wealth or fame,
Though once they would have joyed my carnal sense:
I shudder not to bear a hated name,
Wanting all wealth, myself my sole defense.
But give me, Lord, eyes to behold the truth;
A seeing sense that knows the eternal right;
A heart with pity filled, and gentlest truth;
A manly faith that makes all darkness light:
Give me the power to labor for mankind;
Make me the mouth of such as cannot speak;
Eyes let me be to groping men, and blind;
A conscience to the base; and to the weak
Let me be hands and feet; and to the foolish, mind;
And lead still further on such as thy kingdom seek.

Unitarian and transcendentalist Theodore Parker, little known to most Americans today, was a great influence in the lives of some of America's greatest leaders. The phrase he used in a speech to abolitionists, "of all the people, by all the people, for all the people," inspired Abraham Lincoln in writing his Gettysburg Address. More than a hundred years after he declared that "the arc of the moral universe is long, but it bends toward justice," Martin Luther King Jr. would echo the same words in a major speech he delivered in Atlanta in 1967. In this prayer Parker shows his resolve in setting course for what he called "the higher good."

Prayer of the Confederacy

We humbly beseech Thee be present with us in all the course and passages of our lives, but especially in the Secession we have undertaken, and the hostilities in which it has involved us. . . . Defeat, we implore Thee, the designs and confound the machinations of our enemies; abate their pride and assuage their fury; soften their hearts and change their unnatural hatred into Christian love, and forgive them all their sins against Thee and against us. Grant that their ships may find no way in our seas, nor any path in our floods; may their spies be speedily detected and effectually banished from our midst; preserve us from war and tumult; from battle, murder, and sudden death; guard us from sedition, conspiracy, and rebellion; defend our soil from invasion, our ports from blockade—that we may glorify Thee for these deliverances.

As in all of America's wars, churches of all denominations printed prayer books during the Civil War to be distributed to soldiers and the general population as a means to persevere toward victory. This was the prayer that was part of the devotional published in the South that framed the war for the Confederacy at the outset of the war.

The Rock

Thou art, there is no stay but in Thy love;
Thy strength remains; it built the eternal hills;
It speaks the word forever heard above,
And all creation with its presence fills;
Upon it let me stand and I shall live;
Thy strength shall fasten me forever fixed,
And to my soul its sure foundations give,
When earth and sky thy word in one has mixed;
Rooted in Thee no storm my branch shall tear;
But with each day new sap shall upward flow,
And for thy vine the clustering fruit shall bear;
That with each rain the lengthening shoots may grow,
Till o'er Thy Rock its leaves spread far and wide,
And in its green embrace its Parent hide.

Jones Very, a Unitarian minister from Salem, Massachusetts, and one of the most prolific spiritual writers of the nineteenth century, was both a mystic and an absolutist when it came to his notion of God. As this prayer shows, he believed that personal fortitude could be best sustained by continuous communion with the Almighty.

For a Stronger Back

Lord, I do not pray for a lighter load, but for a stronger back.

This one-sentence prayer, from a sermon delivered by Episcopal bishop Phillips Brooks, became the inspiration for Theodore Roosevelt and John Kennedy, and would be echoed in speeches they delivered during their presidencies. In its simple way, it asks only for the ability to handle the burdens, no matter what they may be, throughout life.

Not in Dumb Resignation

Not in dumb resignation
We lift our hands on high;
Not like the nerveless fatalist,
Content to do and die;
Our faith springs like the eagle,
That soars to meet the sun,
And cries exulting unto Thee,
"O Lord, Thy will be done!"

When tyrant feet are trampling
Upon the common weal,
Thou dost not bid us cringe and writhe
Beneath the iron heel;

In Thy name we assert our right,
By sword and tongue and pen.
And ev'n the headsman's axe may flash
Thy message unto men.

Thy will, it bids the weak be strong,
It bids the strong be just:
No hand to beg, no lip to fawn,
No brow to kiss the dust;

Wherever man oppresses man
Beneath the liberal sun,
O Lord, be there, Thine arm made bare,
Thy righteous will be done!

John Hay, the private secretary to President Abraham Lincoln and later secretary of state under Presidents William McKinley and Theodore Roosevelt, was a particularly religious man. An adherent of the "muscular Christianity" that blossomed in the late nineteenth century, he expressed in this prayer his unwavering trust in God's sustaining help.

An Incident True

If you'll listen I'll tell you an incident true,
Which occurred in a high license place,
Where five thousand saloons pay a large revenue,
For the right to breed crime and disgrace

In the city of Chicago, a poor drunken man,
In his wrath, seized his dead infant child;
With its body he beat his own poor dying wife;
Licensed rum made him frantic and wild.

But who sold him the drink? Who enacted the laws?
That allowed the saloonist to sell?
And who made him saloonist?
And who was the cause of this horrible deed,
Can you tell?

Shall we say that the man who elects by his vote,
Those who make just such laws ev'ry time.
And supports party platforms that license denote,
Has no part in this terrible crime?

Can we tell at what price all that's dear shall be sold,
And just what is the worth of a soul?
Can the sum that would meet all the damage be told—
That would make ev'ry broke heart whole?

Oh, what shall we do with this terrible curse,
And when shall deliverance come?
O God, we turn our eyes to Thee,
Protect, protect our home.

The temperance movement in the late nineteenth and early twentieth centuries took on with a vengeance the battle against "the sin of liquor indulgence." Women's groups in particular believed that tenacity, forceful activism, and prayer were the ideal weapons in their cause. One of the most famous hymns composed for the movement was this piece, which told the story of a family that had fallen victim to alcohol abuse, asking God to deliver all of America's families from the curse of alcohol.

Prayer of the Brotherhood

Almighty and eternal Father, without whom nothing is strong, nothing is holy, we beseech Thee, to inspire and sustain the prayers and efforts of the members of our Brotherhood and to hallow their lives; and grant that young men everywhere be brought into the Kingdom of Thy Son, and may be led from strength to strength until they attain unto the fullness of eternal life, through the same, Thy Son, Jesus Christ our Lord.

In late-nineteenth-century America, "muscular Christianity" became the blueprint for spiritual steadfastness for many Protestants, particularly men. Believing that recently composed prayers and hymns were too soft and did not go far enough in encouraging spiritual, mental, and physical toughness, adherents to the movement composed their own works. This particular prayer was the cornerstone to the Fellowship of St. Andrew, an organization that counted tens of thousands of members.

A Prayer

O LORD, the hard-won miles
Have worn my stumbling feet:
Oh, soothe me with thy smiles,
And make my life complete.

The thorns were thick and keen
Where'er I trembling trod;
The way was long between
My wounded feet and God.

Where healing waters flow
Do thou my footsteps lead.
My heart is aching so;
Thy gracious balm I need.

The son of ex-slaves and a classmate of aviation pioneer Orville
Wright, Paul Laurence Dunbar was the first African American to
gain widespread fame as a poet. His ability to use different con-
versational dialects made his works accessible to a vast audience. This particular prayer was written as a personal
retrospection not long before he died at the age of thirty-four, in
1906, from tuberculosis.

Lift Ev'ry Voice and Sing

Lift ev'ry voice and sing,
Till earth and heaven ring.
Ring with the harmony of Liberty;
Let our rejoicing rise.
High as the list'ning skies,
Let it resound loud as the rolling sea.
Sing a song full of the faith that the
dark past has taught us,
Sing a song full of the hope that the
present has brought us;
Facing the rising sun of our new day begun,
Let us march on till victory is won.

Stony the road we trod.
Bitter the chast'ning rod,

Felt in the days when hope unborn had died;
Yet with a steady beat, have not our weary feet,
Come to the place for which our fathers sighed?
We have come over a way that with tears has been
watered,
We have come, treading our path through the blood
of the slaughtered,

Out from the gloomy past,
till now we stand at last
Where the white gleam of our bright star is cast.

God of our weary years,
God of our silent tears,
Thou who has brought us thus far on the way;
Thou who has by Thy might led us into the light,
Keep us forever in the path, we pray.
Lest our feet stray from the places,
our God, where we met Thee,
Lest our hearts, drunk with the wine of the world,
we forget thee,
Shadowed beneath thy hand, May we forever stand,
True to our God,
True to our native land.

In honor of the anniversary of Abraham Lincoln's birth, James Weldon Johnson, the principal of the Edwin M. Stanton Grammar School in Jacksonville, Florida, wrote this composition in 1900 to be performed at a school assembly. He wanted to portray the struggles and perseverance of African Americans whom Lincoln had emancipated as well as to speak to their pride and aspirations for the future. He turned to his brother J. Rosamond Johnson to set his words to music. Practically overnight the piece became known as the "Negro National Hymn" as it was pasted to the back of church hymnals from one African American congregation to the next.

Grit

In the midst of life and deeds it is easy to have endurance and
strength and determination, but Thy Word, O Lord, teaches us that
this is not enough to bring good to the world—to bring happiness
and the worthier success. For *this* we must endure to the end—
learn to finish things—to bring them to accomplishment and full
fruition. We must not be content with plans, ambitions, and
resolves; with part of a message or part of an education, but be
set and determined to fulfill the promise and complete the task
and secure the full training. Such men and women alone does God
save by lifting them above and raising them to higher worlds and
wider prospects. Give us then, O God, to resist today the
temptation of shirking, and the grit to endure to the end. Amen

Early in his teaching career at Atlanta University, author, lecturer, and political activist W. E. B. Du Bois was called upon regularly to lead the student body in prayer during chapel services.
While his own religious faith seemed to be continuously in flux,
he realized that his invocations held significant meaning for the
young people under his care. He made sure that he provided his
students with lessons for life, as he does in this prayer for perseverance.

The Challenge

> The gray hills taught me patience,
> The waters taught me prayer;
> The flight of birds unfolded
> The marvel of Thy care.
>
> The calm skies made me quiet,
> The high stars made me still;
> The bolts of thunder taught me
> The lightening of Thy will!

Thy soul is on the tempest,
Thy courage rides the air!
Through heaven or hell I'll follow;
I must—and so I dare!

Dozens of hymnals were produced after the Civil War for schools and colleges to use at chapel services. This inspirational hymn, written by the very erudite educator Eastman Cross, was included in many of those devotionals. Much of the inspiration for his hymns came from his experience on the college campuses of New England and his commitment to the spiritual development of students everywhere.

God Will Take Care of You

Be not dismayed whate'er betide,
God will take care of you;
Beneath His wings of love abide,
God will take care of you.

God will take care of you,
Through every day, o'er all the way;
He will take care of you,
God will take care of you.

Through days of toil when heart doth fail,
God will take care of you;
When dangers fierce your path assail,
God will take care of you.

All you may need He will provide,
God will take care of you;
Nothing you ask will be denied,
God will take care of you.

No matter what may be the test,
God will take care of you;
Lean, weary one, upon His breast,
God will take care of you.

This poignant hymn was composed in 1904 by Civilla and W. Stillman Martin, a married couple who had long worked for the Disciples of Christ. Many years after its publication it made a profound impact on retail giant J. C. Penney. Suffering a deep depression marked by a crushing sense of loneliness and despair over financial setbacks, Penney sought treatment at the Kellogg Sanitarium in Battle Creek, Michigan, in 1929. Minutes before he was prepared to take his own life (all of the clinic's treatments having failed him), he heard a small group of patients and staff singing "God Will Take Care of You" at a morning religious service, just steps away from his room. As he would later describe, he experienced an overwhelming sense of the presence of God, and despite his problems he knew he would be able to survive anything if he only turned to Divine Providence.

To Do More Than Is Expected

Help me to love mercy, to go beyond what is acceptable in earthly society, and to do more than is expected.

Known by friends and competitors alike for his honesty and hard work, retail magnate James Cash Penney never forgot the plight of the less fortunate or the personal travails he had faced at one low point in his life. Consequently he set up several charities to support such diverse causes as helping farmers improve their crops and livestock, and establishing a residential community for retired clergy. As this prayer shows, he was dogged in his belief in the need for moral steadfastness.

Personal Renewal

Oh God, I ask not for easier tasks. I ask for stronger aptitudes and greater·talents to meet any tasks which may come my way. Help me to help others so that their lives may be made easier and happier. Strengthen my confidence in my fellow men in spite of what they may do or say.

Give me strength to live according to the Golden Rule, enthusiasm to inspire those around me, sympathy to help lighten the burdens of those who suffer, and a spirit of joy and gladness to share with others.

Help me to make a worth-while contribution in the world. Give me courage and confidence to meet adversity with a smile and wisdom to see the good in all things. Renew in me the resolve to do Thy will honestly and fearlessly and grant to me a peaceful mind.

Harry Amos Bullis, the U.S. industrialist who served as chief executive officer and chairman of General Mills from 1943 to 1959, focused a great deal of his personal attention on assisting others. He was particularly instrumental in supporting the reconstruction of Europe after World War II. In this piece he renews his commitment to God and others, asking for the strength to put his words and good intentions into action.

I'll Overcome Some Day

This world is one great battlefield
With forces all arrayed,
If in my heart I do not yield
I'll overcome some day. . . .

I fail so often when I try
My Savior to obey;
It pains my heart and then I cry,
Lord, make me strong some day. . . .

Both seen and unseen powers join
To drive my soul astray,
But with His Word a sword of mine,
I'll overcome some day. . . .

Though many a time no signs appear,
Of answer when I pray;
My Jesus says I need not fear,
He'll make it plain some day. . . .

This spiritual call for fortitude would become the inspiration for the civil rights anthem "We Shall Overcome." Written by American gospel music pioneer Charles Albert Tindley, it reinforces the Christian notion of faith and ultimate triumph in the midst of human toil and trial.

Prayer of Waiting

Lord Jesus, You want honest words on my lips: no thought of mine is hidden from You anyway . . . but Lord, why does Your providence have to move so slowly?

I know the seasons come and go in majestic sequence. The earth rotates on its axis in a predetermined rhythm. No prayers of mine could change any of this. I know that Your ways are not my ways; Your timing is not my timing. But Lord, how do I, so earthbound, come to terms with the pace of eternity?

I want to be teachable, Lord. Is there something You want to show me, some block You want removed, some change You want in me or my attitudes before You can answer my prayer? Give me the gift of eyes that see, of ears that hear what You are saying to me.

Come Lord Jesus, and abide in my heart. How grateful I am to realize that the answer to my prayer does not depend on me at all. As I quietly abide in You and let Your life flow into me, what freedom it is to know that the Father does not see my threadbare patience or insufficient trust, rather only Your patience, and Your confidence that the Father has everything in hand. In Your faith I thank You right now for a more glorious answer to my prayer than I can imagine.

Catherine Marshall included this "prayer of waiting" as part of a collection of works she called *Adventures in Prayer.* After the sudden death of her husband, legendary U.S. Senate chaplain Peter Marshall in 1949, she poured herself into writing more than twenty books on spirituality.

Precious Lord, Take My Hand

Precious Lord, take my hand.

Lead me on. Let me stand.
I am tired. I am weak. I am worn.
Through the storm, through the night,
Lead me on to the light.
Take my hand, precious Lord, lead me home.
When my way grows drear,

Precious Lord, linger near.

When my life is almost gone,
Hear my cry, hear my call,

Hold my hand, lest I fall;
Take my hand, precious Lord, lead me home.

One of the most recognizable gospel songs of all time was written by Thomas Dorsey, the son of a revivalist preacher from
Georgia. While he was on a national music tour in 1932, Dorsey
learned that his wife had died in childbirth and that his baby boy
had died shortly thereafter. Grief stricken, he instinctively began to pour out his emotions by composing this hymn, which
was set to the music of an 1844 American religious tune.
"Precious Lord, Take My Hand" would propel his career to new
heights and solidify his reputation as "the father of gospel music."

Still Standing, Lord

I'm standing, Lord.
There is a mist that blinds my sight.
Steep jagged rocks, front, left, and right.
Lower, dim, gigantic, in the night.
Where is the way?

I'm standing, Lord.
The black rock hems me in behind.
Above my head a moaning wind
Chills and oppresses heart and mind.
I am afraid!

I'm standing, Lord.
The rock is hard beneath my feet.
I merely slipped, Lord, on the sleet.
So weary, Lord, and where a seat?
Still must I stand?

He answered me, and on His face
A look of ineffable grace,
Of perfect, understanding love,
Which all my murmuring did remove.

I'm standing, Lord.
Since Thou hast spoken, Lord, I see
Thou hast beset; these rocks are Thee;
And, since Thy love encloses me,
I stand and sing!

Reminiscent of the spirituals of early America, this prayer was written by Elizabeth Alden Scott Stam, who served as a missionary with her husband in China in 1934. This entreaty, which conveyed both faith and anxiety, was found as packing material used by a faithful cook to cover her ceramics after she and her husband were brutally murdered by Chinese Communist soldiers.

Stablish Our Hearts

Save us and deliver us from the hands of our enemies; abate their pride, assuage their malice, and confound their devices; that we, being armed with thy defense, may be preserved ever more from all perils, to glorify Thee, who art the only giver of all victory.

Stablish our hearts, O God, in the light of battle, and strengthen our resolve, that we fight, not in enmity against men, but against the powers of darkness enslaving the souls of men; till all enmity and oppression be done away, and the people of the world be set free from fear to serve one another; as children of our Father, who is above all and through all and in all, God for ever and ever. Amen

Before the United States entered into World War II, Prime Minister Winston Churchill and President Franklin Roosevelt met aboard a British destroyer in the middle of the Atlantic Ocean to conclude a secret agreement of mutual support that would become known as the Atlantic Charter. During the conference several hundred men joined the leaders in a Sunday worship service. This prayer was taken from that ceremony. Churchill later recounted the emotion of all those men praying together and mourn the fact that nearly half of them would die in the war.

In Search of Victory

God of our fathers, who by land and sea have ever lead us to victory, please continue your inspiring guidance in this the greatest of all conflicts. Strengthen my soul so that the weakening instinct of self-preservation, which besets all of us in battle, shall not blind me to my duty to my own manhood, to the glory of my calling, and to my responsibility to my fellow soldiers. Grant to our armed forces that disciplined valor and mutual confidence which insures success in war. Let me not mourn for the men who have died fighting, but rather let me be glad that such heroes have lived. If it be my lot to die, let me do so with courage and honor . . . and please, oh Lord, protect and guide those I shall leave behind. Give us the victory, Lord.

Although he had a gruff exterior and an intense personal constitution, General George Patton was deeply religious. In this prayer, which he composed while commanding the Third Army during World War II, he begs God for complete victory over Hitler's forces. This was one of dozens of poems that he wrote over his lifetime.

Eddie's Prayer

O Lord, I thank thee for the strength and blessings thou hast given me, and Even though I have walked through the valley of the shadow of death, I feared no evil, for thy rod and thy staff comforted me even unto the four corners of the world. I have sinned, O Lord, but through thy mercy thou hast shown me the light of thy saving grace.

In thy care we are entrusting our boys and girls in the Services scattered throughout the entire world, and we know that in thee they are finding their haven of hope. Be with our leaders, Lord; give them wisdom to lead us to a spiritual victory, as well as a physical one. And until that day, be with those at home— strengthen them for whatever may lie ahead. Be with our enemies, O Lord, and through the light of thy divine grace, may they reconsecrate themselves to thy service as we are reconsecrating ourselves, so all peoples of the world will sing in unison "Glory to God in the Highest," as only through thee can we realize our hopes for peace everlasting. In Jesus' name I ask it. Amen

One of America's true heroes, World War I flying ace Eddie Rickenbacker had a rich and diverse career after he retired from active military service. Months after the bombing of Pearl Harbor, he agreed to help the war effort by inspecting U.S. air bases throughout the Pacific. Taking off from Hawaii to meet up with General Douglas MacArthur, Rickenbacker's aircraft malfunctioned, taking him and his team off course by hundreds of miles. With little fuel left, the plane went down, and the men floated on wreckage in the Pacific Ocean for twenty-four days. Throughout the ordeal the men offered daily prayers, asking for fortitude and rescue. After he and the other six survivors were found alive, the fifty-two-year-old Rickenbacker wrote these words as a way to memorialize his faith in the Almighty.

Conquering the Spirit

Almighty God,
Upon You I call.
Don't let evil spirits
Possess my soul.
Don't let hatred
Strangle my love.
Or despair
Crush my hope.
Tie me with the rope
Of patience
To the pillar of strength
When anger erupts
In my mind.
Don't let emotion
Blind my reason.
Teach me the psalm
Of faith
And restore my calm.
Dispel my doubts and fears
While the bells of life
Toll my years.
Let the warm rays
Of affection and compassion
Conquer my spirit.
O Lord, our God.
Please disperse
The seeds of peace and brotherhood
Upon the earth.
As time rolls
On the wheels
Of the universe.

This devotional poem was inspired by the life experiences of Magda Herzberger, a survivor of three death camps during the Nazi Holocaust. One of the early settlers in the new state of Israel, she would later become a citizen of the United States. She attributed her survival to her faith in God and the ability to pray.

PART TWO

FAMILY

Entrega De Novios

Ayuda pido a Jesús
y a la Reina soberana,
para entregar estos novios
a las dos de la mañana.

Ya los padres de estos novios
esto ya les voy a hablar,
si en algo me equivoco
me deben de dispensar.

Esta mañana salieron
cuatro rosas de la iglesia,
el padrino y la madrina
el novio con la princesa.

Y el padre les preguntó
—Si quieren casarse, di,
y la iglesia los oyó
y ambos dos dijerón—Sí

My Request for the Newlyweds
(English Translation)

I request help from Jesus
and the sovereign Queen,
to deliver these newlyweds
at two in the morning.

The parents of these newlyweds,
this I am going to tell them,
if I make any mistakes
they should forgive me.

This morning four roses
came out of the church,
the godfather, the godmother,
the groom with the princess.

And the father asked them,
—If you would be wed, say so,
and the church heard them
and both of them said—We do.

This *alabado,* or hymn, from early Hispanic America, was passed down from generation to generation and finally recorded for posterity just before World War II. A specially chosen individual, known as a *poeta,* would have sung this traditional blessing accompanied by guitar and violin. It would have been performed at the end of the day's wedding Mass and reception, reminding the couple as well as their family and friends of the serious commitment of marriage.

This Is the Day

Now this is the day,
Our child,
Into the daylight
You will go out standing.
Preparing for your day,
We have passed our days,
When all your days were at an end,
When eight days were past,
Our sun father
Went in to sit down at his sacred place.
And our night fathers
Having come out standing to their sacred place,
Passing a blessed night
We came to day.
Now this day
Our father,
Dawn priests
Have come out standing to their sacred place.
Our sun father
Having come out standing to their sacred place.
Our child,
It is your day.
This day,
The flesh of white corn,
Prayer meal,
To our sun father
This prayer meal we offer.
May your road be fulfilled
Reaching to the road of your sun father,
When your road is fulfilled
In your thoughts (may we live).
May we be the ones whom your thoughts will embrace,
For this, on this day
To our sun father.

We offer prayer meal.
To this end:
May you help us all to finish our roads.

The Zunis, whose territory encompassed today's southeastern
United States, had a strictly observed ritual to mark the addition
of a new soul to the tribe. When a newborn reached eight days
of age, a ceremony equivalent to a christening took place at
dawn. The child's "aunts" would chant the words of this prayer
while sprinkling cornmeal over the infant. In addition to herald-
ing the birth of the child, the ceremony stood as a reminder to
the Zunis of the renewal of the cycle of life.

Savior, Who Thy Flock Art Feeding

Savior, who thy flock art feeding
with the Shepherd's kindest care,
all the feeble gently leading,
while the lambs thy bosom share:

Now, these little ones receiving,
fold them in thy gracious arm;
there, we know, thy word believing,
only there, secure from harm.

Never, from thy pasture roving,
let them be the lion's prey;
let thy tenderness so loving
keep them through life's dangerous way.

Then within thy fold eternal
let them find a resting-place;
feed in pastures ever vernal,
drink the rivers of thy grace.

These lyrics, set to the tune "O Sanctissima," were written by William Augustus Muhlenberg as a baptism hymn in 1826. Muhlenberg came from a distinguished American family. His great-grandfather founded the Lutheran Church in America, and his grandfather served as the first Speaker of the U.S. House of Representatives. Despite his Lutheran roots, Muhlenberg was ordained as an Episcopal minister and went on to become a leading American religious voice for more than sixty years.

Now I Lay Me Down to Sleep

Now I lay me down to sleep,
I pray the Lord, my soul to keep;
If I should die before I wake,
I pray thee, Lord, my soul to take.

Even today this prayer is known to children and their parents across the country. Initially published in London in a slightly different form, and later included in the *New England Primer,* which was first printed in Boston in 1690, it became an instant classic. In the eighteenth century alone more than two million copies of the book were sold, most of which were passed down from generation to generation.

Now I Wake and See the Light

Now I wake and see the light:
'Tis God who kept me through the night.
To him I lift my voice and pray
That he would keep me through the day:
If I should die before 'tis done,
O God, accept me through thy Son.

Less known but also an important part of the *New England Primer,* this prayer was recited by children at the beginning of each day. Facing high child mortality rates in the American colonies, parents made sure that their offspring were prepared to meet their death at any time.

Keep Me in the Right Way

O Lord, my God, though Thou art in heaven and I on earth, yet thou seest me and observest all I do and say. . . . Wilt Thou, O Lord, bless me, and keep me in the right way? Make my duty plain, and assist me to do all that is good and virtuous. Give me food and raiment while I live in Thy world. Forgive all my offenses against Thee, and help me to forgive my enemies, and to wish them well. . . . May I walk in all virtue and honesty in this world, so that I may be prepared to dwell in Thy heavenly kingdom when Thou shalt close my eyes in death; all which I would ask in the name and for the sake of my divine Redeemer.

This much longer prayer appeared at the end of the *New England Primer,* which also served as America's primary school text-book in all thirteen colonies. Geared for older children, this prayer provided a detailed blueprint for living a virtuous life, echoing the sentiments of the "Lord's Prayer."

Worthy Art Thou

Worthy art Thou, O Lord, of praise,
But ah! It's not in me.
My sinking heart I pray Thee raise
So shall I give it Thee.

My life as spider's web's cut off,
Thus fainting have I said,
And living man no more shall I see
But be in silence laid.

My feeble spirit Thou didst revive,
My doubting Thou didst chide,
And though as dead mad'st me alive,
I here a while might 'bide.

Why should I live but to Thy praise?
My life is hid with Thee.
O Lord, no longer be my days
Than I may fruitful be.

Anne Bradstreet's voice was one of the most eloquent of the colonial period. In her writings Bradstreet chronicled her struggles and her joys in the wilderness of the New World. She dedicated her life and her heart to God in this prayer, believing that in serving God she would find the full meaning and purpose of her existence.

Four Simple Graces

God is great, God is good.
Let us thank Him for our food. Amen

Thank you for the world so sweet,
Thank you for the food we eat,
Thank you for the birds that sing,
Thank you, God, for everything. Amen

Come Lord Jesus, be our guest,
and let these gifts to us be blessed. Amen

> Bless to us, O Lord, these thy good creatures,
> which we are now about to receive.
> Give them strength to nourish us,
> and us grace to serve thee,
> through Jesus Christ our Lord. Amen

Very little is known about the origins of these four prayers except that they derive from the earliest days of the republic. In the fourth blessing, reference is made to "these thy good creatures, which we are now to receive." Most likely this is an echo of King David's cry in Psalm 145: "The eyes of all wait upon thee; and thou givest them their meat in due season." Over the generations millions of families have recited these graces.

Prayer on the Eve of the Wedding

On this eve, the night before these two young people enter into the covenant of marriage, we turn to You for Your special blessing. As they exchange their vows tomorrow, we ask that You instill within them, and every day thereafter, the true meaning of unqualified love.

Tomorrow will mark the beginning of a long and challenging road that will require patience, persistence, and mutal understanding. Let Kenneth and Carolyn as individuals realize that in this extraordinary journey they are about to take, their union makes them one, not simply a percentage of the whole.

Married life will call for sacrifice and for acceptance of one another's virtues and faults. But in that acceptance, Lord, let them appreciate how much stronger and more loving they will become as they forge that life together.

Through Your graciousness, may they reach their twilight years and look back on a life that was fuller, more meaningful, and better lived because of their commitment to one another. Help them to recognize that as long as they have each other, their glass will always be half full.

Let them also know that those of us who stand in witness tomorrow are ready to sustain them in the days ahead. We simply are not passive observers but part of Your human family who see their success as part of our own.

It will be a great and glorious day, and we thank You, Lord, for having brought them together in matrimony. But then, again, You knew it would happen on that day, so very long ago, when they first set eyes on one another. Once again, we are reminded that You work in rather profound and mysterious ways.

We ask Your favor upon them and upon us, in Your name.

With the complexities of the twenty-first century and the high divorce rate facing America, this prayer was written and delivered by James P. Moore Jr. for a young couple on the eve of their wedding. Keeping in mind both the challenges and opportunities they will face, the piece recognizes that the journey they take together will be far greater in the end because they had one another.

In the Midst of Delivery

Save, Lord, and hear me, O King of heaven! Now I call upon thee in this time of my trouble.

Thou art my helper and Redeemer, make no long tarrying, O my God, nor suffer me to sink under the burdens of my pain.

Oh! Be thou my help in this time of my trouble; for without thee, vain is the help of man.

O Lord, let it be thy pleasure to deliver me; make haste, O Lord, to help me.

Given the difficulties that women faced at childbirth in the nine-teenth century, devotionals of the time included prayers for expectant mothers. This prayer was usually recited by the mother-to-be or by a close female friend. At the conclusion of the petition, other prayers were offered for the new baby or for a baby delivered stillborn.

A Child's Prayer

What does every good child say when at peep of day?
"Jesus, blessed Saviour keep me safe from harm I humbly
    pray."
Jesus answers, "I'll be near thee, I'll protect thee, I will
    cheer thee.
When thou prayest I will hear thee; I will keep thee safe
    this day."
Jesus, blessed Saviour, keep us safe from harm, I humbly
    pray.

Nineteenth-century composer Stephen Collins Foster often found himself in debt, even after writing such marketable and popular songs as "Swanee River" and "Jeanie with the Light Brown Hair." With churches and families at the time looking for new expressions of their faith, writing spiritual songs was both popular and lucrative. Foster wrote this comforting prayer for a child just at the outbreak of the Civil War.

Mother's Hymn

Lord who ordainst for mankind
Benignant toils and tender cares,
We thank thee for the ties that bind
The mother to the child she bears.

We thank thee for the hopes that rise
Within her heart as, day by day,
The dawning soul, from those young eyes,
Looks with a clearer, steadier ray.

And grateful for the blessing given
With that dear infant on her knee,
She trains the eye to look to heaven,
The voice to lisp a prayer to thee.

Such thanks the blessed Mary gave
When from her lap the Holy Child,
Sent from on high to seek and save
The lost of earth, looked up and smiled.

All-Gracious! grant to those who bear
A mother's charge, the strength and light
To guide the feet that own their care
In ways of Love and Truth and Right.

A lawyer by profession and a convert to the Unitarian Church, William Cullen Bryant was one of the great names in publishing in the early years of the new republic, serving as owner and editor in chief of the *New York Evening Post* for half a century. He was also one of the most widely read and influential American writers of the time. Here, he weaves Christ's Mother, Mary, into a poem about a mother's gratitude to God for the gift of her child.

For Parents

> Father, I believe that a home not built on the rock of faith
> hasn't a chance. Help give my children a chance.

Dale Evans Rogers, country singer and Western movie costar
with her real-life husband, Roy Rogers, was religiously devout.
She and her husband were parents to nine children, most of
them adopted. It was on behalf of her children that she wrote
this short prayer and would speak across the country on the
virtues of joining God and family together.

A Mother's Evening Prayer

> O gentle presence, peace and joy and power;
> O Life divine, that owns each waiting hour,
> Thou Love that guards the nestling's faltering flight!
> Keep Thou my child on upward wing tonight.
>
> Love is our refuge; only with mine eye
> Can I behold the snare, the pit, the fall:
> His habitation high is here, and nigh,
> His arm encircles me, and mine, and all.
>
> O make me glad for every scalding tear,
> For hope deferred, ingratitude, disdain!
> Wait, and love more for every hate, and fear
> No ill,—since God is good, and loss is gain.
>
> Beneath the shadow of His mighty wing;
> In that sweet secret of the narrow way,
> Seeking and finding, with the angels sing:
> "Lo, I am with you always,"—watch and pray.

No snare, no fowler, pestilence or pain;
No night drops down upon the troubled breast,
When heaven's aftersmile earth's tear-drops gain,
And mother finds her home and heav'nly rest.

Christian Science founder Mary Baker Eddy loved children and was bereft when her only child was taken away from her by family and friends who believed she was too ill to raise her son, George. This prayer conveys the depth of her affection for the bond between mother and child.

The Husband's Prayer

Accept my humble thanks, O Lord my God, who has provided a help meet for me, to be my partner in the nearest of all relations. O teach and enable me, in all things, to conduct myself towards her as it becomes me in this station. May I be enabled to cherish her as my own flesh. Let me never on any account despise her or be bitter against her; but may I bear with her infirmities, and forbear her in love and all gentleness. Nor let insult over her, as an inferior; but mildly use my authority, in treating her as my dear yoke-fellow and companion. O make me meek and patient, faithful, and kind, respectful and tender in all my conduct towards her; and may I show myself on all occasions well pleased and satisfied with her, that she may find comfort in fellowship with me, and never have reason to regret that she has forsaken all others for my sake. And while, in Thy good providence, we are separated from each other, be Thou her protector and almighty friend. O blessed Lord, espouse my dear friend to Thyself, in loving-kindness, and faithfulness, and tender mercies. Bless her and love her, and make her lovely in Thy sight, and in the eyes of all. And grant, O Lord our God, that we may be lovers of one another's souls, and that we may be

lovers of each other's salvation; so that after a short season of
fellowship here, we may meet again with rejoicing there, where
we shall never part, even in that fullness of joy which is in Thy
presence; where, though there be no marrying nor giving in
marriage, yet is there greater festivity and gladness, than in any
day of espousals; and where those who are united together in
Thy fear and love, shall be blessed together in everlasting
fellowship with Thee, and with Thy dear Son Jesus Christ. Amen

In response to the outbreak of the Mexican War in 1846, several
Protestant churches published devotionals for use by U.S. troops
and their families. This prayer, from the Presbyterian Church's
Manual of Devotion for Soldiers and Sailors, spoke to the duties
of a husband toward his wife, particularly when they are separated from each other. This prayer expresses the aspiration and
commitment for complete love for one's spouse.

The Perspective of Family

> When little things would irk me, and I grow
> Impatient with my dear one, make me know
> How in a moment joy can take its flight
> And happiness be quenched in endless night.
> Keep this thought with me all the livelong day
> That I may guard the harsh words I might say
> When I would fret and grumble, fiery hot,
> At trifles that tomorrow are forgot—
> Let me remember, Lord, how it would be
> If these, my loved ones, were not here with me.

In this brief "perspective" written just after the Civil War,
Wisconsin writer Ella Wheeler Wilcox uses straightforward language to express the small daily frustrations of a wife and
mother. After confronting a series of setbacks in her life, she

translated her struggles into poetry and prose. Her work was acclaimed for bringing comfort to thousands of Americans by allowing them to understand more clearly the human dimensions of their own hardships.

Bless This House

May nothing evil cross this door,
And may ill fortune never pry . . .
About these windows, may the roar,
And rain go by.

By faith made strong, the rafters will
Withstand the battering of the storm.
Your heart, though all the world grow chill,
Will keep you warm.

Peace shall walk softly through your rooms,
Touching your lips with holy wine.
Till every casual corner blooms . . .
Into a shrine.

With laughter drown the raucous shout,
And, though your sheltering walls are thin.
May they be strong to keep hate out.
And hold love in.

Written by Louis Untermeyer, poet laureate at the Library of Congress in the early 1960s, this popular blessing has been recited often at the dedication of both homes and public buildings. It was part of an anthology he published in 1923 called *This Singing World.* At the dawn of television Untermeyer's face became familiar to Americans everywhere when he appeared as a regular panelist on *What's My Line?*

For Home and Hearth

Oh, thou, who dwellest in so many homes, possess thyself of this. Bless the life that is sheltered here. Grant that trust and peace and comfort abide within, and that love and life and usefulness may go out from this home forever.

Lady Bird Johnson found this prayer hanging in a frame at a friend's home and jotted it down in shorthand. Although she would never know who had composed these words, she would later recount that she took great comfort in reciting it throughout the rest of her life.

Two Prayers of a Father

> Last night my little boy confessed to me
> Some childish wrong;
> And kneeling at my knee
> He prayed with tears—
> "Dear God, make me a man
> Like Daddy—wise and strong;
> I know you can."
>
> Then while he slept
> I knelt beside his bed,
> Confessed my sins,
> And prayed with low-bowed head.
> "O God, make me a child
> Like my child here—
> Pure, guileless,
> Trusting Thee with faith sincere."

Known as "The Two Prayers" this work was the creation of Andrew Gillies, a young Scottish immigrant. From the moment

this poignant introspection was published, just before the outbreak of World War I, it took immediate root and for years
would be read from church pulpits across the country on
Father's Day. Later in life Gillies would be named pastor of the
Third Presbyterian Church in Rochester, New York, and become
a leading voice in the New York Presbytery.

For the Little Children

Thou great Father of the weak, lay thy hand tenderly on all the
little children of the earth and bless them . . . But bless with a
sevenfold blessing the young lives whose slender shoulders are
already bowed beneath the yoke of toil, and whose glad growth
is being stunted forever. Suffer not their little bodies to be
sapped, and their minds to be given over to stupidity and the
vices of an empty soul. We have all jointly deserved the
millstone of thy wrath for making these little ones to stumble
and fall. Grant all employers of labor stout hearts to refuse
enrichment at such a price. Grant to all the citizens and officers
of states, which now permit this wrong the grace of holy anger.
Help us to realize that every child of our nation is in very truth
our child, a member of our great family. By the Holy Child that
nestled in Mary's bosom; by the memories of our own childhood
joys and sorrows; by the sacred possibilities that slumber in
every child, we beseech thee to save us from killing the
sweetness of young life by the greed of gain.

Christian theologian and Baptist minister Walter Rauschenbusch
was a formidable figure in forcefully addressing the working
conditions of sweatshops that relied on child labor. His work
and writings had an enormous influence on Dr. Martin Luther
King Jr. as he began his own ministry. In this particular prayer,
one of many he wrote over his lifetime, he emphasized the need
for members of society to embrace the cause of child workers

so as to protect them from exploitation. Child labor was abolished by law in the United States in 1938.

My Soldier

Now I lay me down to sleep
I pray the Lord my soul to keep.
God bless my brother gone to war
Across the seas, in France, so far.
Oh, may his fight for Liberty,
Save millions more than little me
From cruel fates or ruthless blast,
And bring him safely home at last.

During World War I the U.S. Treasury Department urged Americans to buy savings bonds and thrift stamps to help pay for the war. One of its most memorable advertising posters showed a mother seated with her daughter's head bowed against her lap as the child recites these words.

Build Me a Son

Build me a son, O Lord, who will be strong enough to know when he is weak, brave enough to face himself when he is afraid, one who will be proud and unbending in honest defeat, and humble and gentle in victory.

Build me a son whose wishbone will not be where his backbone should be; a son who will know Thee—and that to know himself is the foundation stone of knowledge.

Lead him, I pray, not in the path of ease and comfort, but under the stress and spur of difficulties and challenge. Here, let him learn to stand up in the storm; here let him learn compassion for those who fail.

Build me a son whose heart will be clear, whose goal will be high; a son who will master himself before he seeks to master other men; one who will learn to laugh, yet never forget how to weep; one who will reach into the future, yet never forget the past.

And after all these things are his, add I pray, enough of a sense of humor, so that he may always be serious, yet never take himself too seriously. Give him humility, so that he may always remember the simplicity of true greatness, the open mind of true wisdom, the meekness of true strength. Then I, his father, will dare to whisper, "I have not lived in vain."

At the outbreak of World War II, while he was stationed in the Philippines, General Douglas MacArthur received word that his wife, Jean, had given birth to a baby boy. Upon learning of the news, the fifty-eight-year-old MacArthur sat down at his desk and wrote these words.

For My Son Off to War

Dear God, please help my little boy to play the part of a man in this infectious blood poisoning of nations we call war. Give him the gift of thine own forgiveness that he in turn may forgive me and the rest of my generation who stood smugly by and permitted this senseless and insane thing to come about. Give him the strength to hold fast to his little-boy dreams and hopes and aspirations while all the forces of international evil seek to turn him into an efficient and deadly killer. And if thou dost decree that he shall not come back, then let his end be quick and sudden and sharp and not like that of thine only begotten Son who hung upon a cross for long hours far off in Calvary. And give him the inspiration of thine own divine wisdom that he may protect and preserve the lives of the men he commands who are fathers of children and the husbands of young wives and the sons of mothers of most of whom are older in years than he. For please remember, God, that he is only nineteen and a Second Lieutenant of Infantry in the Army of our United States.

This petition to God, written by a despairing father during World War II, could have been composed in any war. It was written and set aside, only to be discovered many years later. In the end his son did return from the war.

A Prayer for Mother

Lord Jesus, Thou hast known a mother's love and tender care, and Thou wilt hear while for my own mother most dear I make this Sabbath prayer. Protect her life, I pray, who gave the gift of life to me; and may she know from day to day, the deepening glow of joy that comes from Thee. I cannot pay my debt for all the love that she has given; but thou, Love's Lord, wilt not forget her due reward—Bless her in earth and heaven.

Composed by the prolific and prodigious educator Henry van Dyke, these words were adapted from a prayer he wrote in 1903 as a tribute to mothers on their birthdays. The piece became so popular that by World War I it was included in prayer books printed by the U.S. government for use by troops in the field.

For Wayward Children

Today, O Lord, we pray for wayward sons and daughters. We join our prayers to the prayers of sorrowing parents, who know their children will be lost forever if they do not repent and return to God. May we never add to their heavy burden by our undue criticism. Keep us humble and loving, O Lord. We thank Thee for the prodigals who have returned. May we ever be ready to welcome them and to forgive, as Thou art ready to forgive. We remember that we have all been prodigals.

This plea on behalf of parents with troubled teenage children was written by Esther Eby Glass, a prominent Mennonite writer from Lancaster, Pennsylvania, just after World War II. She and her husband raised two sons, but much of her experience with adolescents came from teaching Sunday school. She had a life-long passion to try to understand the motivations, anxieties, and problems facing teenagers.

A Student Prayer at the Beginning of a New Term

Lord, we thank Thee for the rest we have had from our tasks; for the joys of home, for games and walks, the rush of the wind, and the sound of the sea. O Thou, who givest to the old to dream dreams and to the young to see visions, grant that this term we may never come short of the dreams of our parents for us, or fail in the vision Thou requirest of youth. Grant us to help the lonely and timid, to support those who find it hard to keep their good resolutions. Give to those who teach sympathy and patience; to those who learn, perseverance and endurance; that we may daily grow more like Thee; through Jesus Christ our Master.

Among the prayers that have appeared in the college devotionals published throughout much of the country's history, this prayer from the early twentieth century was offered for students at the start of a new semester. Educators always felt the need to educate their young men and women in mind, body, and soul. This particular piece would have set the tone for the new semester ahead.

For Self-Control

O God, whose Apostle hath taught us that he that striveth for the mastery is temperate in all things; Grant to us, who are seeking to grow in strength of mind and body, such power of self-control that we may never give way to intemperance in food, drink, or pleasure, but may wisely order our lives so that work and recreation, rest and labor, may have their due share, and no wrongful self-indulgence mar our lives in Thy sight; through Jesus Christ our Lord.

This invocation by an unknown author was written almost a hundred years ago to remind young people of the need for moderation and self-control in their daily lives. Academic administrators hoped that communal prayers like this one, invoked in chapels and meeting halls on high school and college campuses, would allow students to reflect on the consequences of their actions.

COMMUNITY

An American Muslim Prayer in Remembrance of September 11, 2001

Dear God, as our country remembers the heartbreaking events of September 11th, 2001, we humbly turn to You in prayer. At a time where our nation is facing unprecedented challenges, we need Your Spirit, Mercy, and Strength, now more than ever, to guide us down the right path.

Dear Lord, we pray that you have taken under Your Merciful wings those who innocently perished on that tragic day. We are grateful they were once a part of our lives. We thank You for the love and joy they gave their parents, spouses, children, friends, and coworkers. We thank You for the testimony of their faith in their churches, mosques, synagogues, and temples. We thank you for the comfort and courage they extended to others in their last moments. Dear God, with Your compassion, please answer our prayer.

Dear Almighty, shower Your comfort upon the families of the victims. We pray for all who searched the streets and hospital rooms and rubble with fading hopes of finding a dear one alive. Replace the pain in their hearts with the knowledge that their loved ones are in an abode of peace. We pray their tears of grief are replaced with a tranquility of the soul that only You can bestow. Dear God, with Your compassion, please answer our prayer.

O our Sustainer, bless the children of the victims. Bless them with bountiful lives, with direction and remembrance, with discipline and virtue. Bless them with all that is good, and protect them from all that is evil. May the loss of one or both parents be replaced by Your Merciful and Blessed guidance. For You are the best of all guides. May the country do what it must to ensure their future. Dear God, with Your compassion, please answer our prayer.

Dear God, we pray for the rescue workers and volunteers from across the nation, who worked faithfully and tirelessly to find survivors and cleared the debris. Sustain them all, dear God, and please answer our prayer.

O Lord strengthen our nation and protect us from evil. Guide our leaders, elevate our society, and enrich the fabric of the country. Dear God, with Your compassion, please answer our prayer.

O Most Merciful, we have seen the very worst that we are capable of—vengeance, greed, and murder. But we have seen the very best that we are capable of—courage, compassion, service, faith, heroism, community, love. Strengthen us and make us better people who will choose the latter and better way.

Dear God, it is in You that we place our ultimate trust; it is to You that we pray; it is to you that we ask for guidance.

Dear Almighty, please bless the victims; Dear Sustainer, please bless the families; Dear God, please bless America.

This invocation was written by Omar Ricci and Khadijah Abdullah, both American Muslims, in the aftermath of the terrorist attacks of September 11, 2001. Ms. Abdullah, a high school student at the time, was concerned that non-Muslims would see Islam as a fanatic religion, so she began to organize neighborhood prayer groups in Los Angeles to create greater understanding. She read this prayer, condemning the atrocities of 9/11, before an ecumenical audience at the Roman Catholic Cathedral of Our Lady of the Angels in Los Angeles.

Thy Peace Be with Us Evermore

Thou gracious Power, whose mercy lends
The light of home, the smile of friends,
Our families in Thine arms enfold
As in the peaceful days of old.

For all the blessings life has brought,
For all its sorrowing hours have taught,
For all we mourn, for all we keep,
The hands we clasp, the loved that sleep.

The noontide sunshine of the past,
These brief, bright moments fading fast,
The stars that gild our darkening years,
The twilight ray from holier spheres.

We thank Thee, Father; let Thy grace
Our narrowing circle still embrace,
Thy mercy shed its heavenly store,
Thy peace be with us evermore.

Poet Oliver Wendell Holmes Sr. composed this prayer for his Harvard classmates on the anniversary of their fortieth class reunion in 1869. Parts of this work have been used on other special occasions to appeal for God's blessings on both family and community.

Shall We Gather at the River

> Shall we gather at the river,
> Where bright angels he has brought,
> With its crystal tides forever
> Flowing by the throne of God
>
> Ere we reach the shining river
> Lay we every burden down,
> Praise our spirits will deliver
> And provide our robe and crown.
>
> Soon we'll reach the shining river,
> Soon our pilgrimage will cease,
> Soon our happy hearts will quiver
> With the melody of peace.
>
> Yes, we'll gather at the river.
> The beautiful, the beautiful, river.
> Gather with the saints at the river,
> That flows by the throne of God.

Robert Lowry, pastor of the Hanson Place Baptist Church in Brooklyn, New York, was in a state of physical and mental exhaustion when he wrote this hymn. It was 1864 and he had just finished reading about the latest casualties from the Civil War and how thousands were dying across the country from typhoid. Trying to find a way to bring people together in the midst of their troubles and help them find solace in turning to God, he came up with a memorable tune to accompany the lyrics.

Rutgers Prayer

> We, men of Rutgers, bow in prayer, to ask Thy blessing,
>   loving care,
> provision for our many needs, thy guidance in our daily
>   deeds.
> Protect us, God, as we go on to meet the challenge of the
>   dawn.
>
> We, men of Rutgers, turn to Thee to make our hearts beat
>   pure and free,
> To see the glimmer of the Light that leads men into paths
>   of right.
> As we trudge old Rutgers sod, keep us ever near Thee
>   God.

In the late nineteenth century colleges began to compose their own hymns and prayers to bind their students, faculty, and alumni together as a community. Sung or recited at chapel services or at graduation and other formal ceremonies, these invocations became time-honored traditions in the halls of academia. This hymn from Rutgers College, memorably arranged by Rutgers professor F. Austin Walter, was composed when the school was an all-male bastion.

Where Cross the Crowded Ways of Life

> Where cross the crowded ways of life,
> Where sound the cries of race and clan
> Above the noise of selfish strife,
> We hear Thy voice, O Son of man!
>
> In haunts of wretchedness and need,
> On shadowed thresholds dark with fears,

From paths where hide the lures of greed,
We catch the vision of Thy tears.

From tender childhood's helplessness,
From woman's grief, man's burdened toil,
From famished souls, from sorrow's stress,
Your heart has never known recoil.

The cup of water given for Thee,
Still holds the freshness of Thy grace;
Yet long these multitudes to view
The sweet compassion of Your face.

O Master, from the mountainside
Make haste to heal these hearts of pain;
Among these restless throngs abide;
O tread the city's streets again.

Till sons of men shall learn Your love
And follow where Your feet have trod,
Till, glorious from Your heaven above,
Shall come the city of our God!

This prayer, recalling the social gospel movement, was one of the most popular invocations of the time. Written in 1903 by Frank Mason North, a minister of the Methodist Episcopal Church, it reflected the greater consciousness of the ills that were befalling inner cities and communities across the country.

Prayer for New York City

"Help!"

In 1975 the economic plight of New York City became a worldwide story. When the federal government refused to bail the city

out of its financial woes, Mayor Abraham Beame was at his wit's
end. During a visit to Jerusalem with other U.S. mayors, he made
a point of visiting the Western Wall. Wearing a yarmulke and
with his head bowed in prayer, he slipped a piece of paper into
one of the cracks of the ancient edifice with this one-word
prayer for New York City.

A Prayer for the City

Dear God,

We thank You for the gift of life
and for the cycle of blessing that holds the world in being.
We thank You for those who are alive to the fact that they
    are blessed
and bless others in return, for people of vision with
    generous hearts
who understand their obligation to give back to the world
    from the
abundance they have received.

We ask You to bless this city and its leadership in these
    times of
challenge and stress.

We ask that You raise up among us people of generosity
    and imagination
who help make the world a place of fulfillment and
    celebration
for all Your children.

May the leadership of this city call us out of the fortress
    into the
banquet of life where we are both hosts and guests,

welcoming all creatures to a table where no one is turned
   away
and there is enough for all.

Help us to choose.
Help us to act.
Help us to be.
The world is one.

This plea for assistance and community awareness was written by the Very Reverend Alan Jones, dean of the Episcopal Grace Cathedral of San Francisco. Given the beauty and relative wealth of the city on the bay, this prayer reminds people to consider their less fortunate neighbor, no matter where he or she might be.

STATES

A Prayer for Alabama

Timeless rolls the streams while man moulds their course and
wrests his sufficient margin of life from Thy scattered benefice;

> Shapes the flint to arrow point;
> Nurses seed to cotton, bale and cloth;
> Carves the wood to cabin logs
> and bakes his cities from the clay;
> mines the ore and makes the steel;
> catches the surging flood upon his
> shining wheels and makes the river
> yield light and power for Thy people all.

Praise Thee, wondrous God, for the blessed watershed that is
Alabama, pliant to man's need, gracious to his questing spirit.
May her sons not forget Thy bounty, nor fail to deserve
benediction. Amen

A Prayer for Alaska

Bless, Lord, the land that Thou hast spread to the North, the necklace of isles in the cold sea; mountains and tundra and great rivers, and the valleys where Thy people dwell.

As Thou dost light shining Borealis across the dark heavens of night, so may Thy glory adorn the day, that those who behold Thy splendor may lift their lives to Thee, and ever know the liveliness of Thy wondrous grace. Amen

A Prayer for Arizona

O God, who hast hid such plentiful treasure in the age-hewn soil of Arizona, and etched the timeless calendar of Thy patience upon her rocks and canyons, liberate now Thy blessing to all who live within the shadow of his grandeur.

Consecrate, O Lord, the phoenix birth of seed from dry suspense,

> rain to the yellow flowers,
> the fleece of sheep for
>   an Indian's loom,
> and the bread of life
>   to Thy needful people.

By crowning of the dawn refresh their spirit; in the brightness of the day and the cool of the night let all in peace come to the rising of Thy light. Amen

A Prayer for Arkansas

Mid all wonder of Thy glory, O God, we thank Thee most for the familiar places where Thou dost come to meet our lowly love and our unspoken hope.

Blessed be the quiet hallows where Thy people have found peace, and the steeples they have built to crown the circle of their friendship in Thy Word. Bless their homes along the rivers Red and White and muddy brown; deck their lives with the homely comfort of humor, with proportion, and the silent pride of valiant struggle.

So may the common web of life in Arkansas be ennobled by that holiness and help which is Thine alone to give, and our grateful destiny to reflect. Amen

A Prayer for California

Golden gate, Golden state,
Who posts the watch on Farallon's isle?
Who lifts up Shasta's snowy crown
And keeps the high passes of Sierra Nevada?

'Tis Thee, O Lord, who hath ringed a
royal valley with such ramparts
that within, blessing may lie among
the palms and poppies, the orchards
and vineyards and man-made waterways.

Praise the good monks in their missions;
Drake in his ship; pioneers and settlers;
all who sought life in Thy Name

from Tahoe's emerald blue to the surf
dancing upon the breathless coast.

Hallow, O Father, our questing too; that
we may behold the beauty of Thy truth;
far off among the stars and close
in the charters we devise
that peace and friendship may endure
upon the lovely face of earth. Amen

A Prayer for Colorado

Bless, high and holy Lord, the people who live
under the eaves of our continent.

Bless the rocky peaks of their golden roof-land,
which pluck crystal snow from heaven to refresh
the earth on every side with water pure.

Guard, O God, the mountain passes, the spruce
and lovely aspen sentinels upon their crests;
protect the lowly sheep and patient cattle in their
verdant valleys; prosper the seed by man's labor planted.

So, loving Father, do Thou keep Thy Colorado children
in the beauty of their lofty clime, and the joy of their
unspoiled hope; through Jesus Christ our Lord. Amen

A Prayer for Connecticut

Have in Thy keeping, O God, the strong hills and homely rocks of
Connecticut, and the undaunted folk who live among them. As by
mighty glacier Thou didst shape and furnish the land, so by
grace and labor did Thy servants clear it, meeting the bounds

with boulders, and measuring themselves against the stern beauty of Thy handiwork. Thus molded to Thy majesty, may Thy people ever rejoice in the bounty of their valleys, the refreshment of the sea, and Thy changing glory at each season of the year. Bless their towns and government; bless their commerce; bless their rest; that in turn they may endow their progeny with that hard and humble hope which is learned of Thee. Amen

A Prayer for Delaware

Bless, Lord, the peaceable homes and steady lives which from early times have looked to a wide and quiet river to be their highway and their harbor. As the estuary opens to the sea, so may the hope of Thy people be borne to the wideness of Thy glory and Delaware be ever sanctified: Lovely among her fields of green; first to wear the Constitution of American freedom; alert to the needs of all, and in all things faithful. Amen

A Prayer for the District of Columbia

Sanctify anew, Thou Ruler of Destiny, this bit of Federal soil which our forefathers set apart from any State to nourish the high mission of our common government. Bless, O Lord, the precious branches planted here:

> The deep-rooted responsibility of Law,
> the even measure of justice,
> and the leadership fitly chosen and
> held aloft before our people.

Grant to all who serve in this District the same vision that drew
Columbus to a new world, and a kindred steadiness of purpose
to that of the first president whose name and flag we bear.

So by Thy grace may we be worthy of that special place given to
a capital city in Thy holy Name. Amen

A Prayer for Florida

> Place of rest, place of work;
> Place of water upon the land
> And land upon the water;
> Place of straight horizon
>
> Edged in green upon the strand,
> Laughing birds, bright-hued fish,
> Store of fruit and fatling calves,
> and sun-warmed rows of vegetables.

May God's bright grace be given Thee, that all who dwell on
Florida's happy peninsula may be secure in her bounty, and
forget not to keep clear those sweet channels where Thy spirit
moves and the living water softly flows. Amen

A Prayer for Georgia

Cherish, Lord, the hardy spirit of Thy servants whose lives are
rooted in the tawny earth of Georgia. Nurture in them the
precious fiber of freedom wrested by their fathers from the
upland clearings and workworn fields. Visit now upon the sons,
in their towns and cities and burgeoning affairs, such fresh
vision of Thy destiny that they may ever be knit together in

fruitful life and liberty, planting deep the seed of courage by their abounding streams, and winning Thy blessing upon the goodly land. Amen

A Prayer for Hawaii

Praise be to Thee, O God:

> For mighty fire deep in earth
> lifting up the aisles from ocean floor;
> for steady wind wafting seed to the shore;
> and rain to bless her mantle green
> and fill the cisterns of life.

Thanks be to Thee, O Father: For all men who have traveled here, bearing in every race Thy image upon their brows; for the sea-girt commonwealth which they fashioned of courage and forbearance and the imagination of peace.

May the fire of Thy Holy Spirit ever burn in the hearts of Thy people, and Thy benediction be the lively hope of all who dwell in Hawaii. Amen

A Prayer for Idaho

Great Father, by whose timeless love the ages are adorned, we thank Thee for Thy splendor strewn upon the earth, and deeded free to all who seek Thy glory in the fresh land of Idaho.

From the peaked wall towering by the sunrise to the winding shadows of the mighty gorge to the West, Thou hast bounded her sundry treasure with light. Bless, Lord, the settled valleys and the wild places in between; that the lives of Thy people may be suffused by Thy radiance from on High. Amen

A Prayer for Illinois

O God, forasmuch as many have sought their destiny upon the level soil of Illinois, grant that they may be ever nourished by Thy good Spirit. Let the skein of commerce cast upon the prairies yield its fruitfulness as openly and equally as Thy blessing upon the seed and sowers of this uncommon land. And if the winds blow cold or very hot, then from that seasoning do Thou sift out the souls of great leaders, whose gifts of conscience and unbroken vision may serve Thy cause in the emancipation of all. Amen

A Prayer for Indiana

Forasmuch, O God, as in open Indiana Thou hast matched the boundless sky upon the wide unfettered earth, allow the spirits of those who dwell there the same unbroken vision. Fruitful hast Thou made her soil; let Thy people's lives be equally endowed. Firm as the limestone undergirding, so let her building be. Thus may Thy benediction come to her learning and her life, and to all whose livelihood is cast inside the Hoosier boundary. Amen

A Prayer for Iowa

To our hands, Great Pastor of Creation, hast Thou committed the abounding yield of earth; grant that as we receive, so we may share that mantle to brimming nourishment which thou hast spread upon the breast of the continent. In seeds and sowing, in cooling rain and patient care, in welcome reaping and fallow rest—Thou dost plant Thy goodness.

Give us also gladness in the blessed land of Iowa, cradled in fertility between her river boundaries. Amen

A Prayer for Kansas

> Open sky, open land;
> Open face, open heart;
> So hast Thou made Kansas
>   And her children, Lord.
>
> Homesteads for weather,
> Hands for work;
> Fiber of human souls
>   Thou hast winnowed on the prairie.
>
> Bless that free soil, O God,
> Her hills of flint,
> Her miles of wheat,
> Her flowers in the sun;
> And steady servants of Thine
>   unswerving truth. Amen

A Prayer for Kentucky

O God, who makest dawn to rise upon the mist and spreadest light in all the world, may we follow where Thy brightness beckons.

As of old Thou didst steady the eye and temper the sinew of those who sought fresh life upon the wooded land, keep now a like daring, and equal courage in our Kentucky homes. Let Thy glory summon each new day:

> In cabins by the winding brooks;
> On fields of blue where horses dance;
> Among Thy people
> In their uniformed cities.

Thou who hast blessed our roots in willing earth, illumine too the homestead of the spirit when shall spring vision of a nobler commonwealth. Amen

A Prayer for Louisiana

Bless, gracious Lord, the bright state of Louisiana; her pine hills and river bluffs, her bayous and coastal plains. In many shades of green does she deck the tawny flood that brings her life.

Praise be to Thee for the churning wheels of ships which have threaded that curling channel, assorted fate upon their sails. Bless in fertile peace the counterpoint of hope that here planted, farmers to the north and boatmen in their waterways.

May Thy goodness fall upon all the parishes of this delta-land, that her people, following the course of Thy grace, may be nourished by Thy love. Amen

A Prayer for Maine

Thank you, God, for the State of Maine, reaching ever for the first light of day. As Thy people wake to the Eastern rays, what chowder of nourishment dost Thou prepare for body and soul: concocted so delectably of pine needles and potatoes; of herring and clams and lobsters in their rocky lairs, of blueberries and new-mown hay and a thousand lakes and little boats brave upon the deep.

Of such blessing did our fathers distill their rugged liberty: Grant us grace to win the same, along the country roads and on the fringed and tasseled coast of our wooded land. Amen

A Prayer for Maryland

Blow, Lord, Thy clean winds upon the shores and shoals of Maryland. Blow gentle breeze of blessing across the earth, atop her stalwart hills, and over the greening fields. Blow, Holy Spirit, the freshness of liberty through the hearts of Thy people whose domain named for a queen, yet worships the King who is the Father of us all.

So may Thy children catch upon their hopes the breath of glory which Thou doth send to fill the spangled sky, the loft sails of ships, and faithful lives of men.

Fulfill then, O God, the promise once borne upon the wings of a dove and a land of peace and companionship, and courage enough ever to follow after Thee. Amen

A Prayer for Massachusetts

Bless, O Lord, the fish in the sea, emblems of Thine own Son, and like Him given for the sustenance of life. Bless the crook of sandy cape curving out upon that sea to fold in safety the Pilgrims who crossed the deep for salvation.

Bless the harbors and hills to which they came, who fled starvation or oppression or a mean spirit. Bless, O Heavenly Father, the goodly land that was their refuge; the farms and schools and lofty ships builded there, and the golden dome presiding over the brave heritage of patriot fathers.

Bless the commonwealth thus established, that her people, daring ever to venture in Thy Name, may not fail to reach the haven of Thy mercy and be renewed in the quest of life. Amen

A Prayer for Michigan

Guard in beauty, O God, the two great juts of land bowered in the unsalted sea, all garlanded with bays and decked with riches, which we call Michigan. From Royale Isle to Lake St. Clair is Thy bounty strewn, whence man could fashion his livelihood with furs and farms and furnaces.

Consecrate the labor, Lord, and hallow the thoughtful minds that seek to civilize the raw gifts of earth, organizing and refining them to the massive use of mankind. So may industry be yoked to human need, and the great engines of manufacture made to serve the common weal.

In the print of Thy feet, O Father, may then our footsteps be; and if we fit our foot to a wheel, then bless the little chariots of our making, that they may carry us to the wide places of Thy splendor. Amen

A Prayer for Minnesota

O God, by whose timeless care earth is furnished; we praise Thee for livelihood and leisure so amply framed in welcome Minnesota.

> For sheer delight hast Thou spangled her land
>> with ten thousand mirrors of glory;

> For the need of life dost Thou bring forth sturdy
>> grain for the millers' grist, to bind
>> thy love to our bread;

> And if after Thee we would builders be, then
>> thanks for the mountains of iron that
>> we may exchange for sinews of steel.

Where Thou hast gone before, O blessed Father, let us follow after: to the headwaters of Thy mercy and the harbor of Thy might. Amen

A Prayer for Mississippi

Hark, O Lord, the whisper of hope upon fallow land, that they who wait for Thy dawning may rejoice in the freshness of Thy blessing.

> Send, God, light upon the level horizon;
> Wash, God, the waiting earth with goodness;
> Fill, God, the hearts of Thy people with friendship and
>> faith;

That remembered upon the levees, the fields and beaches, and in every town, Thy spirit may preside to the health and peace of the citizenry of Mississippi. Amen

A Prayer for Missouri

Great God whose plough is weather and whose season is Time itself, we thank Thee for the earth Thou hast fashioned in Missouri:

> Smoothing the glacial plain with
>   great blades of ice;
> Irrigating the land with burnished
>   streams and
> Bounding it with Ozark beauty.

When Thou wast ready, Thy spirit stood by the Gate, inviting all mankind to the heart of Thy goodly continent.

Bless us now as we seek to retrace the mighty sweep of Thy making:

> Possessing our inheritance to
>   the little step of mules,
> Or the roar of city wheels;
> by the flutter of a steamer
>   upon the river,
> by the sound of sweet blues
>   upon the lips of a trumpet,
> or the cry of some distant
>   train across the night.

At every turn may we find the door; beyond learning to wisdom; beyond living to Life; beyond receiving to the happier joy of giving. And so, as river threads the prairie, may our hearts be open to Thy truth and blessed independence. Amen

A Prayer for Montana

Lord, this wild and sturdy state we call Montana, let it be Thy place of openness and peace enduring. Lift there man's little spirit to the infinitude of Thy glory, imprinted upon the glaciered peaks, the glistening streams and arid plains of Thy making.

Let herders by their wagons have Thee for company; men lonely in the mines, and ranchers at their corrals know Thy boundless presence. Forfend that townsmen should be sheltered from the neigh of horses, the coyote's cry, or the silent respect of furry neighbors; but grant that they, rejoicing in Thy creation, may ever reflect in their own affairs the freedom by which Thou hast surrounded them. Amen

A Prayer for Nebraska

O God, whose splendor unfettered, whose mercy unbounded rests upon the wide plain of Nebraska, let the soul of Thy people be open too. May they hark Thy call gently upon the wind, poignant as a whistle cry haunting the prairie night.

Nurture, Lord, the great course of flat water which once bore the questing pioneer across our nation's heart, and now dispenses life to the fields of corn and farmers' homes.

So may blessing come, O Father, to children schooled to Thy glory, whose eyes shall reflect the distant hills of faith. Amen

A Prayer for Nevada

Thou Lord who pleased to pierce the sky and furrow earth in such wild abandon, give Thy servants to endure the pursuit of

Thy glory, which Thou hast tumbled upon the untamed vastness of Nevada.

Bless the liveliness of water stored upon her snow-clad slopes and melted in her shining reservoirs. Bless the veins of treasure girt within her rocky soil. Bless Thy children all, who come seeking peace as a cool draught in a dry land. Amen

A Prayer for New Hampshire

O God, how hast Thou favored Thy children who are given to perceive Thy splendor upon the wooded terrain of New Hampshire!

> For hemlock and spruce and sweet maple
> dancing down the valleys; for
> granite uplifted, unmoved, eternal,
> for myriad lakes like eyes
> in the forest where shines
> the image of the lively sky;
> for the silent peace of snow,
> the cool verdure of summer,
> and autumn's gorgeous praise:
> Accept our thanksgiving for
> Thy abounding glory.

May our lives too reflect Thy grace: As free as a deer upon the mountain, yet humble enough to seek Thy way and no other. So shall we dwell with Thee and one another, taking the place in Nature's harmony which Thou hast appointed to be our blessing. Amen .

A Prayer for New Jersey

Grant, gracious Lord, that we may find grace ever to plant gardens alongside the busy marts of commerce;

> By the roadside.
> A window-box of beauty;
> At the door of a city,
> A fertile plot of nourishment
> And growing things;
> By the gate of a nation,
> A placement of settlement and welcome
> And the roots of a new home.

So, O Father, may blessing fall upon Thy people in New Jersey; and upon their coastlands and riverbanks and wooded hills; and upon their souls within. In their sowing, let hope be never dim, and in their reaping no defilement, but rather thanksgiving for the bloom of glory which is Thine alone to give. Amen

A Prayer for New York

Praise be to Thee, O God, for courage to dream and strength to build.

Thanks be to Thee for empires won and kingdoms yet to come; and for lakes and coursing rivers on which has passed the commerce of a continent.

Bless, Lord, these generous valleys and ancient hills; and the harbor at their edge where ocean and earth are married in so great a portal, where ebbs and flows the rhythm of exchange between the Old World and the New.

Grant only, O Father, that those who are posted at such a gate, may match to their tall towers the hope of their spirit; and ever to keep open the sacred path to a country wider than their own. Amen.

A Prayer for North Carolina

Preserve unto us, good Lord, the precious treasure bequeathed to us by those silent eons when Thou wast preparing earth for our inheritance. May we cherish, and not despoil, the cup of loveliness entrusted to our hands for a space.

So may the green land be blessed, whose smoky highlands yield their mineral riches to the soil below, and whose surf-bound coast is protected by necklaces of sand. Guard the peaceful sounds; protect the forest mantle, the pliant ploughlands; and let Thy grace abound among Thy Carolina people whose lives are rooted in this place of promise. Amen

A Prayer for North Dakota

We thank Thee, Lord, for the hard and healthy country of North Dakota, where all is tempered by the sweeping power of Thy creating hand.

By wind Thou dost scour the rocks; by weather etch Thy children's fate: as with tornado or hail, baking sun or driven ice Thou dost chisel the profile of mesa and of man.

Bless then the pliant clay of Thy stout fashioning: the black beds of ancient lakes, little hills left by glaciers, and the untold patience of farmers' lives so humbly bowed to soil and season.

By such winnowing is purest vision born; praise be ever Thine,
Creator God, for this open province of Thy cleansing grace.
Amen

A Prayer for Ohio

O God, at whose behest we are given to be weavers at Thy great
loom, grant that our labor may be worthy of Thy design. Blessed
was the sketch Thou didst imprint upon the land, when hawk and
squirrel, whitefish and chestnut tree celebrated together the
holy concert of life.

Bless now the human hands that would elaborate Thy plan:

> Planting where earth gives promise.
> building where water warrants hope,
> and combining the bare elements
> into countless goods convenient
> and useful for our common welfare.

Of many climes is gathered the skein; of many colors the coat is
woven; knit all together in honest Ohio, giving purpose in her
prosperity and glory to her praise of Thee. Amen

A Prayer for Oklahoma

River Red, and soil, and Indian brother before us: tawny is Thy
canvas, Creator God, whereon by touch of light Thou hast
daubed the bluestem grass, rich black earth and white-tailed
flash of deer.

Grant that they who sojourn in Oklahoma's land may deserve Thy rainbowed blessing gilding the arch of heaven, and fish below, and every creature in his special mode of life.

Thine the painting, Lord; ours to pursue Thy beauty and truth in the various errands of our common cause. Amen

A Prayer for Oregon

Author of all majesty, how bright is Thy glory upon the land of Oregon! Blessed be the trees upon their hills, the valleys in their verdure, and the dry places waiting their turn of fertility.

Praise be to Thee for the precious gift of rain: Drawn into heaven from the sea. Caught again upon the snowy peaks, returning fruitfully down the strong rivers giving life to Thy people in their orchards and city places. May their lives be likewise lifted to Thee, and blessed, and sent again to do Thy service upon earth.

So may the land be renewed, and the souls of Thy servants. Amen

A Prayer for Pennsylvania

Bless, Lord, the hilly ramparts, the steep valleys and generous plains where by Thy Providence Thou didst settle a sturdy race, destined for freedom. By inwardness of faith, in openness of spirit was the soil prepared, where independence might take root, and liberty baptize a nation fit for the New World. Grant, O Heavenly Father, that they to whom such riches have come down may ever be chosen of Thee to be builders of Thy commonwealth and bearers of Thy peace. Amen

A Prayer for Rhode Island

Praise be to Thee, O God, for the little prism where men have seen the splendor of Thy glory:

> In the conscience of a single
> man who ventured to settle
> his life under Thy Providence
> alone;

> In the coastal towns where
> faith was planted in open
> companionship and none was
> barred;

> By the sparkling bays where
> spirit grew because there is
> no limit of Thy love.

Bless, O Lord, the smallest state of our fellowship, that her people may ever nourish the widest of our hopes. Amen

A Prayer for South Carolina

Grant, great Creator, that we too may love what Thou hast blessed so well: The Southland soil of Carolina.

Praise Thee, Lord, for the blue of upcountry hills, and their grassy apron falling toward the sea; praise Thee for islands and salt marshes and birds which nest in the sand; praise and thanksgiving for the fruitful earth that cherishes a magnolia or laurel upon the mountain, or cotton for raiment.

Soft is the wind, soft the speech of men, gentle Thy Grace where the roots of Thy children are hid. May they in Thy goodness grow, reaching up their spirits toward heaven, until they shall have fulfilled Thy purpose for them. Amen

A Prayer for South Dakota

Red man, white man,
Who shall sing for thee
Of the great ocean of grass, thy tawny home?
Of badland draws and lookout hills?
Of coyotes and bison and friendly beasts of the barn?

Hark, O Lord, the night chant of the Sioux,
The rising hymn of settlers' hope,
The prayer Thy people make upon the Dakota plain;

That they may grow in peace and goodness
Until Thy praises resound in every heart. Amen

A Prayer for Tennessee

Praise be to Thee, Father of myriad waters, for coursing life gushing upon the land of Tennessee:

For prancing freshets reviving the earth;
For sweet streams to slake man's thirst;
For swift rivers carving paths for hunters' feet;
For that majestic tide which collects them all to make
    A highway for the continent.

After Thy leading, clean and cool have Thy people followed, resting only where beaver or man has caused the flood to pause.

Grant to Thy servants in their blessed valleys the spirit still to seek and to find that living water which is the prize of life that is more than mortal. Amen

A Prayer for Texas

Republic within a republic, may the Lord endow they strength with freedom doubly bold: Hallow the proud star of thy destiny; cherish the light of each man's liberty; until the Texas plain be bright with the galaxy of God's blessing. Then by heaven's high design, may her sons dare to choose their way, true to the glory that ever summons them to life. Amen

A Prayer for Utah

O God, who day by day doth pierce the desert with the brightness of Thy presence, lead us 'neath the heights and across the great salt flats to the temple of Thy holiness. In storm or danger, in drought or plague, send O Father sweet birds of mercy to keep Thy Utah folk in safety upon the promised land.

Guard the painted cliffs, the vermillion spires and rocky spans; keep too the watered furrows and well-kept streets where springs Thy blessing to our homes in love and hope. Amen

A Prayer for Vermont

Abide, dear Lord, with the steady folk who choose to dwell in the gentle valleys of Vermont. Thy goodness doth her land proclaim:

by waters dancing in her streams,
    pure in the ponds;
by the silence of winter cold and
    the sweetness of Spring in
    the maple sap;
by granite sentinels against the sky,
    and the greenness of life below.

By such blessing surrounded may thy frugal people, sturdy and
free, sanctify their hands for work and their hearts to Thee.
First to march for liberty, first to outlaw slavery, first to count
the vote of every man: Thou didst teach Thy people well. Guard
now their peace, and forever the openness of truth. Amen

A Prayer for Virginia

Renew Thy grace, O Thou ruler of destiny, upon the
Commonwealth of Virginia, that she may ever rejoice in the
dominion of Thy Providence. Bless the gracious land where thou
hast unfolded such a measure of Thy purpose for mankind.

For each step on the highway of history we lift our thanksgiving:
For those who wrested welcome from the wilderness; who
planted peace along the inland avenues of the sea; who saw Thy
glory upon the mountain heights and likened it to freedom.
Praise be to Thee, mighty Lord, for the sturdy quest which
generation by generation sought out the noble mark of
independence and distilled that brave wisdom into the
instruments of a nation's governance.

Cherish, O Father, that generous spirit which has raised up such
leaders of liberty; and sanctify to thy people still the vision of
Thy great design for them and for all men. Amen

A Prayer for Washington

O Thou Creator Divine, who dost fashion our lives by the rhythm of Earth, we thank Thee for that wide span of glory we call Washington.

Hardy the wagons that first came there, and the little ships, which were met by shining salmon striving, upstream leaping that life might be sown.

Bless, O God, our struggle too, that fresh bounty may come of our hands and hearts, and goodness like unto Thine.

Then Lord, after work, in peace let Thy people be. Let them abide as great trees rooted in the embracing soil, their branches spread to heaven's promise.

Thus upon the plains, by ocean's teeming sound and 'round the snowy sentinels that guard these timbered hills, may Thy people live ennobled by Thy grace. Amen

A Prayer for West Virginia

Shine, O Lord, upon the homely mosaic of West Virginia's land: Upon her step-hewn hills and angled draws, her maple-strewn valleys and ridges clad in mountain rhododendron.

Shine, Lord, upon her citizens, armed only with freedom, scrappers all for such measure of dignity as fearlessness and faith may win.

Shine, O God, into those deep recesses where Thou hast hidden abundant riches, that those who dig in the earth, and those who watch for their return, may know the radiance of Thy light and the safety of Thy love.

Bright be the cleansing fire of Thy truth in the hearts of the people, and in the public weal of their common life. Amen

A Prayer for Wisconsin

Cherish, Lord, by Thy steady grace, the State of Wisconsin; her trim and serried fields, her frost-scoured shores, the lively marts of her trade.

Fresh springs her teeming life; clear and clean may its coursing be; in government, in learning and sport and in the heart of every citizen.

Where once trees grew in quiet grace upon the rolling land, now let Thy children stand, blessed in their kith and their kine; peaceful by their barns, and eager still for the day Thou hast in store for them. Amen

A Prayer for Wyoming

Guide, O Lord, the feet that seek to follow in the trail of Thy bright passing: on burnished peaks of light, or scoured beds of rushing water, and quietly by the sheltering folds of sheep. In wide places and in small, haste Thy blessing upon the Wyoming land, that her people faithful be, their lives attuned to Thy generous splendor upon the buttes and grassy pasture, the wooded home of elk or bear, and the hearths of human friendship at the ending of the trail. Amen

Few individuals would seem to be more uniquely qualified to compose these unusual prayers than the Reverend Frances B. Sayres. The grandson of President Woodrow Wilson, he was born in the White House in 1915 and served as the dean of Washington National Cathedral, known to many as the "Nation's House of Prayer," from 1951 to 1978. Merging his deep spirituality with great affection for the United States, he composed this series of invocations to represent each of the fifty states and the District of Columbia, trying to represent in some meaningful way the unique character of each one.

The lush language of these prayers is reminiscent of another era, yet they continue to charm and inspire. Dean Sayres hoped that children in particular would be spiritually moved and intrigued by the clues he left behind in these prayers to find out more about their country.

Since 1972 the cathedral has dedicated one Sunday during the year to each of the states and the District of Columbia, and the relevant prayer is recited by the entire congregation during services. In the dedication of his devotional Dean Sayres wrote, "Please God that in praying we might be united, rather than divided!"

COUNTRY

In Love of Philadelphia

And thou, Philadelphia, the Virgin settlement of this province named before thou wert born, what love, what care. What service and what traveil have there been to bring thee forth and preserve thee from such as would abuse and defile thee.

O that thou mayest be kept from the evil that would overwhelm thee. That faithful to the God of thy mercies, in the Life of Righteousness, thou mayest be preserved to the end. My soul prays to God for thee, that thou mayest stand in the day of trial, that thy children may be blest of the Lord and thy people saved by His Power.

William Penn, the founder of the Pennsylvania colony, took great efforts to lay out his vision for a new kind of city in Philadelphia, which he affectionately called "the city of brotherly love." In this prayer, written in 1684 and engraved on a prominent bronze plaque in the north portico of Philadelphia's City Hall, he expressed his hopes for the city's future.

A First Prayer

Be Thou present O God of Wisdom and direct the counsel of this Honorable Assembly; enable them to settle all things on the best and surest foundations; that the scene of blood may be speedily closed; that order, Harmony, and peace may be effectually restored, and Truth and Justice, Religion and Piety, prevail and flourish among the people.

Preserve the health of their bodies, and the vigor of their minds, shower down on them, and the millions they here represent, such temporal Blessings as Thou seest expedient for them in this world, and crown them with everlasting Glory in the world to come. All this we ask in the name and through the merits of Jesus Christ, Thy Son and our Saviour, Amen

When delegates from the original thirteen colonies met in Philadelphia for the first time on September 5, 1774, most of them had never met one another before. At the time rumors were rife that British troops were shelling the homes of those "traitors" who had come to the meeting from Massachusetts. Before they began to address matters of substance, the delegates decided to open their daily sessions with prayer as a means to bond together and to ask for God's blessing upon their cause. This was the first invocation that was offered by Reverend Philip Duche, the local pastor of Christ's Church. The practice of opening legislative sessions with a prayer established a precedent that has continued to this day in both the U.S. House and Senate.

American Patriot's Prayer

Parent of all, omnipotent
In heav'n and earth below,

Thro' all creation's bounds unspent
Whole streams of goodness flow.

But chief to hear my country's voice,
May all my thoughts incline,
'Tis reason's law, 'tis virtue's choice,
'Tis nature's call and thine.

Throughout the pages of Thomas Paine's pivotal 1776 treatise *Common Sense,* he spoke strikingly of how prayer can express the most private aspirations of human beings. In most editions of his pamphlet, he added this prayer, believing that it would have a catalytic effect on the colonists.

In Praise of Freedom

Let Tyrants shake their iron rod,
And slavery clank her galling chains.
We fear them not; we trust in God;
New England's God forever reigns.

When God inspired us for the fight
Their ranks were broke, their lines were forced;
Their ships were shattered in our sight
Or swiftly driven from our coast.

The foe comes on with haughty stride;
Our troops advance with martial noise.
Their veterans flee before our youth,
And generals yield to beardless boys.

What grateful offerings shall we bring?
What shall we render to the Lord?
Loud hallelujahs let us sing.
And praise his name on every chord.

William Billings composed the lyrics and music for this hymn in 1778 to give voice to American resolve during the Revolutionary War. At the time, this song was almost as popular as "Yankee Doodle." Considered by many to be America's unofficial composer laureate, Billings created both spiritual and patriotic anthems expressing the hopes of Americans throughout the original thirteen colonies.

Petition to God and to the States United

> My prayer is unto the Lord.
> May the people of the states rise up as a great and young lion.
> May they prevail against their enemies.
> May the degrees of honor of his Excellency the President of the Convention George Washington, be extolled and raised up.
> May everyone speak of his glorious exploit.
> May God prolong his days among us in this land of liberty.
> May he lead armies against his enemies as he has done hereuntofore.
> May God extend peace to them and their seed after them so long as the sun and moon endureth, and
> May Almighty God of our Father Abraham, Isaac, and Jacob endue this noble assembly with wisdom, judgment, and unanimity in their councils, and
> May they have the satisfaction to see their present toil and labor for the welfare of the united States . . .

Jonas Phillips was a wealthy Jewish merchant from Philadelphia who strongly supported the Revolutionary War. On September 7, 1787, he submitted a petition to the Constitutional Convention asking the delegates, in the midst of their deliberations, to remember the patriotic Americans of the Jewish faith, and not to alienate them by creating an exclusively Christian republic.

A Jewish Call for American Prayer

When we call on Thee, O righteous God, answer us.
Hearken to the voice of our cry and show us grace.
Have compassion on us and hearken to your prayer.
For thou, Most High God, hast removed distress far from us.

O gracious God, Thou hast delivered us from our enemies;
Thou hast redeemed us from those who rose up against
    us;
Thou has girded us with strength to smite the pride of our
    enemies;
In shame and disgrace they fell beneath our feet.

O God of Hosts, Thou has set peace and tranquility in our
    palaces
And has set the President of the United States as our head
    [ruler?],
And in prayer we humble ourselves before Thee, oh, our
    God.
Unto our supplications mayest Thou hearken and deliver us.

A *mind* of wisdom and understanding set in the heart of
    the head of our country;
May he *judge* us with justice; may he cause our hearts to
    rejoice and be glad.
In the *paths* of the upright may he lead us;
Even unto old age may he administer and judge in our
    midst.

Pure and upright be the heart of the one who rules and
    governs us.

May God Almighty hearken to our voice and save us.
We will prolong our prayer before God, our Redeemer.
May he guard and keep the Vice President, senators, and
    representatives of the United States.

May he give good sense and understanding to the officers
    of the courts.
May the hearts of our governors be upright and faithful.
May he prosper and bless our country,
And deliver us from the hand of outside enemies.

May our sons in their youth be like a growing plant,
May our daughters be like [cornerstones?]
May our storehouses be full and bursting from end to end,
    multiplying in our streets.
May our cattle be fat and may there be no breach . . . in
    our broad places.

May our God bless all friends of our country and their
    judges,
And give glory to the Lord God, our Redeemer.
May Judah be saved and Israel dwell securely,
And may the Redeemer come to Zion, and let us say, Amen.

In the early days of the republic Jewish communities from north
to south were quite small but very vocal in their desire to be integrated into the mainstream of the new nation. This composition, entitled "A Prayer for the *Medina*," was written by
mercantilist Jacob Cohen for the Beth Shalom Congregation in
Richmond, Virginia. The occasion was a celebration of the first
officially declared Thanksgiving by George Washington in 1789.
The word "medina" in Hebrew refers to "new land," and this
prayer became for the Jewish people an expression of pride.

On the Occasion of George Washington's Birthday

Almighty and eternal God,
You have revealed your glory to all nations.
God of power and might, wisdom and justice,
Through you authority is rightly administered,
Laws are enacted, and judgment is decreed.

Assist with your spirit of counsel and fortitude
The President of these United States,
That his administration
May be conducted in righteousness,
And be eminently useful to your people
over whom he presides.
May he encourage due respect for virtue and Religion.
May he execute the laws with justice and mercy.
May he seek to restrain crime, vice, and immorality.

We, likewise, commend to your unbounded mercy
All who dwell in the United States
Bless us and all people with the peace
Which the world cannot give.

We pray to you, who are Lord and God, forever and ever.
  Amen.

Bishop John Carroll, the first Roman Catholic bishop in the United States and the founder of Georgetown University in 1789, wrote this invocation in 1794 in honor of the birthday of President George Washington. He composed this and other prayers for the new republic and its leaders, directing that they be recited in every Catholic church across the country. Carroll hoped that these prayers would help integrate Catholics into the larger mainstream of the United States.

Blessings upon This House

I pray to heaven to bestow the best of blessings on this house, and all that shall hereafter inhabit it. May none but honest and wise men ever rule under this roof.

On the second night that John Adams lived in the White House, he sat down to write to his wife, Abigail. Awed by his new surroundings, still in the process of being built, and facing reelection, Adams ended the letter with the preceding verse. Franklin Roosevelt had this blessing engraved on a plaque that he installed next to the fireplace in the East Room.

The National Anthem

> Oh, say, can you see, by the dawn's early light,
> What so proudly we hail'd at the twilight's last gleaming?
> Whose broad stripes and bright stars, thro' the perilous
>   fight,
> O'er the ramparts we watch'd, were so gallantly
>   streaming?
> And the rockets' red glare, the bombs bursting in air,
> Gave proof thro' the night that our flag was still there.
> O say, does that star-spangled banner yet wave
> O'er the land of the free and the home of the brave?
>
> On the shore dimly seen thro' the mists of the deep,
> Where the foe's haughty host in dread silence reposes,
> What is that which the breeze, o'er the towering steep,
> As it fitfully blows, half conceals, half discloses?
> Now it catches the gleam of the morning's first beam,
> In full glory reflected, now shines on the stream:
> 'Tis the star-spangled banner: O, long may it wave
> O'er the land of the free and the home of the brave!

And where is that band who so vauntingly swore
That the havoc of war and the battle's confusion
A home and a country should leave us no more?
Their blood has wash'd out their foul footsteps' pollution.
No refuge could save the hireling and slave
From the terror of flight or the gloom of the grave:
And the star-spangled banner in triumph doth wave
O'er the land of the free and the home of the brave.

O, thus be it ever when freemen shall stand,
Between their lov'd homes and the war's desolation;
Blest with vict'ry and peace, may the heav'n-rescued land
Praise the Pow'r that hath made and preserv'd us as a
    nation!
Then conquer we must, when our cause it is just,
And this be our motto: "In God is our trust."
And the star-spangled banner in triumph shall wave
O'er the land of the free and the home of the brave!

As generations of schoolchildren have come to know, Frances Scott Key wrote "The Star-Spangled Banner" during the War of 1812 as he watched the British bombard Fort McHenry in Baltimore. What is less well known is that in the fourth verse of the national anthem he spoke of God's guiding hand in the affairs of the nation and promoted the need to adopt the motto "In God is our Trust." Historians believe that this line prompted the government to institutionalize the motto "In God We Trust," even having it engraved on the nation's currency.

My Country 'Tis of Thee

My country 'tis of Thee,
Sweet land of liberty,
Of thee I sing.
Land where my fathers died!

Land of the Pilgrim's pride!
From every mountainside,
Let freedom ring!

My native country, thee
Land of the noble free,
Thy name I love.
I love thy rocks and rills,
Thy woods and templed hills;
My heart with rapture fills
Like that above.

Let music swell the breeze
And ring from all the trees
Sweet freedom's song.
Let mortal tongues awake;
Let all that breathe partake;
Let rocks their silence break,
The sound prolong.

Our father's God to Thee,
Author of Liberty,
To Thee we sing.
Long may our land be bright
With freedom's holy light
Protect us by Thy might,
Great God, our King!

When he was a student at the Andover Theological Seminary in Massachusetts in 1832, Samuel F. Smith was convinced that the new republic needed a national hymn. "In a brief period of time at the close of a dismal afternoon," as he would later write, he penned the lyrics and matched them to the tune of Great Britain's "God Save the King" and America's "God Save the President." The piece was premiered by a choir of five hundred children on July 4, 1832, at the Park Street Church in Boston.

Commissioning Prayer

O Eternal God, creator of the Universe and Governor of Nations: Most Heartily we beseech Thee with Thy favor to behold and bless Thy servant, the President of the United States, and all the officers of our Government, and so replenish them with the grace of Thy Holy Spirit that they may always incline to Thy will and walk in Thy ways. Bless the Governors of the several states, and all who are in authority over us; give them grace to execute justice and maintain truth that peace and happiness, religion and piety, may be established among us for all generations.

May the vessels of our navy be guarded by Thy gracious Providence and care. May they not bear the sword in vain, but as the minister of God, be a terror to those who do evil and a defense to those who do well.

Graciously bless the officers and men of our navy. May love of country be engraven on their hearts and may their adventurous spirits and severe toils be duly appreciated by a grateful nation; may their lives be precious in Thy sight, and if ever our ships of war should be engaged in battle, grant that their struggles may be only an enforced necessity for the defense of what is right. Bless all nations and kindreds on the face of the earth and hasten the time when the principles of holy religion shall so prevail that none shall wage war any more for the purpose of aggression, and none shall need it as a means of defense.

All of which blessings we ask through the merits of Jesus Christ our Lord.

First invoked at the Philadelphia Shipyard in 1843, this prayer with slight variations has been used in the commissioning of U.S. naval vessels ever since. Although it opens with a petition asking for God's blessings on the navy and on America's leaders, it becomes much broader toward the end, embracing "all nations."

Battle Hymn of the Republic

Mine Eyes have seen the glory of the coming of the Lord:
He is trampling out the vintage where the grapes of wrath
    are stored;
He has loosed the fateful lightning of his terrible swift
    sword:
His truth is marching on.

I have seen Him in the watch fires of a hundred circling
    camps;
They have builded Him an altar in the evening dews and
    damps;
I can read His righteous sentence by the dim and flaring
    lamps:
His day is marching on.

I have read a fiery gospel writ in burnish'd rows of steel,
"As ye deal with my contemners, so with you my grace
    shall deal";
Let the Hero, born of woman, crush the serpent with his
    heel
Since God is marching on.

He has sounded forth the trumpet that shall never call
    retreat;
He is sifting out the hearts of men before his judgment
    seat:
O, be swift my soul, to answer Him! Be jubilant, my feet!
Our God is marching on.

In the beauty of the lilies Christ was born across the sea;
With a glory in his bosom that transfigures you and me:
As he died to make men holy, let us die to make men free,
While God is marching on.

While accompanying her husband to Washington, D.C., on government business during the Civil War, Julia Ward Howe was struck by the massive number of Union troops she encountered along the way. She was profoundly moved by the sacrifices the young men were making for their families and for their country. From the desk of her room at Washington's Willard Hotel, she penned the words to the "Battle Hymn of the Republic." The lyrics, set to the popular tune of the time "John Brown's Body," was published in newspapers in both the North and the South.

The Centennial Hymn

Our fathers' God! From out whose hand
The centuries fall like grains of sand,
We meet today, united free,
And loyal to our land and Thee,
To thank Thee for the era done,
And trust Thee for the opening one.

Here, where of old, by Thy design,
The fathers spake that word of Thine
Whose echo is the glad refrain
Of rended bolt and falling chain,
To grace our festival time, from all
The zones of earth our guests we call.

Be with us while the New World greets
The Old World thronging all its streets,
Unveiling all the triumphs won
By art or toil beneath the sun;

And unto common good ordain
This rivalship of hand and brain

Beneath our Western skies fulfil
The Orient's mission of good-will,
And freighted with love's Golden Fleece,
Send back its Argonauts of peace.

For art and labor met in truce,
For beauty made the bride of use,
We thank Thee; but, withal, we crave
The austere virtues strong to save,
The honor proof to place or gold,
The manhood never bought or sold!

Oh make Thou us, through centuries long,
In peace secure, in justice strong;
Around our gift of freedom draw
The safeguards of Thy righteous law:
And, cast in some diviner mould,
Let the new cycle shame the old!

Quaker poet James Greenleaf Whittier was commissioned in 1876 to write "The Centennial Hymn" to celebrate the anniversary of American independence. Set to the music of German composer J. Max Mueller, the work was first performed by the Philadelphia Orchestra and a choir of a thousand voices. It would be the only hymn ever written by the eminent Whittier, who would have preferred a much less dramatic setting for this prayer.

America the Beautiful

O beautiful for spacious skies,
For amber waves of grain,

For purple mountain majesties
Above the fruited plain!
America! America!
God shed his grace on thee
And crown thy good with brotherhood
From sea to shining sea!

O beautiful for pilgrim feet
Whose stern impassioned stress
A thoroughfare of freedom beat
Across the wilderness!
America! America!
God mend thine every flaw,
Confirm thy soul in self-control,
Thy liberty in law!

O beautiful for heroes proved
In liberating strife.
Who more than self their country loved
And mercy more than life!
America! America!
May God thy gold refine
Till all success be nobleness
And every gain divine!

O beautiful for patriot dream
That sees beyond the years
Thine alabaster cities gleam
Undimmed by human tears!
America! America!
God shed his grace on thee
And crown thy good with brotherhood
From sea to shining sea!

Once referred to as "the national heartbeat set to music," these
lyrics of Katharine Lee Bates, combined with the music of

Samuel Augustus Ward, continue to capture the spiritual essence of the country more than a hundred years after this hymn was written. "America the Beautiful" came to Bates while she was hiking along Pike's Peak in Colorado during the summer of 1893. On the evening of September 11, 2001, members of Congress stood on the front steps of the U.S. Capitol for a press conference and spontaneously began to sing this spiritual and patriotic anthem to show their unity and defiance in the face of the terrorist attacks that had taken place that morning.

America's National Hymn

God of our fathers, whose almighty hand
Leads forth in beauty all the starry band
Of shining worlds in splendor through the skies
Our grateful songs before Thy throne arise.

Thy love divine hath led us in the past,
In this free land by Thee our lot is cast,
Be Thou our Ruler, Guardian, Guide and Stay,
Thy Word our law, Thy paths our chosen way.

From war's alarms, from deadly pestilence,
Be Thy strong arm our ever sure defense;
Thy true religion in our hearts increase,
Thy bounteous goodness nourish us in peace.

Refresh Thy people on their toilsome way,
Lead us from night to never ending day;
Fill all our lives with love and grace divine,
And glory, laud, and praise be ever Thine.

Written by the Reverend Daniel C. Roberts in 1876, this work was meant to honor the nation's hundredth anniversary at a celebration in Brandon, Vermont. It was so well received that Roberts anonymously sent it to the General Convention of the Episcopal Church, which embraced it wholeheartedly and adopted it as America's "national hymn." It was set to the tune of "Pro Patria" from the Episcopal Church's hymnal. It has been performed on numerous occasions, from national celebrations to the funerals of presidents.

America First

America first, not only in things material,
But in things of the spirit.
Not merely in science, invention, motors, skyscrapers,
But also in ideals, principles, character.
Not merely in the calm assertion of rights,
But in glad assumption of duties.

Not flouting her strength as a giant,
But bending in helpfulness over a sick and wounded world
    like a Good Samaritan.
Not in splendid isolation,
But in courageous cooperation.

Not in pride, arrogance, and disdain of other races and
    peoples,
But in sympathy, love, and understanding.
Not in treading again the old, worn, bloody pathway which
    ends inevitably in chaos and disaster,
But blazing a new trail along which, please God, other
    nations will follow into the new Jerusalem where wars
    shall be no more.

Some day, some nation must take that path—unless we are
    to lapse into utter barbarism—and that honor I covet for
    my beloved America.

And so in that spirit and with these hopes, I say with all
my heart and soul, "America First."

First published at the beginning of the twentieth century, this
prayer expressed the ideals that America had come to represent
to its people and to the world. Its message is as relevant today as
it was when it was written. It was composed by George Ashton
Oldham, a British immigrant who had chosen to come to the
United States as a young man largely because of the country's
ideals. He was later ordained an Episcopal priest, ultimately being consecrated the bishop of Albany, New York.

America Befriend

O Lord our God, Thy mighty hand Hath made our country
free;
From all her broad and happy land may worship rise to
Thee;
Fulfill the promise of her youth, her liberty defend;
By law and order, love and truth, America befriend!

The strength of every state increase in union's golden
chain;
Her thousand cities fill with peace, her million fields with
grain.
The virtues of her mingled blood in one new people blend;
By unity and brotherhood, America befriend!

O suffer not her feet to stray; but guide her untaught
might;
That she may walk in peaceful day, and lead the world in
light.
Bring down the proud, lift up the poor, unequal ways
amend;
By justice, nationwide and sure, America befriend!

Through all the waiting land proclaim Thy gospel of
   goodwill;
And may the joy of Jesus' name in every bosom thrill.
O'er hill and vale, from sea to sea, Thy holy reign extend;
By faith and hope and charity, America befriend!

Poets at the outset of the twentieth century turned out numerous
prayers, many of them set to music, asking for God's help in
guiding the future course of America. One of the most engaging
works was composed by clergyman Henry van Dyke in 1912. Van
Dyke, who became a close friend of President Wilson during
their days working at Princeton together, would later be elected
to the prestigious American Academy of Arts and Letters.

A Cadet's Prayer

O God, our Father, thou Searcher of men's hearts,
help us to draw near to thee in sincerity and truth.
May our religion be filled with gladness and
may our worship of thee be natural.

Strengthen and increase our admiration
for honest dealing and clean thinking,
and suffer not our hatred of hypocrisy
and pretense ever to diminish.

Encourage us in our endeavor
to live above the common level of life.

Make us to choose the harder right
instead of the easier wrong, and
never to be content with a half truth
when the whole can be won.

Endow us with courage that is born of loyalty
to all that is noble and worthy,
that scorns to compromise with
vice and injustice and knows no fear
when truth and right are in jeopardy.

Guard us against flippancy and
irreverence in the sacred things of life.
Grant us new ties of friendship and
new opportunities of service.

Kindle our hearts in fellowship with
those of a cheerful countenance,
and soften our hearts with sympathy
for those who sorrow and suffer.

Help us to maintain the honor of the
Corps untarnished and unsullied and to
show forth in our lives the ideals of West
Point in doing our duty to thee and to our Country.

All of which we ask in the name of the
Great Friend and Master of men.

Written by Colonel Clayton Wheat, chaplain and professor of English at the U.S. Military Academy, this prayer has been invoked by West Point cadets since 1920, when General Douglas MacArthur served as the school's commandant. Several generations of the academy's graduates have recited this prayer on the battlefield, and for some these words would be the last they would ever utter.

Eternal Father, Strong to Save

Eternal Father, Strong to save,
Whose arm hath bound the restless wave,
Who bid'st the mighty Ocean deep
Its own appointed limits keep;
O hear us when we cry to thee,
for those in peril on the sea.

O Christ! Whose voice the waters heard
And hushed their raging at Thy word,
Who walked'st on the foaming deep,
and calm amidst its rage didst sleep;
Oh hear us when we cry to Thee
For those in peril on the sea!

Most Holy Spirit! Who didst brood
Upon the chaos dark and rude,
And bid its angry tumult cease,
And give, for wild confusion, peace;
Oh, hear us when we cry to Thee
For those in peril on the sea!

O Trinity of love and power!
Our brethren shield in danger's hour;
From rock and tempest, fire and foe,
Protect them wheresoe'er they go;
Thus evermore shall rise to Thee,
Glad hymns of praise from land and sea.

In 1860 these words were written by William Whiting of
Winchester, England, in honor of a young man who was about to
cross the Atlantic Ocean for America. A year later John B. Dykes,
an Anglican clergyman, wrote music to accompany the lyrics,
and the piece in time became the hymn for both the British and
U.S. navies. This life-affirming piece was performed at the fu-

nerals of Presidents Franklin Roosevelt, John F. Kennedy, and Ronald Reagan.

For Our Nation

Almighty God, ruler of all the peoples of the earth, forgive, we pray, our shortcomings as a nation; purify our hearts to see and love truth; give wisdom to our counselors and steadfastness to our people; and bring us at last to the fair city of peace, whose foundations are mercy, justice, and goodwill, and whose builder and maker you are.

This prayer was offered by America's twenty-eighth president, Woodrow Wilson, as World War I was unfolding. The son of a Presbyterian minister from Staunton, Virginia, Wilson fervently believed that daily prayer was absolutely key to a person's well-being. These words would be included in the *Book of Common Worship* of the Presbyterian Church.

What I Owe America

Dear God . . .

Please help me repay the debt I owe America, the land of the Free and the Home of the Brave. And make me able to help those who need help.

Eddie Cantor, one of the country's most famous comedians in the early twentieth century, wrote down this petition at the height of his career after enduring a particularly difficult life's journey from rags to riches. Known as the "Apostle of Pep," he was beloved by the millions of Americans who listened to his

top-rated radio shows. Here he makes clear that the country af-
forded him opportunities for which he was grateful and that he
should always be mindful to support the less fortunate.

In Service of God and Country

Almighty God: May those who have given their lives in the
service of this nation rest in Thy care.

May those who are wounded in body find spiritual comfort
under Thy guidance in the knowledge that through their services
a great cause has been served.

May those who offer their lives in support of that cause, by land
and sea and air, find strength in Thy divine guidance.

May those of us who serve this nation in its great purpose to
secure freedom for all peoples be sustained by Thy blessings.

Give us strength, O Lord, that we may be pure in heart and in
purpose to the end that there may be peace on earth and good
will among men.

May we be mindful this Easter morning "still stands Thine
ancient sacrifice, an humble and a contrite heart." Amen.

General George C. Marshall was called upon to speak at an ecumenical sunrise service on Easter morning of 1945 as World War
II was coming to a close. His wife, Katherine Tupper Brown,
would later recount that the emotions of the crowd ran high as
he read this prayer. As she sat there, she realized how the years
of loss and sacrifice on the battlefront and home front seemed
to well up all at once.

Recovery from War

Our Heavenly Father, if it be Thy will that America should assume world leadership, as history demands and the hopes of so many nations desire, make us good enough to undertake it. We consider our resources in money and in men, yet forget the spiritual resources without which we dare not and cannot lead the world.

Senate Chaplain Peter Marshall opened the proceedings of the U.S. Senate on June 5, 1947, with these words. He knew that later that day George Marshall, the U.S. secretary of state, would be delivering his historic speech at Harvard University, outlining the Marshall Plan to help rebuild Europe.

President Eisenhower's First Inaugural Address

My friends, before I begin the expression of those thoughts that I deem appropriate to this moment, would you permit me the privilege of uttering a little private prayer of my own? And I ask that you bow your heads.

Almighty God, as we stand here at this moment my future associates in the Executive Branch of government join me in beseeching that Thou will make full and complete our dedication to the service of the people in this throng, and their fellow citizens everywhere.

Give us, we pray, the power to discern clearly right from wrong, and allow all our words and actions to be governed thereby, and by the laws of this land. Especially we pray that our concern shall be for all the people regardless of station, race, or calling.

May cooperation be permitted and be the mutual aim of those who, under the concepts of our Constitution, hold to differing political faiths; so that all may work for the good of our beloved country and Thy glory. Amen

Minutes before he emerged from his Washington hotel room on January 20, 1953, the day he was to be sworn in as president, Dwight Eisenhower jotted down this prayer. He became the first president to deliver an invocation at his inauguration.

The Regents' Prayer

Almighty God, we acknowledge our dependence upon Thee, and we beg Thy blessings upon us, our parents, our teachers, and our country.

These words were carefully composed in 1951 by the Board of Regents for the State of New York for children to recite daily in public school classrooms. Reaction against this prayer brought about the landmark case before the U.S. Supreme Court on the question of prayer in public schools. The Court ruled on June 25, 1962, in *Engel v. Vitale,* that "it is not part of the business of the government to compose official prayers for any group of the American people to recite as part of a religious program carried by the government." The decision would become one of the most controversial in the history of the Court.

A Bicentennial Prayer

My fellow Americans, I once asked you for your prayers, and now I give you mine:

May God guide this wonderful country, its people, and those they have chosen to lead them. May our third century be illuminated by liberty and blessed with brotherhood, so that we and all who come after us may be the humble servants of thy peace. Amen.

During his last address before a joint session of Congress, President Gerald Ford ended his remarks with a prayer for the nation, using the occasion to look ahead to the new century. In bringing an end to the Vietnam War and closure to President Richard Nixon's legal culpability in the Watergate scandal, Ford became known as the "great healer."

Dedication of the Vietnam War Memorial

O Lord our God and God of generations past, help us, we pray, make this the beginning of the time of healing that we all seek. Help us ease the terror and the pain of all who suffered because of war. And help them and help us find the way to peace.

God, let this monument and this dedication forever remind us that we will come together to mourn our dead. We will come together to reach out to our wounded. We will come together to remember and to honor our brave. Only then may we have the vision to dream our dreams again. May we have the faith to pray our prayers again. May we have the courage to march along together again and, together, help make this the kind of country and the kind of world for which we pray.

May we all join together and say, Amen

This prayer, offered by Rabbi Arnold E. Resnicoff on the occasion of the dedication of the Vietnam War Memorial in Washington, D.C., in November 1982, reflects on one of the more difficult and divisive chapters in U.S. history. Rabbi Resnicoff was a decorated veteran of the war and a mentor to numerous U.S. military chaplains during his tenure at the Pentagon.

On Democracy's Front Porch

We meet on democracy's front porch, a good place to talk as neighbors and as friends. For this is a day when our nation is made whole, when our differences for a moment are suspended. And my first act as President is a prayer—I ask you to bow your heads.

Heavenly Father, we bow our heads and thank You for Your love. Accept our thanks for the peace that yields this day and the shared faith that makes its continuance likely. Make us strong to do Your work, willing to heed and hear Your will, and write on our hearts these words: "Use power to help people." For we are given power not to advance our own purposes nor to make a great show in the world, nor a name. There is but one just use of power and it is to serve people. Help us remember, Lord. Amen.

Minutes after he was sworn into office on January 20, 1989, President George H. W. Bush began his inaugural address with these words. He had been struck by how his predecessor President Dwight Eisenhower had offered a similar invocation during his inauguration. Although Bush was quite private when it came to speaking about his religious faith, he also considered it imperative that he begin his presidency with a prayer.

Blessings for America

Our Creator, the merciful benefactor, the merciful Redeemer who opens for all people a way to have good conscience and a good life:

Grant to this Nation that Americans continue to live as a prosperous nation of "many in one" and as a people of faith taking pride in human decency, industry, and service.

Let us pray that this great Nation's two centuries of national life may inspire other nations to move toward social and economic justice for all.

Grant that her big heart for charity, compassion, repentance, and mercy continues to beat strongly within all of us. Grant that Americans always have more hope than troubles and ever grow in goodness and in wisdom.

Bless Americans to always cherish our freedom and the noble essence of the American people.

Grant that we Americans understand better our brothers and sisters around the world and reject unsuitable national pride for a global community of brotherhood and peace.

Bring all citizens and governments together, those of great means and small means, to appreciate more our Nation's solemn pledge of liberty, peace, and justice for all.

Bless our homes and our schools.

Bless the parents, our troubled youth, our burdened inner cities to never be without hope or direction. Bless Americans to keep to the best of our ways.

Bless Americans to cherish more the pride of industry.

Bless the efforts of the President and all other efforts in progress for more jobs and more opportunity to be in this great society for more of us.

Bless matrimony and families here and in all the world.

Increase for the President of the United States, for every Member of the Senate, and for every Member of the House of

Representatives, the excellence of man's spirit and the excellence of the intellect of the statesmen so that they may build a better America for us all. Amen.

This invocation, delivered by Imam Warith Deen Muhammad before the U.S. Senate on February 6, 1992, was the first prayer to be offered by someone of the Islamic faith. Although he is the son of the late controversial leader of the Nation of Islam Elijah Muhammad, Warith Deen Muhammad later rejected the notion of the religion's black separatist views, opting instead to support the ideal of an inclusive America.

The Cabinet's Prayer

Ever-faithful God, in death we are reminded of the precious birthrights of life and liberty you endowed in your American people. You have shown once again that these gifts must never be taken for granted.

> We pledge to those whom you have called home, and ask
>   of you—
> Patience, to measure our lust for action;
> Resolve, to strengthen our obligation to lead;
> Wisdom, to illuminate our pursuit of justice, and
> Strength, in defense of liberty.

We seek your special blessing today for those who stand as sword and shield, protecting the many from the tyranny of the few. Our enduring prayer is that you shall always guide our labors and that our battles shall always be just.

We pray this day, heavenly Father, the prayer our nation learned at another time of righteous struggle and noble cause—

America's enduring prayer: Not that God will be on our side, but always, O Lord, that America will be on Your side.

Like several of his predecessors, President George W. Bush began most of his cabinet meetings with a prayer. He would invite a particular secretary to offer an invocation. In this case, the prayer was offered by Secretary of Defense Donald Rumsfeld at the first cabinet meeting held after the terrorist attacks of September 11, 2001.

Prayer for America

Dear Lord,

We're still hoping we'll wake up. We're still hoping we'll open a sleepy eye and think, What a horrible dream.

But we won't, will we, Father? What we saw was not a dream. Planes did gouge towers. Flames did consume our fortress. People did perish. It was no dream and, dear Father, we are sad.

There is a ballet dancer who will no longer dance and a doctor who will no longer heal. A church has lost her priest, a classroom is minus a teacher. Cora ran a food pantry. Paige was a counselor and Dana, dearest Father, Dana was only three years old. (Who held her in those final moments?)

We are sad, Father. For as the innocent are buried, our innocence is buried as well. We thought we were safe. Perhaps we should have known better. But we didn't.

And so we come to you. We don't ask you for help; we beg you for it. We don't request it; we implore it. We know what you can do. We've read the accounts. We've pondered the stories and now we plead, Do it again, Lord. Do it again . . .

We thank you, dear Father, for these hours of unity. Disaster has done what discussion could not. Doctrinal fences have fallen. Republicans are standing with Democrats. Skin colors have been covered by the ash of burning buildings. We thank you for these hours of unity.

And we thank you for these hours of prayer. The Enemy sought to bring us to our knees and succeeded. He had no idea, however, that we would kneel before you. And he has no idea what you can do.

Let your mercy be upon our President, Vice President, and their families. Grant to those who lead us wisdom beyond their years and experience. Have mercy upon the souls who have departed and the wounded who remain. Give us grace that we might forgive and faith that we might believe.

And look kindly upon your church. For two thousand years you've used her to heal a hurting world.

Do it again, Lord. Do it again.

Through Christ, Amen

Max Lucado, best-selling author and one of the country's most influential ministers at the turn of the twenty-first century, responded to the terrorist attacks of September 11, 2001, with a prayer. In this excerpt from that prayer, he looks to God for healing America's wounds.

9/11 Prayer Before the House of Representatives

O God, come to our assistance.

O Lord, make haste to help us.

Yesterday we were stunned, angry and violated. Today, Lord, we stand strong and together. Yesterday changed our world. Today we are changed.

We have humbly prayed to You, O Lord God of Heaven and Earth, yesterday and through the night. Now we turn to You for Your guidance and sense of eternal truths which built this Nation as we begin a new day of building security and peace through justice.

We mourn our dead and reach out with prayer and acts of compassion to all those families splattered with blood and exhausted by tears. Heal the wounded. Strengthen all civil servants, medical and religious leaders as they attempt to fill the gaping holes left in the fabric of our Nation.

Send forth Your Holy Spirit, Lord, upon all the Members of Congress, the President, and all government leaders across this Nation. Free them of fear, any prejudice whatsoever, remove all doubt and confusion from their minds. With clear insight which comes from You and You alone, reveal all that is unholy, and renew the desire of Your people to lives of deepening faith, unbounding commitment, and lasting freedom here where liberty has made her home.

We place our trust in You now and forever.

This invocation was offered by the Reverend Daniel Coughlin, the fifty-ninth chaplain of the U.S. House of Representatives, to open the chamber's deliberations twenty-four hours after the events of September 11, 2001. Father Coughlin was the first Catholic priest to serve in that capacity.

9/11 Prayer Before the U.S. Senate

Almighty God, source of strength and hope in the darkest hours of our Nation's history, we praise You for the consistency and constancy of Your presence with us to help us confront and battle the forces of evil manifested in infamous, illusive, cowardly acts of terrorism. We turn to You with hearts filled with dismay, anger, and grief over the terrorist attacks on the World Trade buildings in New York City and the Pentagon here in Washington. We pray for the thousands of victims who lost their lives as a result of these violent acts against our Nation. We intercede for their loved ones; comfort them and give them courage. In particular, we pray for the loved ones of the fire fighters and police who died seeking to help others. Quiet our turbulent hearts. Remind us of how You have been with us in trouble and tragedies of the past and have given us victory over tyranny. Bless the women and men of this Senate today as they join with President Bush in decisive action. Guide them as they seek justice against the perpetrators of yesterday's evil destruction and seek to devise a long-range solution to the insidious problem of terrorism. Thank You in advance for the courageous leadership You will provide through this Senate. You are our Lord and Savior.

Reverend Lloyd John Ogilvie, the chaplain of the U.S. Senate, de-livered this invocation before a hushed chamber the day after the terrorist bombings of September 11, 2001. The Presbyterian minister served the body from 1995 to 2003.

A Commander-in-Chief's Prayer

We are here in the middle hour of our grief. . . . On this national day of prayer and remembrance, we ask almighty God to watch over our nation, and grant us patience and resolve in all that is to come. We pray that He will comfort and console those who now walk in sorrow. We thank Him for each life we now must mourn, and the promise of life to come.

As we have been assured, neither death nor life, nor angels nor principalities nor powers nor things present nor things to come, nor height nor depth, can separate us from God's love. May He bless the souls departed. May he comfort our own. And may He always guide our country.

God bless America.

President George W. Bush memorialized the tragedy of September 11 with these words, which he offered at the National Day of Prayer and Remembrance at Washington National Cathedral on September 14, 2001. The service included religious leaders of different faiths from across the country, as well as members of the diplomatic corps and U.S. government officials.

Muslim Prayer After September 11

In the name of God, most gracious, most merciful.

Lord, you said and your words are true: If any do seek for glory and power, to God belongs all glory and power. To Him mount up all words of purity. He exalts all righteous deeds. But those that lay the plots of evil, for them is a terrible penalty; and the plotting of such will He not abide.

Goodness and evil are not equal. Repel the evil with the good. Then will he between whom and you was hatred become as it were your friend and intimate. But no one will be granted such goodness except those who exercise patience and restraint, none but persons of the greatest good fortune.

In the aftermath of the September 11 attacks, members of Muslim communities from across the United States strove to counteract negative perceptions of their faith based on the actions of a handful of radical terrorists. They joined together two prayers adapted from the Koran to deliver at the Washington National Cathedral and at other services of remembrance.

WORLD

Give Us Hearts to Understand

Give us hearts to understand;
Never to take from creation's beauty more than we give;
never to destroy wantonly for the furtherance of greed;
Never to deny to give our hands for the building of earth's
    beauty;
never to take from her what we cannot use.

Give us hearts to understand
That to destroy earth's music is to create confusion;
that to wreck her appearance is to blind us to beauty;
That to callously pollute her fragrance is to make a house
    of stench;
that as we care for her she will care for us.

We have forgotten who we are.
We have sought only our own security.
We have exploited simply for our own ends.
We have distorted our knowledge.
We have abused our power.

Great Spirit, whose dry lands thirst,
Help us to find the way to refresh your lands.

Great Spirit, whose waters are choked with debris and
   pollution,
help us to find the way to cleanse your waters.

Great Spirit, whose beautiful earth grows ugly with
   misuse,
help us to find the way to restore beauty to your
   handiwork.
Great Spirit, whose creatures are being destroyed,
help us to find a way to replenish them.

Great Spirit, whose gifts to us are being lost in selfishness
   and corruption,
help us to find the way to restore our humanity.
Oh, Great Spirit, whose voice I hear in the wind,
whose breath gives life to the world, hear me;
I need your strength and wisdom.
May I walk in Beauty.

This Algonquin prayer was composed by Big Thunder, a distinguished chief in the late nineteenth century. In these words he asks the Great Spirit for help in restoring the majesty of earth's beauty, which is being marred by human beings.

Overcoming Oppression

Almighty God! God of Hosts!

Thou who didst strengthen the hearts and guide the arms of our fathers when they were fighting for the sacred rights of their national independence! Thou who didst make them triumph over a hateful oppression, and hast granted to our people the benefits of liberty and peace!

Turn, O Lord, a favorable eye upon the other hemisphere;
pitifully look down upon an heroic nation which is even now
struggling as we did in the former time, and for the same rights.

Thou, who didst create man in the same image, let not tyranny
mar thy work and establish inequality upon the earth.

Almighty God! do thou watch over the destiny of the Poles, and
make them worthy to be free. May thy wisdom direct their
councils, may thy strength sustain their arms!

Shed forth thy terror over their enemies; scatter the powers
which take counsel against them; and permit not the injustice
which the world has witnessed for fifty years to be
consummated in our time.

O Lord, who holdest alike the hearts of nations and of men in
thy powerful hand, raise up allies to the sacred cause of right;
arouse the French nation from the apathy in which its rulers
retain it, that it may go forth again to fight for the liberties of
the world.

Lord, turn not thou thy face from us, and grant that we may
always be the most religious, as well as the freest, people of the
earth.

Almighty God, hear our supplications this day. Save the Poles, we
beseech thee, in the name of thy well-beloved Son, our Lord
Jesus Christ, who died upon the cross for the salvation of all
men. Amen.

"The religious atmosphere of the country was the first thing that
struck me on arrival in the United States," wrote Alexis de
Tocqueville in *Democracy in America*. While visiting the Midwest in 1831 the Frenchman was invited to a political rally where
two to three thousand mainly poor people were gathered to dis-

cuss how to help the people of Poland in their struggle against Russian occupation. Tocqueville recorded this prayer offered by the local priest who led the assembly. A collection was then taken up to help the Poles. Tocqueville was almost reverential in describing the extraordinary compassion shown by Americans, whether of Polish extraction or not, in helping those beyond their borders who were struggling against oppression.

He's Got the Whole World in His Hands

He's got the whole world in His hands
He's got the whole world in His hands
He's got the whole world in His hands
He's got the whole world in His hands

He's got the itty bitty baby in His hands
He's got the itty bitty baby in His hands
He's got the itty bitty baby in His hands
He's got the whole world in His hands

He's got a-you and me brother in His hands
He's got a-you and me brother in His hands
He's got a-you and me brother in His hands
He's got the whole world in His hands

He's got a-you and me sister in His hands
He's got a-you and me sister in His hands
He's got a-you and me sister in His hands
He's got the whole world in His hands

He's got the whole world in His hands
He's got the whole world in His hands
He's got the whole world in His hands
He's got the whole world in His hands

Originally a spiritual sung in the South in the early nineteenth century, this hymn hit the top of the music charts in 1958 after a thirteen-year-old British boy named Laurie London recorded it as an upbeat song. In turn, performing artists from a wide variety of musical genres gave it their own interpretation, and it took on a new life and following of its own.

America: The Fifth Stanza

> Lord, let war's tempest cease,
> Fold the whole world in peace
> Under Thy wings,
> Make all the nations one,
> All hearts beneath the sun,
> Till Thou shalt reign alone,
> Great King of Kings.

Prior to the Civil War, "My Country 'Tis of Thee" was performed at numerous religious and civic functions as a way to stir national pride and unity. Just before the outbreak of hostilities between the North and South, Henry Wadsworth Longfellow added his own stanza to the beloved piece. Since then his words have been added to Samuel Smith's original work.

Jesus Loves the Little Children

> Jesus calls the children dear,
> "Come to me and never fear,
> For I love the little children of the world;
> I will take you by the hand,
> Lead you to the better land,
> For I love the little children of the world."

Jesus loves the little children,
All the children of the world.
Red and yellow, black and white,
All are precious in His sight,
Jesus loves the little children of the world.

Jesus is the Shepherd true,
And He'll always stand by you,
For He loves the little children of the world;
He's a Savior great and strong,
And He'll shield you from the wrong,
For He loves the little children of the world.

Jesus loves the little children,
All the children of the world.
Red and yellow, black and white,
All are precious in His sight,
Jesus loves the little children of the world.

I am coming, Lord, to Thee,
And Your soldier I will be,
For You love the little children of the world;
And Your cross I'll always bear,
And for You I'll do and dare,
For You love the little children of the world

Jesus loves the little children,
All the children of the world.
Red and yellow, black and white,
All are precious in His sight,
Jesus loves the little children of the world.

This is one of the most recognizable children's hymns, originally written as a Civil War ballad. A generation after the war, a
preacher from Chicago by the name of Clare Herbert Woolston
adapted his words to the popular melody of "Tramp, Tramp,

Tramp" to express God's unconditional love for children of all color.

In Praise of the World, O God

O God, we thank Thee for this universe, our great home; for its vastness and its riches; and for the manifoldness of the life which teems upon it and of which we are part. We praise Thee for the arching sky and the blessed winds, for the driving clouds, and the constellations on high. We praise Thee for the salt sea and the running water, for the everlasting hills, for the trees, and for the grass under our feet. We thank Thee for our senses by which we can see the splendor of the morning, and hear the jubilant songs of love, and smell the breath of the springtime. Grant us, we pray Thee, a heart wide open to all this joy and beauty, and save our souls from being so steeped in care or so darkened by passion that we pass heedless and unseeing when even the thorn bush by the wayside is aflame with the glory of God.

Enlarge within us the sense of fellowship with all the living things, our little brothers, to whom Thou hast given this earth as their home in common with us. We remember with shame that in the past we have exercised the high dominion of man with ruthless cruelty, so that the voice of the Earth, which should have gone up to Thee in song, has been a groan of travail. May we realize that they live, not for us alone, but for themselves and for Thee, and that they love the sweetness of life, even as we, and serve Thee in their place better than we in ours.

When our use of this world is over and we make room for others, may we not leave anything ravished by our greed or spoiled by our ignorance, but may we hand on our common heritage fairer and sweeter through our use of it, undiminished in fertility and joy, that so our bodies may return in peace to the great mother who nourished them and our spirits may round the circle of a perfect life in Thee.

The son of an Orthodox German preacher, Walter Rauschenbusch became preoccupied with carrying out the message of Christ's Gospels during his years studying at Rochester Theological Seminary. He believed that through prayer and social work, men and women could make the world, or at least their little part of it, a better place.

Places of Vision

Almighty God, supreme Governor of all men, incline Thine ear, we beseech Thee, to the prayer of nations; and so overrule the imperfect counsel of men, and set straight the things they cannot govern, that we may walk in paths of obedience to places of vision, and to thoughts that purge and make us wise; through Jesus Christ our Lord.

Woodrow Wilson firmly believed that God and prayer had been key to every success he enjoyed in life. Indeed, he was one of the most religious men ever to occupy the Oval Office. In this short piece, he contemplated a world torn apart by war.

Standing Up to Oppression

Let us pray for the invaded countries, in the grief and havoc of oppression; for the upholding of their courage; and the hope for the speedy restoration of their freedom. O Lord God, whose compassions fail not, support, we entreat Thee, the peoples on whom the terrors of invasion have fallen; and if their liberty be lost to the oppressor, let not this spirit and hope be broken, but stayed upon Thy strength till the day of deliverance. Through Jesus Christ our Lord. Amen.

Prior to the country's formal entry into World War II, President Franklin Roosevelt and British prime minister Winston Churchill met secretly on the battleship HMS *Prince of Wales* off the coast of Newfoundland to discuss how the United States could support Great Britain's defenses against the German onslaught. During the time they were together, the two leaders, along with their staffs and the sailors present, participated in an ecumenical Sunday service. The chaplains from both countries compiled a series of prayers, of which this was one, to forge a spiritual alliance with one another.

For the Freedom of Mankind

God of the free, we pledge our hearts and lives today to the cause of all free mankind.

Grant us victory over the tyrants who would enslave all free men and Nations. Grant us faith and understanding to cherish all those who fight for freedom as if they were our brothers. Grant us brotherhood in hope and union, not only for the space of this bitter war, but for the days to come which shall and must unite all the children of earth.

Our earth is but a small star in the great universe. Yet of it we can make, if we choose, a planet unvexed by war, untroubled by hunger or fear, undivided by senseless distinctions of race, color, or theory. Grant us that courage and foreseeing to begin this task today that our children and our children's children may be proud of the name of man.

The spirit of man has awakened and the soul of man has gone forth. Grant us the wisdom and the vision to comprehend the greatness of man's spirit, that suffers and endures so hugely for a goal beyond his own brief span. Grant us honor for our dead who died in the faith, honor for our living who work and strive for the faith, redemption and security for all captive lands and peoples. Grant us patience with the deluded and pity for the betrayed. And grant us the skill and the valor that shall cleanse the world of oppression and the old base doctrine that the strong must eat the weak because they are strong.

Yet most of all grant us brotherhood, not only for this day but for all our years—a brotherhood not of words but of acts and deeds. We are all of us children of earth—grant us that simple knowledge. If our brothers are oppressed, then we are oppressed. If they hunger, we hunger. If their freedom is taken away, our freedom is not secure. Grant us a common faith that man shall know bread and peace—that he shall know justice and righteousness, freedom and security, an equal opportunity, and an equal chance to do his best, not only in our own lands, but throughout the world. And in that faith let us march toward the clean world our hands can make.

Six months after the bombing of Pearl Harbor, when the future seemed particularly fragile, President Franklin Roosevelt spoke to the nation in a radio address on Flag Day. He wanted to deliver a very different message, so he asked Pulitzer Prize winner Stephen Vincent Benet to draft a speech that would include an appropriate prayer. This earnest plea brings to mind his call a year earlier for a world based on "four freedoms"—freedom of speech and expression, freedom of religion, freedom from want, and freedom from fear. This prayer was also offered at the United Nations.

Symphony of Life

Father, we call Thee Father because we love Thee. We are glad to be called Thy children, and to dedicate our lives to the service that extends through willing hearts and hands to the betterment of all mankind. We send a cry of Thanksgiving for people of all races, creeds, classes, and colors the world over, and pray that through the instrumentality of our lives the spirit of peace, joy, fellowship, and brotherhood shall circle the world. We know that this world is filled with discordant notes, but help us, Father, to so unite our efforts that we may all join in one harmonious symphony for peace and brotherhood, justice, and equality of opportunity for all men. The tasks performed today with forgiveness for all our errors, we dedicate, dear Lord, to Thee. Grant us strength and courage and faith and humility sufficient for the tasks assigned to us.

Born into a family of seventeen children whose parents had once been slaves, Mary McLeod Bethune became one of the most indefatigable voices for global equality and understanding in the immediate years before and after World War II. She was a self-assured educator, activist, and columnist and found in prayer one of life's great comforts. Here she expresses her firm belief in the beauty of diversity throughout the world.

The Simple Prayer of a Carpenter

May I, who have the privilege of constructing this ballot box, cast the first vote? May God be with every member of the United Nations organization and through your noble efforts bring lasting peace to us all—all over the world!

In the fall of 1949 a slip of paper was found in the ballot box of the newly constructed chambers of the United Nations Security

Council. On it was written this message, signed simply, "Paul Antonio, the carpenter."

Prayer for the United Nations

> Father in Heaven, God of all nations,
> Bless Thou America, bless Thou the world!
> Bless Thy people whose representatives here assemble,
> Bless them with Thy truth, that they be all-truthful,
> Bless them with Thy mercy, that they may be all-merciful
> Bless them with Thy spirit of peace, that they may know
>   peace
> And foster peace upon the earth for the sake of Thy glory.

This prayer was prepared by Francis Cardinal Spellman for delivery on United Nations Day not long after the organization had come into existence in 1945. As one of the most prominent Catholic clergymen of the twentieth century, he had seen his share of the horrors of war as Apostolic Vicar for the U.S. Armed Forces during World War II. He came away from the experience as a champion for world peace before assuming his place as the archbishop of New York City until his death in 1967 at the age of seventy-eight.

Send Our Minds and Hearts Abroad

God of our life, who meetest us on every hand in the beauty and bounty of nature, in the love which binds us to the living and the dead, in glimpses of truth, and in the calls of duty: Draw aside the veils and set our spirits face-to-face with Thee. Thine eyes are in every place, for Thy thought and love go out to all men. Send our minds and hearts abroad until we too feel our kinship with the world-wide brotherhood of Thy children, and carve for all, as for ourselves, health of body, education that frees us from superstition and ignorance, liberty to think and live as sons and daughters of God, a chance to work and a chance to rest, a conscience made sensitive by the ideals of Christ, and a soul that trusts and serves Thee in his Spirit; through the same Jesus Christ our Lord.

Henry Sloane Coffin, a distinguished theologian, was a student of evangelical preacher L. Dwight Moody, whose desire to spread the message of Christianity around the world was tireless. Although Coffin would come to represent a more liberal strain of his religious faith, he did share with Moody a sense of spreading the message of Christ around the world, as this prayer conveys.

From the Heavens to Earth

Give us O God, the vision which can see Thy love in the world in spite of human failure. Give us the faith, the trust, the goodness in spite of all our ignorance and weakness. Give us the knowledge that we may continue to pray with understanding hearts, and show us what each of us can do to set forth the day of universal peace. Amen.

This prayer was the first ever to be transmitted from space to earth. *Apollo 8* commander and astronaut Frank Borman was scheduled to serve as lay reader at his Episcopal church in Seabrook, Texas, but was unable to attend because of his moon mission. Fellow parishioner and NASA engineer Rob Rose suggested that he read the prayer, transmit it, and have it replayed at his church. While orbiting the moon on December 24, 1968, Borman read the prayer. In a later Christmas eve television broadcast from *Apollo 8,* he and astronauts James Lovell and William Anders read from the book of Genesis on the creation of the world.

Prayer for Peace at Camp David

Conscious of the grave issues that face us, we place our trust in the God of our fathers from whom we seek wisdom and guidance. As we meet here at Camp David, we ask people of all faiths to pray with us that peace and justice may result from our deliberations.

On September 5, 1978, President Jimmy Carter, Egyptian president Anwar Sadat, and Israeli prime minister Menachem Begin began their deliberations at Camp David, which would lead to a historic accord in the Middle East. Before any substance was brought up, all three leaders wanted to pray. As President Carter would recount, "I spent several hours negotiating the text of the prayer. . . . I made some edits, Sadat approved it, Begin made some changes, and we issued the prayer the first day."

A Christmas Prayer

Dear God,
The world awaits for the coming of the Prince of Peace.
Our hearts ache for justice for the poor and carefree
safety for our children; for laughter in our homes—the
singing and dancing native to the human spirit.

We thank you for the glorious sounds of Christmas—
tokens of our longing and signs of your love.

We ask to bless the families represented here:
the whole ones; the broken ones; the scattered ones.

We commend into your gracious keeping all those caught
in the spiral of violence and poverty—here at home—and
in other cities—Jerusalem, Baghdad, Kabul.

Especially protect the children, and in your spirit, help us
to rebuild the world for them so that your joy may fill their
hearts and your peace heal the nations.

Let's switch off the world's distorting noise until we hear
our own heart beating. Let's listen to its inner rhythm,
whispering, "God is with us."

Revelation is all around, showing us that every baby is
well-connected and every one the dwelling place of God.

Thanks be to God!

This prayer was written for a Christmas service by the Very
Reverend Alan Jones, dean of San Francisco's Episcopal Grace
Cathedral. It addresses the need for ecumenical understanding
and world peace through the prism of little children everywhere.

TITLE INDEX

PERMISSIONS ACKNOWLEDGMENTS

Grateful acknowledgment is made to the following for permission to reprint previously published and unpublished material:

Alfred Publishing: George Gershwin, "I'm On My Way" from *Porgy and Bess*. Copyright © 1935 by George Gershwin Estate. Thomas Dorsey, "Precious Lord, Take My Hand." Copyright © 1938 by Unichapell Music, Inc. Reprinted by permission of Alfred Publishing.

Belknap Press of Harvard University Press: Emily Dickinson, "Saviour, I've No One Else to Tell" from *The Poems of Emily Dickinson*, Thomas H. Johnson, ed. Copyright © 1951, 1955, 1979, 1983 by the President and Fellows of Harvard College. Reprinted by permission of the President and Fellows of Harvard College.

Big Sky Music: Bob Dylan, "Father of Night." Copyright © 1970 by Big Sky Music. International copyright secured. Reprinted by permission of Big Sky Music.

Bug Music and Carlin America: Stephen Schwarz, "Day by Day" from *Godspell*. Copyright © 1971 by Stephen Schwarz. Reprinted by permission of Bug Music and Carlin America.

Cesar E. Chavez Foundation: "Cesar's Prayer." Copyright © 2008 by the Cesar E. Chavez Foundation www.chavezfoundation.org. Reprinted by permission of the Cesar E. Chavez Foundation.

Crosswicks, Ltd.: Madeleine L'Engle, "Lines Scribbled on an Envelope While Riding the 104 Broadway Bus." Copyright © 1969 by Crosswicks, Ltd. Reprinted by permission of McIntosh & Otis.

Curtis Brown, Ltd.: Ogden Nash, "Prayer at the End of a Rope" from *I'm a Stranger Here Myself*. Copyright © 1938 by Ogden Nash, renewed. Reprinted by permission of Curtis Brown, Ltd.

Kate Donohue: "Eleven Addresses to the Lord" from *Collected Poems, 1930–1978*. Copyright © 1989 by Kate Donohue. Reprinted by permission of Kate Donohue.

Doubleday: Eddie Rickenbacker, "Eddie's Prayer" from *Seven Came Through: Rickenbacker's Full Story*. Copyright © 1943 by Doubleday and Duran Company. Reprinted by permission of Doubleday.

W. E. B. Du Bois: "Grit" and "Give Us Grace" from *Prayers for Dark People*, Herbert Apetheker, ed. Copyright © 1980 by University of Massachusetts Press. Reprinted by permission of the Estate of W. E. B. Du Bois.

Marie Gallo: "Good Morning, God." Reprinted by permission of Marie Gallo.

Father Benedict Groeschel, C.F.R.: "Prayer After a Suicide." Reprinted by permission of Father Benedict Groeschel, C.F.R.

Henry Holt and Company: Robert Frost, "A Prayer in Spring" from *A Boy's Will*. Copyright © 1913 by Henry Holt and Company. Reprinted by permission of Henry Holt and Company. Random House: *Collected Poems*. Copyright © 1930 by Henry Holt and Company. Reprinted by permission of Random House.

Houghton Mifflin Harcourt Publishing Company: T. S. Eliot, Section VI of "Choruses from the Rock" from *Collected Poems 1909–1962*. Copyright © 1936 by Houghton Mifflin Harcourt Publishing Company and renewed 1964 by T. S. Eliot. Reprinted by permission of Houghton Mifflin Harcourt Publishing Company. Faber and Faber: *The Complete Poems and Plays* of T. S. Eliot. Copyright © 1982 by Faber and Faber. Reprinted by permission of Faber and Faber.

Herald Press, Scottdale, Pennsylvania: Esther Eby Glass, "For Wayward Children" from *Breaking Bread Together*, Elaine Sommers Rich, ed. Copyright © 1958 by Herald Press, Scottdale, Pennsylvania. Reprinted by permission of Herald Press.

Magda Herzberger: "Conquering the Spirit." Reprinted by permission of Magda Herzberger.

Conrad N. Hilton College of Hotel & Restaurant Management, University of Houston: Conrad Hilton, "America on Its Knees." Copyright © 1952 by Conrad Hilton Foundation. Reprinted by permission of the Conrad N. Hilton College of Hotel & Restaurant Management, University of Houston.

Hope Publishing Company: Thomas Chisholm, "How Great Is Thy Faithfulness." Copyright © 1923 and renewed 1951 by Hope Publishing. Words by Jeffery Rowthorn, "Lord, You Give the Great Commission." Copyright © 1978 by Hope Publishing Company, Carol Stream, IL 60188. All rights reserved. Reprinted by permission of Hope Publishing.

Alfred A. Knopf: Khalil Gibran, "Prayer in the Stillness of the Night" and "Essence of Prayer" from *The Prophet*. Copyright © 1923 by Khalil Gibran and renewed 1981 by Administrators of C.T.A. of Khalil Gibran Estate and Mary G. Gibran. Reprinted by permission of Alfred A. Knopf.

Douglas MacArthur: "Build Me a Son." Reprinted by permission of the General Douglas MacArthur Foundation, Norfolk, Virginia.

Catherine Marshall: "Prayer of Waiting" from *Adventures in Prayer* by Catherine Marshall. Copyright © 1975 by Chosen Books. Reprinted by permission of the Estate of Catherine Marshall.

Monastery of the Transfiguration (Ellwood City, Pennsylvania): Mother Alexandra (née Princess Ileana of Romania), "Through Troubled Waters" and "Our Daily Bread." Reprinted by permission of Mother Christopher and the Monastery of the Transfiguration, Ellwood City, Pennsylvania.

Muslim Public Affairs Council: Khadijah Abdullah and Omar Ricci, "An American Muslim Prayer to Remember September 11, 2001." Copyright © 2001 by Khadijah Abdullah and Omar Ricci. Reprinted by permission of the Muslim Public Affairs Council.

Very Reverend Alan Jones: "A Prayer for the City" and "A Christmas Prayer." Reprinted by permission of Very Reverend Alan Jones, Dean of Grace Cathedral, San Francisco.

Max Lucado: "Prayer for America the Day After." Copyright © 2001 by Max Lucado. Reprinted by permission of Max Lucado.

The Millay Society: Edna St. Vincent Millay, "Poem and Prayer for an Invading Army." Copyright © 1940, 1963 by Edna St. Vincent Millay and Norma Millay Ellis. Reprinted by permission of Elizabeth Barnett, literary executor, the Millay Society.

James P. Moore Jr.: "Prayer Before the Texas State," "The Commuter Flight to Rochester," and "Finding Courage in Life." Copyright © 2007 by James P. Moore Jr. Reprinted by permission of James P. Moore Jr.

John G. Niehardt Trust: "Black Elk's Prayer" from *Black Elk Speaks* by John G. Neihardt. Copyright © 1932 by John G. Neihardt Trust. Reprinted by permission of the John G. Neihardt Trust.

Liveright Publishing Corporation: e.e. cummings, "I thank You God for most this amazing" from *Complete Poems: 1904–1962*, George James Firmage, ed. Copyright © 1950, 1978, 1991 by the Trustees for the E.E. Cummings Trust. Copyright © 1979 by George James Firmage. Reprinted by permission of Liveright Publishing Corporation.

Harold Ober Associates: Karl Shapiro, "I Have Seen Too Much" first published in *Poetry*. Copyright © 1943 by Karl Shapiro. Copyright © renewed 1970 by Karl Shapiro. Reprinted with the permission of Harold Ober Associates, Inc.

Professional Publishing Services: Louis Untermeyer, "Bless This House" from *This Singing World*. Copyright © 1923 by Harcourt, Brace and Company. Reprinted by arrangement with the Estate of Louis Untermeyer, Norma Anchin Untermeyer c/o Professional Publishing Services, Kensington, Connecticut. Permission of Laurence S. Untermeyer.

ABOUT THE AUTHOR

James P. Moore Jr. who resides in Washington, D.C., is the author of *One Nation Under God: The History of Prayer in America,* and is consulting producer of the public television miniseries *Prayer in America,* based on his book. He is also the creator of the American Prayer Project, which was launched at a major interfaith concert held at Washington National Cathedral on November 8, 2005. The project has generated the music CD *The Many Voices of One Nation Under God* by PBA Music Publishing of San Francisco, the Random House Audio production of his book, and a five-part middle school and high school program on the importance of prayer in American life. Currently he teaches international business and ethics and serves as the Director of the Global Leadership Initiative at the Robert E. McDonough School of Business at Georgetown University. A graduate of the Kiski School, Rutgers University, and the Graduate School of Public and International Affairs at the University of Pittsburgh, he is the former U.S. assistant secretary of commerce for trade development. He has also been an active member of such government boards as the National Air and Space Museum of the Smithsonian Institution, the U.S. Overseas Private Investment Corporation, the Export Import Bank of the United States, and the Committee on Foreign Investment in the United States. He has received numerous awards at home and abroad, and his writings have been translated into dozens of languages. He has lectured at major universities across the country and has sat on more than two dozen corporate and nonprofit boards around the world.